English Drama before
Shakespeare

Peter Happé

Longman

London and New York

Addison Wesley Longman Limited,
Edinburgh Gate,
Harlow,
Essex CM20 2JE,
United Kingdom
and Associated Companies throughout the world.

*Published in the United States of America
by Addison Wesley Longman Inc., New York*

© Addison Wesley Longman Limited 1999

First published 1999

ISBN 0-582-49375-7 CSD
ISBN 0-582-49374-9 PPR

Visit Addison Wesley Longman on the world wide web at
http://www.awl-he.com

British Library Cataloguing-in-Publication Data

A catalogue record for this book is available from the British Library

Library of Congress Cataloging-in-Publication Data

Happé, Peter.
    English drama before Shakespeare / Peter Happé.
        p.   cm. — (Longman literature in English series)
    Includes bibliographical references and index.
    ISBN 0-582-49375-7. — ISBN 0-582-49374-9 (pbk.)
        1. English drama—Early modern and Elizabethan, 1500–1600—History
and criticism.   2. English drama—To 1500—History and criticism.
    3. Drama, Medieval—History and criticism.   4. Renaissance—England.
    I. Title.   II. Series.
    PR646.H36   1999
    822.009—dc21   98–39771
                                                                  CIP

Set by 35 in 10/11pt Mono Bembo
Produced by Addison Wesley Longman Singapore (Pte) Ltd.,
Printed in Singapore

Contents

English Drama before Shakespeare

Longman Literature in English Series

General Editors: David Carroll and Michael Wheeler
Lancaster University

For a complete list of titles see pages vii–viii

Longman Literature in English Series

General Editors: David Carroll and Michael Wheeler
Lancaster University

Pre-Renaissance English Literature

⋆ English Literature before Chaucer *Michael Swanton*
  English Literature in the Age of Chaucer
⋆ English Medieval Romance *W.R.J. Barron*

English Poetry

⋆ English Poetry of the Sixteenth Century *Gary Waller*
⋆ English Poetry of the Seventeenth Century *George Parfitt*
  (*Second Edition*)
  English Poetry of the Eighteenth Century, 1700–1789
⋆ English Poetry of the Romantic Period, 1789–1830 *J.R. Watson*
  (*Second Edition*)
⋆ English Poetry of the Victorian Period, 1830–1890 *Bernard Richards*
  English Poetry of the Early Modern Period, 1890–1940
⋆ English Poetry since 1940 *Neil Corcoran*

English Drama

⋆ English Drama before Shakespeare *Peter Happé*
⋆ English Drama: Shakespeare to the Restoration, 1590–1660
  Alexander Leggatt
⋆ English Drama: Restoration and Eighteenth Century, 1660–1789
  Richard W. Bevis
  English Drama: Romantic and Victorian, 1789–1890
⋆ English Drama of the Early Modern Period, 1890–1940
  Jean Chothia
  English Drama since 1940

English Fiction

⋆ English Fiction of the Eighteenth Century, 1700–1789
  Clive T. Probyn
⋆ English Fiction of the Romantic Period, 1789–1830 *Gary Kelly*
⋆ English Fiction of the Victorian Period, 1830–1890 *Michael Wheeler*
  (*Second Edition*)

★ English Fiction of the Early Modern Period, 1890–1940
Douglas Hewitt
English Fiction since 1940

English Prose

★ English Prose of the Seventeenth Century, 1590–1700 *Roger Pooley*
English Prose of the Eighteenth Century
English Prose of the Nineteenth Century

Criticism and Literary Theory

Criticism and Literary Theory from Sidney to Johnson
Criticism and Literary Theory from Wordsworth to Arnold
Criticism and Literary Theory from 1890 to the Present

The Intellectual and Cultural Context

The Sixteenth Century
★ The Seventeenth Century, 1603–1700 *Graham Parry*
★ The Eighteenth Century, 1700–1789 *James Sambrook* (*Second Edition*)
The Romantic Period, 1789–1830
★ The Victorian Period, 1830–1890 *Robin Gilmour*
The Twentieth Century: 1890 to the Present

American Literature

American Literature before 1880
★ American Poetry of the Twentieth Century *Richard Gray*
★ American Drama of the Twentieth Century *Gerald M. Berkowitz*
★ American Fiction since 1940 *Tony Hilfer*
★ Twentieth-Century America *Douglas Tallack*

Other Literatures

Irish Literature since 1800
★ Scottish Literature since 1707 *Marshall Walker*
Australian Literature
African Literature in English: East and West
★ Southern African Literatures *Michael Chapman*
★ Caribbean Literature in English *Louis James*

★ *Already published*

Editors' Preface

The multi-volume Longman Literature in English Series provides students of literature with a critical introduction to the major genres in their historical and cultural context. Each volume gives a coherent account of a clearly defined area, and the series, when complete, will offer a practical and comprehensive guide to literature written in English from Anglo-Saxon times to the present. The aim of the series as a whole is to show that the most valuable and stimulating approach to the study of literature is that based upon awareness of the relations between literary forms and their historical contexts. Thus the areas covered by most of the separate volumes are defined by period and genre. Each volume offers new and informed ways of reading literary works, and provides guidance for further reading in an extensive reference section.

In recent years, the nature of English studies has been questioned in a number of increasingly radical ways. The very terms employed to define a series of this kind – period, genre, history, context, canon – have become the focus of extensive critical debate, which has necessarily influenced in varying degrees the successive volumes published since 1985. But however fierce the debate, it rages around the traditional terms and concepts.

As well as studies on all periods of English and American literature, the series includes books on criticism and literary theory and on the intellectual and cultural context. A comprehensive series of this kind must of course include other literatures written in English, and therefore a group of volumes deals with Irish and Scottish literature, and the literatures of India, Africa, the Caribbean, Australia and Canada. The forty-four volumes of the series cover the following areas: Pre-Renaissance English Literature, English Poetry, English Drama, English Fiction, English Prose, Criticism and Literary Theory, Intellectual and Cultural Context, American Literature, Other Literatures in English.

David Carroll
Michael Wheeler

Abbreviations

Bullough	G. Bullough, *Narrative and Dramatic Sources of Shakespeare*, 11 vols (London, 1958).
Briscoe and Coldewey	M.G. Briscoe and J.C. Coldewey, eds, *Contexts for Early English Drama* (Bloomington and Indianapolis, 1989).
Chester	*The Chester Mystery Cycle*, ed. David Mills and R.M. Lumiansky, 2 vols, EETS SS 3 and 9 (Oxford, 1974 and 1986).
Companion	*The Cambridge Companion to the Medieval English Theatre*, ed. Richard Beadle (Cambridge, 1994).
Cox and Kastan	J.D. Cox and D.S. Kastan, eds, *A New History of Early English Drama* (New York, 1997).
Coventry	*Two Coventry Corpus Christi Plays*, ed. Hardin Craig, EETS, ES 87 (Oxford, 2nd edn 1952).
EETS	Early English Text Society.
ES	E.K. Chambers, *The Elizabethan Stage*, 4 vols (Oxford, 1923).
Harbage	A. Harbage, *Annals of English Drama*, London, 1940, rev. S. Shoenbaum, 1964.
Kolve	V.A. Kolve, *The Play Called Corpus Christi* (Stanford, 1966).
Lancashire	Ian Lancashire, *Dramatic Texts and Records of Britain: A Chronological Topography to 1558* (Cambridge, 1984).
Macro plays	*The Macro Plays*, ed. Mark Eccles, EETS 262 (Oxford, 1969).
METh	*Medieval English Theatre*.
MSR	Malone Society Reprint.
MS	E.K. Chambers, *The Medieval Stage*, 2 vols (Oxford, 1903).
N Town	*The N-Town Play*, ed. Stephen Spector, 2 vols, EETS SS 11 (Oxford, 1991).

OED	*The Oxford English Dictionary.* Prepared by J.A. Simpson and E.S.C. Weiner, Second edition, 20 vols (Oxford, 2nd edn, 1989).
REED	Records of Early English Drama.
REED *Cambridge*	ed. A.H. Nelson, 2 vols (Toronto, 1989).
REED *Chester*	ed. L. Clopper (Toronto, 1979).
REED *Coventry*	ed. R. Ingram (Toronto, 1981).
REED *Devon*	ed. J. Wasson (Toronto, 1987).
REED *Somerset*	ed. J.A.B. Somerset, 2 vols (Toronto, 1996).
REED *York*	ed. Alexandra F. Johnston and Margaret Rogerson, 2 vols (Toronto, 1979).
RORD	*Research Opportunities in Renaissance Drama.*
Towneley	*The Towneley Plays*, ed. Martin Stevens and A.C. Cawley, 2 vols, EETS SS 13 (Oxford, 1994).
Wickham	Glynne Wickham, *Early English Stages, 1300–1610*, 3 vols (London, 1959–81).
Woolf	Rosemary Woolf, *The English Mystery Plays* (London, 1972).
York	*The York Plays*, ed. Richard Beadle (London, 1982).

Introduction

Chapter 1

Historical Continuity and Development: the Scope of Drama, 1350–1590

I

Thousands and thousands of lines of dramatic verse, and a few thousand words in prose, survive in the English language from the untold number of plays which were performed before young William Shakespeare reached London in the early 1590s. Their quality forces us to recognise that he was very lucky to have come into such an inheritance. It is the purpose of this book to explore these riches, to indicate their variety, and to illustrate ideas about the nature of drama and how it could be performed. If Shakespeare had not arrived we should have regarded the drama before him in a rather different light, and difficult though it may be, we shall here try to look at it with as little reference to him as possible: after all, the makers of these early plays had no idea of what Shakespeare would do to his inheritance. As far as this book is concerned he will be used only when he illuminates what went before him. This stance is adopted as a countermeasure to many other works interrogating the early drama primarily to show how Shakespeare's work was foreshadowed.

Chronologically this study deals with a period of great change in England and the British Isles from medieval times through the Reformation and the Renaissance. It has become more acceptable recently to talk about the 'early modern period', perhaps in recognition that the rather divisive older terminology will no longer suffice. Though it is not always clear where this new period begins – and there is no doubt that we should begin here in the fourteenth century – it at least helps us to perceive that the Renaissance and Reformation, and the evolution of humanism, did not constitute an historical unconformity with medieval culture. One of the advantages of the structure of this volume may therefore be that it will give an account of many things which continue throughout the period, or which change very slowly indeed. History does not move exclusively in straight lines, nor in sharp changes, and often, as we shall find in what follows, things are recalled from the past almost in a circular fashion.

It follows that the dates 1350 and 1590 are only convenient approximations. The first relates to the conjectural date of the first surviving English dramatic text, *The Pride of Life*, and the second to the putative advent of Shakespeare.

In 1350 there were plenty of other things going on which are now lost to us, and we may perceive, using a broader European perspective, that drama had long been well established in various forms.[1] As far as England is concerned, plays in Latin as well as Norman French had certainly existed for some time. Three significant examples are within the Church's domain. The liturgical ceremony of *Quem Quaeritis* trope is found in the *Regularis Concordia*, St Aethelwold's code of practice written at Winchester (*c*. 965–75). The liturgical drama which developed in Latin as part of the Church services and can be documented from the tenth century to the Renaissance and beyond will be discussed in Chapter 3. *Le Mystère d'Adam* (*c*. 1160), which is thought to have originated in England, the text being in Latin and Norman French reflecting the close connections between England and Northern France, has strong liturgical elements combined with sensitive dialogue. *La Seinte Resureccion* (*c*. 1175) has similar qualities and develops the symbolic use of space to which we shall return later. In their different ways these examples exhibit a high degree of dramatic expertise. Alongside them there no doubt existed a great deal of paradramatic activity in the form of processions, local or parish festivals and entertainments at court and in the houses of the nobility. These included song and dance and reflected pagan as well as Christian culture, and had strong, even ritualistic conventions controlling them. Dramatic activity of this type undoubtedly existed in large quantities as the investigation of the Toronto-based Records of Early English Drama project (REED hereafter) is making more and more evident, but our awareness of exactly what such activities comprised is handicapped by the absence of texts.[2] No doubt the concentration of literacy and of scribal resources within the Church has been a factor here ignoring or suppressing what lay outside in pagan culture.

The chosen terminal date of 1590 was at a time of expansion when there were a number of new features. The chief of these is the development of professional status for performers, and, associated with it, the arrival of the new type of playhouse, and the evolution of new financial bases for organising plays. These stimulated or were stimulated by an increasing concentration of playwrights in London who produced what can only be described as a flood of plays in response to the increasing demands of the new theatres and the public they generated. It follows necessarily that it will not be possible or desirable to adhere strictly to this particular year. If there was a multiplicity of dramatic experiences in the fifteenth century and the first half of the sixteenth, the pace increased markedly from 1550, especially after James Burbage built the Theatre at Shoreditch in 1576.

The authorship of most surviving medieval drama is obscure. There are very few names before Henry Medwall (*fl.* 1490), though some distinctive unnamed authors can be discerned. Some works like the mystery cycles have composite authorship, and reflect that in medieval times the notion of authorship was different from the modern one. Much drama throughout the period was collaborative, and indeed the role of the author cannot always be confidently demarcated from the work of other possible contributors, especially the performers themselves. By the sixteenth century, however, the identity and even the lives of individual authors are often distinctive. The increased use of printing for disseminating plays may have increased the desirability as well as the possibility of identifying them. In this study a biographical approach will be followed for work which can definitely be ascribed to specific authors; otherwise genres of plays will be considered.

II

To give a brief historical outline is to risk omitting many important aspects of English life, but it is important to recall that the period under review contained enormous changes. At the beginning in the reign of Edward III we find a medieval society dominated by the Roman Catholic Church in which there were few signs of the changes to come. Much of English culture, especially in the upper ranks of society, was closely associated with Europe through Latin and French. In the aftermath of the Black Death in 1348 there was a period of recovery and increasing prosperity, though the population total was slow to recover. There was especially an increasing reliance on sheep farming and the trades associated with it. At this point the guild system for the organisation of trades and industry and a huge range of social and religious activity was prospering. As a further manifestation of this new prosperity we can point to the enormous amount of building in the following century. We still find many examples of cathedrals, castles, houses, colleges and even bridges built in stone at that time. W.G. Hoskins notes that by 1500 the population of England was 2.5 million, and he estimates that there were 8 million sheep.[3] Much of this new wealth was concentrated in the southern half of England, and particularly around the cloth industry in East Anglia, an area which will feature repeatedly in this study.

But in *The Canterbury Tales* (*c.* 1387–1400), Chaucer notices the coming of the Lollards, the derogatory name given to the followers of John Wyclif (*c.* 1320–1384) who began a radical criticism of Catholic theology and practices. Coupled with the satire of the errant ways of the clergy

found in *Piers Plowman* and many other writings, this new way of looking
at belief foreshadowed the Reformation, even though the writers themselves may have wanted to remain loyal churchmen. It produced a coun-
teraction however, which may be characterised as a rise in demonstrative
forms of piety throughout Europe in the fifteenth century. This showed
itself in many devotional practices including the visual arts, one of its
chief features being the intensification of the worship of the Virgin Mary
and the saints. The written manifestations of this is typified by the popularity of Jacob de Voragine's *Legenda Aurea* (mid-thirteenth century) which
was one of the first books reproduced by the newly invented printing
presses of the late fifteenth century. Caxton's translation, *The Golden Legend*,
appeared in 1483 and was reprinted eight times by 1527. The movement
embodied much emphasis upon extremes of emotion in religious experience, and often represented the sufferings of Christ, and the saints and
martyrs, graphically. Mary Magdalene became an important centre of attention and this shows itself in the drama as in other arts. In *The Book of
Margery Kempe* (c. 1438), for example, Margery's own sufferings in childbed
are relieved by Christ with the result that she is enabled miraculously to
ease the sufferings of other women, and a sacramental link is established
between Mary's veil, the swaddling clothes, and Christ's loin-cloth on the
cross.[4] Another strain of devotional drama which has not survived is
represented by records of a *Pater Noster Play* and a *Creed Play* at York:
both would have been manifestations of similar piety.

   The direct continuity of Lollardry into the Reformation has been
much questioned, especially by A.G. Dickens,[5] and it may well be that
the coming of Martin Luther (1483–1546) should be regarded as a new
start in the criticism of the Roman Church because it affected so many
different classes of people. From now on there were many educated
Protestants, and people drawn from all ranks of society and from many
different parts of the country, though it is material to this study that the
old religion held on firmly in the North and West of England. By the
middle of the sixteenth century the Bible had been translated into English
by William Tyndale and Miles Coverdale.[6] This encouraged the study of
it by individual Christians, and incidentally created a thirst for literacy
among previously uneducated people. The evolution of an English liturgy
gave new emphasis in the vernacular to the central Protestant doctrine of
Justification by Faith, stressing that God's grace was a response to faith
rather than good works.

   But the Reformation was also a political change. Henry VIII's assumption of royal supremacy over the English Church in 1534 led to separation
from Rome. There were many associated divisions in the rest of Europe,
and there were many public calamities such as the French wars of religion,
culminating in the notorious slaughter of Protestants in Paris at the Massacre of St Bartholomew (1572). In England, as in many other countries

in Europe, Protestantism produced its own literature, and many changes in the drama.[7] For example, Thomas Cromwell, Henry VIII's chief minister, set up propaganda moves to further Protestant ideas and he commissioned John Bale to write and perform plays in support in the late 1530s. It was perceived by Bale, and many others, that the drama was an effective means of persuasion. John Foxe, the martyrologist (1517–87), wrote that 'players, printers, preachers' were a triple bulwark against the triple crown of the Pope.[8] Drama was a process of entertainment as well as instruction, and it offered a measure of camouflage by its indirectness. Whatever success Bale achieved, however, there was a significant reaction in the parallel realisation by those in power that drama could also encourage subversion. One of the chief reasons given for this was that performances of plays might lead to potentially disruptive public assemblies. From the later years of Henry VIII, who died in 1547, there is an increasing pressure by the government against the production and printing of plays, and licensing thus became an important constraint. Censorship was eventually vested in the Master of the Revels. Official unease is most noticeable in the rather sudden decline of the mystery plays in the 1560s and 1570s, and in the striking phenomenon that most of the surviving interludes from the second half of the sixteenth century are distinctly Protestant, publication of plays with a contrary intention being unacceptable to the authorities.

The pressure against drama is endemic in the period on ideological grounds as well. The fifteenth-century *Tretise of Miracles Playing* is a Wyclifite document inveighing against the immorality of participating in plays. Such anti-theatre prejudice or apprehension may be found much earlier in the medieval Church even before the schism, as, for example, in the writings of Bishop Grosseteste of Lincoln, who condemned a series of dramatic and quasi-dramatic festivities between 1236 and 1244.[9] But it developed greatly in Protestant thinking, and by the later sixteenth century those concerned with the organisation and production of plays had to contend with a strong antipathy in the city of London on religious grounds. As we shall see, the city of London during the reign of Elizabeth I showed itself in two minds about whether to support or condemn.

It is paradoxical that one of the results of the crucial work of Desiderius Erasmus (?1469–1536), who was probably the most influential humanist thinker in Europe and a devoted Catholic, was to give impetus to the secularisation of the drama. His reappraisal of the Bible by means of scholarly analysis was not meant by him to be schismatic, but the effect of his work on incipient Protestantism at the beginning of the sixteenth century was incalculable. At the same time the reappraisal of classical literature, aided by the power of the printing presses to disseminate texts, meant that a whole new range of subjects and particularly narratives came into circulation and could be used by dramatists. The sixteenth-century drama often pursued religious or moral objectives, whether Catholic or Protestant, whilst employing many secular narratives which were potent in other ways. This secular interest found some material in medieval sources, but the coming of humanism saw a marked increase in narratives from elsewhere, especially the classical and later Mediterranean cultures.

The enormous changes in political and religious outlook naturally generated a patriotic interest in the past, and some aspects of medieval life were restored or re-developed as part of the new culture. For example, the search for a historical continuity led to the popularity of chronicles. The *History of the Kings of Britain* (1136) by Geoffrey of Monmouth giving a royal narrative back to the survival of Aeneas at the fall of Troy was pressed into service in poetry and drama. There was also a determined attempt to record contemporary events in chronicle form, as in *The Union of the Two Noble and Illustre Families of Lancaster and York* (1548) by Edward Hall, and *The Chronicles of England, Scotland and Ireland* (1577) by Ralph Holinshed. All three of these writers were used by dramatists in the sixteenth century as a new national identity was established and defended. Such material was used for both secular and religious objectives.

The pressure of public events had other significant effects upon the drama of the sixteenth century. It must have been difficult to find one's way in a time of changing religious and political structures. Violent death was still a feature of the lives of those involved in struggles for power, and religious persecution continued through the century. Deaths were often a public spectacle and this undoubtedly influenced the presentation of violence on the stage. There is also the frequency of religious change under the Tudors. Henry VIII's desire for a divorce in the 1530s accelerated the coming of Protestantism, but in his new position as Head of the English Church he intended to allow only such limited change as suited him. The activities of radical reformers were inimical to him and he showed a strongly conservative attitude. His three children who succeeded him produced a religious zigzag. Edward VI was under stronger Protestant influence than his father had been, and his reign (1547–53) shows many important Protestant traits including Cranmer's English liturgy, and two editions of *The Book of Common Prayer* (1549 and 1552). Queen Mary (1553–58) turned things back towards Rome, but the distribution of wealth following Henry's dissolution of the monasteries (1536–39) was an important factor in preventing the re-establishment of the old Church in spite of her strong wishes. Her sister Elizabeth I (1558–1603) achieved a Protestant settlement which stabilised matters, but she remained long under pressure from extremists of both persuasions. Although the public stance of the authorities in response to these changes was usually more than clear, many people had great personal difficulty in changing to order, and affection for the old religion especially lingered for a long time. Hindsight tempts us to see the coming of Protestantism as inevitable, but it did not seem so to everyone in the sixteenth century. There were plenty who, like Sir

Thomas More, Bishop Stephen Gardiner and John Heywood, the dramatist, found the battle to stop it worth fighting.

III

Against this background of public affairs we should consider here in outline the types of drama which existed in this period. At its beginning there is some evidence of morality plays, and these continue to be produced until the mid-sixteenth century. Initially they were concerned with central issues of religious doctrine, and were didactic in tone often with specific topics for instruction. Thus *Wisdom* (*c.* 1460) praises the *vita mixta*, a middle way between the entirely closed life demanded by some religious orders, and Christian life in the everyday secular community, but it is infused with a strong devotional element and extensive use is made of hymns from the liturgy. These plays depended upon allegory as a means of imaging configurations of doctrine such as the Seven Deadly Sins or the Four Cardinal Virtues, and for representing verbal or physical conflict.

This form of drama had great potential for development because the author had to develop plot as well as work out the doctrine. The use of allegorical structures gave definition to both plot and character as well as dominating strategies of meaning. The moralities shade imperceptibly into the interludes of the sixteenth century. These were usually shorter and the chosen objective, while it may have had a moral content, was often directed towards a particular contemporary situation such as the behaviour of greedy landlords in *Enough is as Good as a Feast* (1560). As time went by there were changes in the number and type of actors which had a considerable effect upon what might be attempted in interludes. We should also not lose sight of the cost of productions: where resources were limited authors and actors had to respond accordingly, particularly in respect of doubling, which enables a small number of actors to attempt sometimes very large casts.[10]

Alongside the moralities there were plays based upon biblical episodes. In these the prime narrative from the Bible was often supported and shaped by doctrine derived from the writings of the Church Fathers and many later poets, commentators and teachers. Such interpretations formed a major part of the Church's teaching of the laity. In some places, from about 1375, these plays were grouped into cycles giving a narrative from Creation to Doomsday. The four surviving examples and the cycle in Cornish have long been seen as one of the glories of the early drama. This evaluation has recently been put into a new critical context, however, which shows that full cycles of this type were not universal in England.[11]

The corresponding drama on the Continent, though often of even greater size, usually concentrated upon the Passion of Christ and dealt more briefly with earlier biblical history. When biblical plays are arranged into cycles in this way they constitute a potent art form. A similar development took place in plays about the lives and deaths of saints partly in response to the affective piety noted above. As most of these were lost at the Reformation, they cannot be of much concern here, though the Digby play of *Mary Magdalene* is comparable as a cycle. Such plays depend heavily upon narrative, and in doing so they encouraged the development of different ways of managing it. This has further implications for the use of character and dialogue, and it is one of the features of the cyclic form that it comprehends a variety of dramatic styles largely because of multiple authorship spread over a number of years. When the cycles were discontinued in about 1575 they had lasted about two hundred years and their disappearance was more on grounds of a change in political and religious ideology than any sense that they had ceased to be effective and popular.[12] Indeed efforts to revive them in spite of official displeasure continued for some time. We owe a good deal to the scribes who preserved the *Chester Cycle* after its performance was no longer possible for political or sectarian reasons.

Most of the plays mentioned so far are in manuscript form, and the questions of how and why plays have survived are of importance. Some of the mystery cycles had to be written down to ensure continuity within the social and religious life of towns and cities. The absence of texts may indicate that the cycles were less common and less uniform than was once supposed. Writing down moralities was an even more arbitrary matter and one for which adequate motivation is quite hard to seek. This may account for the small number to have survived from before 1500. Apparently no one thought it worth while to print mystery cycles with the exception of John Bale, who brought out some of his Protestant versions in 1547.

Once printing arrived, however, there was a much more serious attempt to disseminate texts – in short, to sell them. As a result the English text of *Everyman*, which is originally Dutch, was printed four times between 1510 and 1529. It had a special role as a book of devotion, being concerned with what will help a dying man when death summons: it is called a 'moral treatise'. Most of the surviving sixteenth-century interludes are in printed form. There were probably two objectives in publication, as is suggested by the title-page advertisement: to present wholesome and beneficial moral example in an entertainment, and to appeal to other entrepreneurs who might want to produce the play. That a number of interludes, including some by Heywood and Bale, were reprinted suggests that they were successful ventures, though it has been argued that no one throughout the century could have made much profit out of printing and publishing plays.[13]

Another significant impact of humanism was the adoption of plays within the education system. By the beginning of the sixteenth century, when a new curriculum was developed by men like Colet at St Paul's School, classical studies included the study of comedies in schools, particularly those of Terence (185–159 BC). This meant that many young men learned the plays, especially where acting and watching them formed a compulsory part of the curriculum. Terence had been well known throughout the Middle Ages and the remarkable Latin plays of Christian worship by Hrotswitha, a tenth-century nun of Gandersheim, show how sensitively they could be imitated.[14] As for tragedy, the emphasis was upon Seneca, whose works were thought more suitable for undergraduates. There are instances where plays were offered as part of the requirements for a degree. These studies developed throughout the sixteenth century, and by the end of our period the interest in them burst out of the schools and universities into the repertoire of the newly developed popular theatres. There always remained, however, an academic interest in writing and performing Latin and, more rarely, Greek plays at the universities with an educated audience and amateur actors. Queen Elizabeth's visits to Cambridge (1564) and Oxford (1566) were marked by intensive exposures to drama. The irruption of the classics on to the professional stage open to all classes changed the scope of popular theatre and enormously increased its range. The concepts of comedy and tragedy had existed in the Middle Ages, but late in the sixteenth century the contact with the public theatres proved outstandingly fertile and led to their transformation.[15]

IV

As we have seen, the texts available to us are initially in manuscript form. Some of these manuscripts, such as the *Towneley Cycle*, are elaborate and designed for presentation, and are nearer to being books than playscripts. Others are much closer to performance and carry in them valuable details enabling us to envisage how the plays were done. The coming of printing led to the development of the book trade, and the printed plays which survive were meant to be bought and sold. This implies that the majority of printed texts had an existence some distance from the life of the play in performance. We need to bear in mind that to print and publish a play may be very different acts from performing it. The two events might be some distance apart in time and place, and there was always scope for change in rehearsal as well as in the printing house. The pressure of external factors such as taste, censorship and commercial expectation might also affect what actually appeared in print. The practical effect of this is that the texts we inherit must constantly be regarded in the light of what we can discover about the contexts in which they were generated. They always tell us something about the play concerned, but what they tell us is highly variable, and finding this out is one of the pleasures of studying them.

Outside the texts themselves there is a variety of information which helps us to appreciate the nature of the plays and the ways in which the history of drama developed in this period. We shall have to return to the REED project a number of times as the records which it is uncovering are often all we have to show about where and when dramatic activities were going on. Each volume depends upon a differing variety of local records and upon what has been rediscovered in its particular locality. The primary elements are official civil and religious archives, household and parish records, and legal documents: none of these was originally compiled for the convenience of theatre historians.

The same is true for the other collections which ought to be noted here. There are many details in the monumental collections of state papers edited by Brewer, especially when the drama became part of the propaganda machine in the time of Thomas Cromwell.[16] The Malone Society has published in its *Collections* several series of documents relating to entertainment at the Inns of Court, in the city of London and some counties, especially Kent and Lincolnshire, and in East Anglia. These may be supplemented by the Victoria County Histories. Fortunate survivals are the Revels Documents which were preserved in Loseley House and covered court entertainment of many kinds from the mid-sixteenth century, and the *Stationers' Register* recording from 1557 the plays which the members of the Company intended to publish.[17] Philip Henslowe's *Diary* actually falls just outside our period, being a record of expenses and inventories in connection with the Rose Theatre from February 1592 to March 1604.[18] It is especially valuable, however, for what it implies about costumes, properties, and the process by which playwrights were employed by a theatre manager either for original work or for 'additions' to the work of others.

These primary sources have been and still are being mined to help build up the social context in which plays were performed, and also to indicate at times how expenditure supported productions. We shall now turn to an overview of some of the ways in which plays were presented.

Notes

1. For details see R. Axton, *European Drama of the Early Middle Ages* (London, 1974), and W. Tydeman, *The Theatre in the Middle Ages* (London, 1978).

2. The scope of the REED volumes, concentrating upon individual cities and counties, is musical and dramatic records up to 1642 from civic, religious and household sources. It does not include the liturgical drama.

3. *The Making of the English Landscape* (London, 1957), p. 130. Hoskins notes that the population before the Black Death was 3.7 m, and that it had recovered to only 3.5 m by 1603; *The Age of Plunder* (London, 1976), pp. 4–5.

4. For further examples of late medieval piety see E. Duffy, *Stripping of the Altars* (New Haven and London, 1992), pp. 155–200, 233–98; G.M. Gibson, *Theatre of Devotion* (Chicago, 1989), pp. 1–46. For Mary Magdalene in art and drama, see C. Davidson, *The Saint Play in Medieval Europe* (Kalamazoo, 1986), pp. 71–97.

5. *The English Reformation*, 2nd edn (London, 1989), p. 14.

6. Tyndale's *New Testament* appeared in 1526, and Coverdale's *Biblia* in 1535.

7. For the scope of Protestant writing in England and a bibliography for 1525–75, see John N. King, *English Reformation Literature* (Princeton, 1982), pp. 478–506.

8. *Acts and Monuments of John Foxe*, ed. S.R. Cattley (London, 1877), vol. 6, p. 57.

9. *MS* 1.91.

10. For playing in small troupes, see D. Bevington, *From 'Mankind' to Marlowe*, and for sample doubling schemes see my *Four Morality Plays* (Harmondsworth, 1979), Appendix 1, pp. 677–83.

11. A.F. Johnston, 'What if no text survived?' in Briscoe and Coldewey, pp. 1–19 (10).

12. H.C. Gardiner, *Mysteries End* (Hamden, 1946).

13. P.W.M. Blayney, 'The Publication of Playbooks', in Cox and Kastan, pp. 383–422.

14. Axton, pp. 24–9.

15. See W. Farnham, *The Medieval Heritage of Elizabethan Tragedy* (Berkeley, 1936); B.R. Smith, *Ancient Scripts and Modern Experience on the English Stage, 1500–1700* (Princeton, 1988).

16. *Letters and Papers, Foreign and Domestic, of the Reign of Henry VIII*, edited by J.S. Brewer and others, 21 vols (London, 1862–1932).

17. For the Revels Documents see General Bibliography under Feuillerat; for stationers see E. Arber (ed.) *A Transcript of the Registers of the Company of Stationers in London, 1554–1640*, 5 vols (London, 1875–94).

18. R.A. Foakes and R.T. Rickert (eds) *Henslowe's Diary* (Cambridge, 1989).

Chapter 2
Dramatic Practice, 1350–1590

The varieties of theatrical practice in this period are a reflection of the diverse objectives and techniques which playmakers pursued. It is a time when many skills and many ways of thinking about methods of performance were employed. Changing needs also produced developments in techniques, especially in the light of the intensification of theatrical activity in the last quarter of the sixteenth century. It then came about that there were more and more people available to be entertained or influenced, but the medieval intention of using theatre as a form of moral instruction was never entirely left behind, as the prologue shows in Marlowe's *Dr Faustus*. Indeed there are a number of similar continuities which are striking in spite of innovations, and the use of performance as a means of negotiating political power continued throughout. There persists a concern with the functional use of character and place. There may be a great deal of very close observation of people's behaviour as in that of the rage of Magnyfycence, the king figure in Skelton's play, or in the *Towneley* Shepherds' critique of those who exploited them. Such apparent realism is very entertaining in its recognition of contemporary detail, but the playwrights in general seldom lose an opportunity of showing what a character stands for, and this tendency is often far more important than realistic imitation. Both these examples can be seen a part of the power game. This has distinct implications for the way an actor presents character: in some ways such playing anticipates Brechtian alienation techniques in that the actor is separated from his role.[1]

In the light of this we shall here review some aspects of theatrical practice: the idea and use of theatrical space, different kinds of scene, symbolic elements, including allegory, aspects of theatrical language and verse, and festive entertainment.

Spaces exclusively designed for and dedicated to performance hardly arise until late in the period. We may note, however, that John Rastell, presumably for his private use, built a theatre of some kind in his house in 1524.[2] For the most part, if a playwright needed to make the acting area specific he could do it either by letting the speeches detail a location, or by making use of a physical structure which could be given an identity.

There were conventions for managing these. Because many of the performances were given by itinerant players, there was often a need to begin with a cry to 'make room'. Such a call would concentrate attention and also bring into awareness the demarcation between the space occupied by the performers and that of the spectators. This device would be necessary in a public space, such as a street, as well as in a hall where the spectators might be eating and drinking. There would be an opportunity to be very precise about where the action was to take place and about atmosphere, if these were material.

From some of the earliest plays there are indications that the actors were often itinerant, even if they were probably amateurs. Indeed records are now showing that it was quite common for a group of amateur players to go on a local tour to neighbouring villages and towns in the fifteenth and sixteenth centuries.[3] This custom has implications for the festive entertainments we shall discuss below. Itinerant drama remained a feature throughout the period, and was a resource for the professional companies. Its very nature contributed much to the way space was handled, including its imaginative significance.

Besides the halls of great households and anonymous streets, plays were performed in churches, in churchyards, in schools and colleges, in the Inns of Court in London and ordinary inns. With a play like *Mankind* the text is so adaptable that there is no direct evidence about whether it had to be performed outdoors or indoors: it has been done successfully in modern times in both. Some outdoor performances were hugely spectacular. The playing place for Cornish plays was usually an amphitheatre such as the one which survives today at St Just in Penwith. There were specified locations around the circumference of the acting area, and an identifiable central place.[4] Lindsay's *Ane Satire of the Thrie Estaitis* incorporated a brook as part of the action, and *The Castle of Perseverance* specifies and uses a ditch or moat. For these plays and for a limited number of others it is evident that the idea of an arena-like auditorium is deeply embedded in the writing. Specific locations or structures could be identified with individual characters such as God or Satan, and the anonymous space between them could be used for all sorts of journeys, processions, battles and sieges: it was a major resource precisely because it was unspecified, and because it could be made to contrast with the more specifically designated areas. Thus in *Perseverance* there can be significant movement between the scaffolds of Avarice and Mundus, and it is also possible to have some characters on the scaffolds speak or engage with some on the lower area, giving an important vertical dimension to the spectacle.

Theatrical structures were varied in scope and size. In *Perseverance* the scaffolds, so called in the text and on the diagram in the manuscript, have to be big enough to contain several actors and to suggest festive activity within. In the 1580s at the First Blackfriars Theatre, a rather compact indoor setting, there appear to have been small structures which could represent houses. These may have derived ultimately from the classical theatre, but the Revels accounts show that they could be quite expensive items and valuable enough to be worth taking from the Blackfriars to Greenwich or Hampton Court by boat for royal performances.[5] Nevertheless, the action of the plays in this indoor environment still depended upon the contrast between the designated and visually identifiable structures and the flexible, unidentified space between. For the earlier examples this is sometimes called *place and scaffold*, but the principle remains the same through the period whether indoors or in the open air.

Such a similarity transcends some notable differences between small-scale indoor and large-scale outdoor presentations. For the latter there is the likelihood that the atmosphere was distinctly public, even impersonal. Unless a means could be devised for controlling their entrance, the audience could not be made to pay. The playing times were limited by hours of daylight and the weather, and there must have been considerable acoustic problems which required special acting skills. It is remarkable that when the first purpose-built theatres were constructed they continued to use some features of outdoor playing even though the control of entrances and the frequency of playing before a regular, urban audience meant that much greater wealth was generated for profit or re-investment. As to indoor performances, many would take place in intimate environments, often with the possibility that the actors would be personally known to the audience. In such places the opportunities for suggestive 'in' jokes were many, especially in the court and in halls of closed or selective institutions such as schools, colleges, Inns of Court and livery halls.

The great variety of effects within individual scenes is hard to encompass. Because the plays were meant to be entertaining, and perhaps had to gain the attention of their audiences from other diversions, there was plenty of scope for music, singing, dancing. In some plays such as Pikering's *Horestes* the amount of music is so great that they are musical plays rather than plays with music; but there are others where the musical performances were not necessarily so closely related to plot and action. In many early records it is not always clear whether performers were minstrels or actors: some no doubt were both. Animals appear quite often, and there are a number of episodes in which fools play a major part, as in the negotiations between Fansy and Foly over a dog and a pet owl in *Magnyfycence*. Such fool devices were much developed in the professional theatre by Richard Tarlton (d. 1588). The role of the Vice, a threatening but usually comic figure, became highly popular and effective in interludes after 1550, and a related performer also called the Vice appears in records of some country festival entertainments. There is often a sense that performers did a 'turn' and perhaps created a moment for applause. The dramatists used disguise a great deal, and also aliases. Many early

Vices are quick to conceal their name signifying their sinfulness under an alias, and the actors had ample scope to elaborate fooling upon this. Disguise plays a large part in the romance plays which became popular after 1576. By means of such devices, audiences are allowed to know more than the characters, whether for serious or comic effects.

There are many scenes in which the dramatic effect depends upon a very close interaction between the performers. The Fansy and Foly scene mentioned above may be one example: we may contrast it with three others which are discussed in more detail in later chapters. The character Not Loving nor Loved in John Heywood's *A Play of Love* claims to have got the better of a lover who slighted him, but reveals inadvertently that he was more committed than he boasted; Barabas in Marlowe's *The Jew of Malta* succeeds in speaking to three different listeners within the same speech in a spectacular exhibition of verbal juggling; and the two virgins, played by boys but dressed as men, in Lyly's *Gallathea* gradually realise that they have fallen in love, each thinking the other male in a scene more remarkable for its delicacy than for mockery.

The substance of plays could be communicated by intimate dialogue, by soliloquy, by dumb show and by detached moral comment, quite often using metatheatrical techniques which again had special value in managing the response of the audiences. In many plays there is a conscious use of groups of similar or related characters like the Shepherds in the cycles, or the coarse soldiers Ruf, Huf and Snuf in *Cambises*. Such groups allowed comic effects, but they could also act much more grimly as torturers of Christ, or seriously as in the debate of the Four Daughters of God. Their success depended upon playing closely together. Moral comment and the creation of atmosphere could also be created by framing or choric devices which used abstractions such as Revenge. These last devices form an important link with the principles of characterisation which run through much of the drama of the period.

Just as space might be used for its different meanings, so characters were often closely related to abstract ideas or concepts rather than being simply a mimetic representation of real life. This is often misunderstood by the modern spectator or reader, who tends to look for psychological realism and detailed coherent motivation. The latter perhaps depends largely upon a self-consciousness which developed in the Renaissance, but the preceding tradition was very strong indeed. On the Elizabethan stage it was still quite acceptable and meaningful to mix up abstract characters with apparently realistic ones. Supernatural characters also encountered humans.

As a consequence, motivations continued to defy realistic explanation, and this may be because the dramatists had a firm intention of how the ideas of their plays were to predominate, and how the characters were to be functional to them: a technique developed from the morality plays. It is as well to look upon this common practice as dramatically effective rather than as a failure.[6] The important thing was to excite emotion in the audience – of pity, or remorse or indignation – so as to affect attitudes and ideas rather than to give in-depth portraits. Such effects often depended upon the ingenuity with which allegory was conceived and staged.

However, it is noticeable from the cycles to the plays of Robert Greene that family relationships were a subject of continuing interest and use. Thus the emotional relationship of father to son in the cycle plays about Abraham and Isaac could be made to reflect the obedience necessary to God, and a sense of betrayal could later be developed using the subject of the Prodigal Son. Even in late history plays this remains a persistent technical device.

The language of drama is markedly varied. In broad terms there were still many dialect areas, and for the first century or so many plays, including the mystery cycles, were written in local speech for local audiences: a factor which has helped scholars to identify many local provenances and also to point to some areas such as Cornwall or East Anglia as particularly fertile for drama. This regionalism is found in a large number of the medieval plays, and it has the remarkable result of giving great vigour to many speeches and dialogues. Close to this is the incorporation of proverbial language, which also gives great liveliness to many plays.

But this demotic aspect is complemented by two other features of the linguistic culture: the sermon and the use of rhetoric. Though these two are not completely discrete, the former brought to plays an explanatory mode of expression. It embodied moral display and sometimes pithy illustration. Sermons had to exhort and to relate theoretical moral ideas with convincing examples. The sheer power of words was expected to stir the emotions and also to bring people into a community of repentance aimed at salvation. In many ways the religious drama was a direct extension of such objectives.[7] Though plays were naturally not the voice of one but of many, individual characters such as Mercy in *Mankind* were given speeches directed at the audience in their real lives. This is a kind of metatheatricality, but here it is especially effective because it is interrelated to and contrasted with other ways of influencing the audience practised by other characters in asides and a comic song.

The Church made a deliberate attempt to train its preachers, and some of the manuals no doubt influenced the authors of plays, especially in the selection of illustrative examples which were often narratives or anecdotes. But the impact of humanistic education broadened the perceived function of such spoken arts, and gave a new social context for what could be done by public speech which primarily was meant to be heard. Although the medieval Church and the Renaissance schoolrooms produced many learned men, English society as a whole contained a large proportion of illiterates, and the spoken word had therefore to carry highly complex meanings and experiences. For the elite, and it is apparent that this comprised more and more the moderately prosperous as well as the nobility, the arts of persuasion became essential in commerce, politics and the law; and the expansion of schools like St Paul's, Westminster and Merchant Taylors took account of this in their curricula. The idea of rhetoric today may be that it is hollow and superficial, but in the sixteenth century it was an essential part of communication and thought since it encouraged the ordered presentation of ideas and opinions. It was a kind of heightened speech. Like the discourses of the medieval Church, such humanistic communication was learned in such a way that ideas were enhanced by context, cross-reference and repetition and the patterning of language. Wit had a special function since it often neatly introduced the unexpected and the apparently irrelevant, and it could also help with the management of ideas. It was very useful for lateral thinking. Drama played a special role since it allowed students to practise such uses of language in fictional situations and in play which was really work. Thus the four characters in Heywood's *Play of Love*, which was probably acted by boys, are ingeniously contrasted in their manifestations of the state of love. Part of the pleasure of this play is an appreciation of the way each explains his or her attitudes and emotions in the constantly changing contexts brought about by the plot. Heywood is perhaps a special case because his plays show an unusual interest in balancing views, but the practice of argument and persuasion continued to attract interest in other dramatic contexts.

When we turn to the verse we find a variety of techniques, but it is difficult to avoid the conclusion that to write in verse was a universally accepted method of communicating effectively on stage. This is a bit of a mystery, but we may be able to explain it by links with rhetorical devices which are based upon creating patterns. In any case, the ubiquity of dramatic verse cannot be overlooked. Interestingly, many of the large-scale outdoor plays such as *Perseverance* and some of the mystery cycles use very long stanzas with intricate rhyming schemes. Such is the case with the thirteen-line stanzas which are the hallmark of the Wakefield Master in the *Towneley* plays. The origins of these powerful verse conventions in the biblical plays may lie in the poetic versions of the biblical stories, such as *Cursor Mundi*, as well as in medieval song and lyric. We have already noted that actors and minstrels were often indistinguishable. The versification in these plays often combines stanzaic rhymed verse with alliterative principles. If some of the desired effect of the cycles was a deliberate archaism, then it may explain such choices. Even to modern ears when this kind of verse is spoken in the open air there does seem to be an acoustic value derived from the special sound of the verse. Certainly the speeches often have a great deal of poise and balance and the actors are led to speak them distinctively. Some directors in modern times have felt that complex verse is of particular benefit to inexperienced actors.

But part of the skill lies in variation, as Heywood shows in plays manifesting an acute sense of social rank. In *The Play of the Wether* he uses rhyme royal for Jupiter at the top and gives quatrains and couplets to those lower down. Rhyme royal is demanding prosodically because of its interlinked rhyme scheme (ababbcbc) but its stanza breaks do allow decorum and for the proper relationship between characters to be manifested spaciously. From about the middle of the sixteenth century there were two verse innovations. The use of seven-stress rhyming couplets became very popular in the interludes. These 'fourteeners' were really an adaptation of ballad stanza with a fairly free allowance of unstressed syllables. Unfortunately these couplets look much worse on the page than modern productions have shown them to be in performance. It is a very adaptable measure, and when used well it can add much to the rhetorical devices described earlier. This form proved itself very effective in Thomas Newton's translations of Seneca (1581). The development of blank verse, however, proved a more lasting benefit for the drama as well as for many other types of poetry. Marlowe seized upon it as an expression suitable for the power and ambition of Tamburlaine, consciously rejecting what he called the 'jigging veins of rhyming mother wits'. Other dramatists like Peele and Greene followed Marlowe, but they extended the dramatic tasks blank verse was used for. It was successful for onstage narratives as well as for soliloquies, both of which became more and more important techniques on the Elizabethan stages. Because it did not use rhyme it relied more upon the rhetorical structure of sentences, which could be very complex: a feature of great importance to a listening audience.

The concept of festive entertainment has been much developed of recent years as the REED investigations have increasingly drawn attention to it. Usually these events cannot be tied to specific or ascertainable texts or indeed to modes of performance. The variety of places where drama occurred has already been noted and this too is a factor in coming to terms with the variety of dramatic forms. Nineteenth-century scholarship had identified folk elements which were thought to have preserved in a fragmented fashion the beliefs and practices of pre-Christian cultures. This approach is not entirely discredited, but the festive or carnival element is probably based upon a wide variety of origins and embodies other purposes. Some of it was certainly seasonal, especially as people needed entertainment in the long, dark winters. The Church itself also had to celebrate yearly patterns which derived from biblical narrative and which could interrelate with such survivals. Even the liturgical drama had inversions of its ceremonies in medieval times in the Feast of the Ass and the Feast of Fools.

With the development of civic power and the need to demonstrate or perhaps even to contest authority, street processions and royal entries became a focus for many dramatic elements. These would have strong visual effects by means of the decorative wagons and the costumes and scenery which were incorporated in them. The size and scope of the procession would reflect the power of those promoting it, and the areas it passed through were also important. At Chester, for example, the Midsummer Show rivalled, and indeed at times probably exceeded, the mystery cycle in importance. Apparently it lasted from the late fourteenth century until 1678, had a different route, and took place at a different time from the cycle plays at Whitsun. E.K. Chambers records that the craft guilds were represented by characters in costume from the plays, and that they were accompanied by four giants, an elephant and castle, a unicorn, a camel, a luce (lynx), an antelope, a dragon with six naked boys beating it, morris-dancers, a devil 'in his feathers', and another devil called 'cups and cans'.[8] It appears that for a time it offered the Mayor an alternative choice to the cycle in the sixteenth century when there was a need to exploit opportunities and also to tread warily as the religio–political conflicts demanded.

For events related to specific royal visits the spectacles given by town corporations or by wealthy aristocrats were enhanced by speeches and songs. These, together with costumes, drew upon an eclectic mixture of sources classical, pagan, early British as well as Christian, with a suitable Catholic or Protestant bias as appropriate. Specific allegories and general symbols provided conceptual structures for visual effects. When Elizabeth visited the Earl of Leicester at Kenilworth in 1575 she was greeted from the lake by Triton 'dressed as a mermaid'. He spoke verses by the poet George Gascoigne, who was partly responsible for preparing the 'shows'.[9] Elizabeth's visit lasted three weeks during which there featured a Savage man, a bride-ale (traditional drinking ceremony at a wedding), and the Coventry Hock Tuesday Play. If clowns and fools had a part on these occasions they acted as a means of inverting the established order, and so raise for us the interesting question of whether carnival is an allowed inversion which deliberately seeks to contain, or whether it is really subversive. The line is not easy to draw.

Away from the large urban corporations there also took place a myriad of parish events, with many regional variations. These occurred widely throughout the countryside. The names for such events or characters in them sometimes give hints of what went on, as in the King play, Robin Hood, the Lord of Misrule, or a Rush-bearing. Often these were linked to fund-raising, especially as the Protestant settlement placed more and more financial responsibility upon Church Wardens. The so-called Church Ales happened between May and Midsummer and comprised drinking, dancing and various other entertainments.[10] There was sometimes a delicate balance between disorder and having a good time.

The practices we have discussed here evidence the versatility in performance in this period. They are the activities of amateur as well as professional playmakers and actors, and they imply that we should not talk of 'the audience' since the intentions of the makers were so varied. The audiences were put into many different positions physically, from worship to drinking ale, and what they were required to receive had a wide range of intellectual, moral and emotional subject matter.

Notes

1. J. Willett (ed. and trans.), *Brecht on Brecht* (London, 1957), pp. 69–77.

2. R. Axton (ed.), *Three Rastell Plays* (Cambridge, 1979), p. 8.

3. See, for example, the account of East Anglian drama in J.C. Coldewey, 'The Non-cycle plays and East Anglian Tradition', in *Companion*, pp. 189–210 (204), and more generally in Alexandra F. Johnston and Wim Hüsken (eds) *English Parish Drama* (Amsterdam and Atlanta, 1996).

4. S. Higgins, *Medieval Theatre in the Round* (Camerino, 1994), pp. 23–204.

5. For example, for 1558/59: 'Watercariage with bote hiere: William Cleye and his companye with a barge of 8 ores to carrye and recarye the Revels stuffe and attendaunfes theron betweene the courte and the Blackefryers and waytinge late theron toe sondrye nightes for bothe: 13 shillings and four pence', in A. Feuillerat (ed.) *Documents Relating to the Office of the Revels in the Time of Queen Elizabeth* (Louvain, 1908), p. 89. A few days later when a boat with only four oars was used, Cleye was paid for 'a whirry to carrye the stuffe that woold not into the barge', p. 95.

6. At a Royal Shakespeare Company matinée of *Dr Faustus* recently it was very noticeable that the show performed for Faustus of the Seven Deadly Sins which were given in mime was much appreciated by the young audience consisting, one suspects, largely of examination candidates.

7. G.R. Owst, *Literature and Pulpit in Medieval England* (Cambridge, 1933), pp. 471–547.

8. MS 2.356.

9. ES 1.122–3. The full description in Robert Laneham's *Letter* of 1575 is at 1.457.

10. Johnston and Hüsken, pp. 9–10.

Part I
The Medieval Drama

Chapter 3
Worship, Instruction and Entertainment: Liturgical Drama

Since the bulk of English drama before 1500 is religious, and since a very considerable portion of that surviving from the sixteenth century is either specifically didactic or substantially influenced by religious matters, we shall attempt in this chapter to give an account of the religious contexts in which the plays were written and performed. This will include a consideration of the liturgical drama, which is closely linked.

In describing or contemplating medieval drama we ought not to impose distorting modern norms upon a varied corpus of plays, neither in terms of time, nor in terms of types of play, nor in terms of what the twentieth century has come to see as drama. For us the drama takes place on a stage, or on television, or on film or on radio. We may experience drama in a theatre with a proscenium arch, or in an arena, or in a village hall. Today a large part of the appreciation and understanding of drama also takes place by studying the texts of drama in printed books. All of these modes may help us to come closer to the medieval drama, but they all contain obstacles as well.

Life in medieval times was much more orientated towards religion, both in outward forms like people's occupations and also with regard to the inner life. There was a very strong sense of human impermanence, and religion was seen as a way of meeting many difficulties and misfortunes. Instability in society, and the proximity of life-threatening experiences such as the plague or childbirth are constant themes of preaching as well as of the various forms of consolation and instruction which the Church developed. On the other hand, worship also comprised joy and celebration and gave cause for hope. The work of the Church was concerned with both fear and the hope which transcended it. Thus to regard the religious content of the early plays as being about moral instruction alone is to narrow its scope too far.

The sources of the religious drama may give us some indications about what their authors were aiming at, and one can but express surprise at the wide range of material from which they drew. There was, however, a central store, a sort of cultural bank common to medieval Christendom, which consisted of the Bible, in the form of St Jerome's Vulgate in Latin, many legends about saints and their miracles, and many doctrinal configurations such as the World, the Flesh and the Devil, or the Seven Deadly Sins, which arose largely through patristic elaboration of doctrine derived from teaching in the Bible. The most important writers who helped to build up the body of doctrine were the four doctors of the ancient world: St Augustine of Hippo, St Ambrose, St Jerome in the fifth century, and St Gregory in the sixth. To these must be added St Thomas Aquinas (Dominican) in the thirteenth century. But their work may be supplemented by a network of other writings variously interrelated. Among these Peter Comestor's *Historia Scholastica* (1155–58) and *Cursor Mundi*, the anonymous fourteenth-century poem, gave versions of the Christian narrative, and these were supported by books of guidance such as *The Lay Folks' Mass Book,* and John Mirk's *Festial,* a collection of sermons. Works such as these were available in monastic libraries and were used in the training of priests. It is often quite difficult, however, to pin down an exact source for doctrines embodied in the plays because these writings overlapped in so many ways. The key is that they built up a body of doctrine which was in common for the educated clergy, and which could be made available to the laity. Indeed it is essential to come to terms with the many ways in which the wisdom of the Church accumulated so that the various kinds of clergy, priests, monks and friars – the religious teachers, in essence – could learn and accumulate. Much of this was spearheaded by the preaching of the Franciscans and Dominicans. The latter also played an important intellectual role in the development of theology, as did the Augustinians. At the heart this was a literate process which depended upon a huge industry of scribes whose efforts built up great libraries of texts. But most people were still illiterate and had to experience the consolations of the Church through visual and aural means.

This material was used to instruct the audiences in such matters as moral behaviour, or the sanctity of baptism; to give them such information as to help them how to live their lives in spiritual terms. But there was also a need to make familiar, and to reiterate, and to re-inforce the narrative aspects of belief, which were not stressed merely for moral reasons or moral patterns but because the stories or legends could be used in a variety of ways. These narratives often acquired the power of myths. Part of the effectiveness of the presentation of stories through the biblical plays was that they could be related to other narratives of which the spectators were aware. Thus to dwell upon Christ as a second Adam builds upon a pre-existing knowledge of who Adam was in the first place. We should not assume that audiences were ignorant, or that the level of instruction, even for those who could not read, was necessarily elementary. And again as part of religious experience, which it is often difficult to separate from doctrine, there was also the experience of religious emotions which we should regard as worship. This could include a portrayal of the human position in the world created by God; it could make conscious the grimmer aspects of experience such as illness and death and the relationship of these to the life to come; and it could and did extensively celebrate the greatness of God as manifested in legend and in divine intervention into human history. The drama which we shall be discussing here shares with the liturgy of the Church itself this last aspect of religious experience, and indeed it has been an object of controversy as to how far the liturgy itself is dramatic. We can draw from such controversy the important idea that, just as a congregation in a service through the liturgy is made to share what is being celebrated, so in medieval drama there is often a clear role for the audience as participants in an act of worship. It is a nice point to decide where congregations become audiences.

Another important aspect was meditation. Collections like the *Books of Hours* were meant to give a visual version of biblical incidents such as the Nativity, and each page was accompanied by relevant texts and quotations. Such books were not exactly to be read, but to be used to stimulate an appropriate state of mind based upon ideas and feelings arising from the combination of picture and words, and perhaps to lead to prayer. The so-called *Biblia Pauperum* is another such example.[1] It is thought to have been composed in the thirteenth century, the earliest extant manuscript fragments being dated *c.* 1300, and there are eighty-three surviving examples of the texts originating in several European countries. It was printed in 1460 as a 'block book' or book of woodcuts and reprinted many times thereafter. Each page consists of three central pictures linked thematically. Thus a picture of Christ's Entombment is flanked by Joseph being cast into the well, and Jonas being swallowed by the whale (page g), while the Resurrection is accompanied by Samson removing the gates of Gaza, and Jonas emerging from the whale (page i). The pages are set out in a similar fashion and the accompanying texts are grouped symmetrically at corresponding points on the page. Some of them give fragments of narrative, while others are phrases which embody intentions or observations such as 'On the third Day he shall rise up: we shall know and follow him' (Hosea 3:6) on the Resurrection page. It is thought that this material is too sophisticated to be intended for the illiterate or the ignorant, but the processes of cross-reference, illustration and recollection it implies are clearly related to those which might arise from witnessing the performance of a mystery cycle.

Similarly, *The Holkham Bible Picture Book* gives valuable insight into this visual culture. It dates from *c.* 1325 and it was influenced by the *Historia Scholastica* and the *Cursor Mundi*. It is more specifically cyclic than the *Biblia Pauperum*, and graphically illustrates many of the episodes familiar from the plays, such as Adam and Eve eating the apple while the serpent watches, and the Torturers stretching the limbs of Christ to fit the holes in the cross, as the York play enacts. Many of the gestures and actions seem highly mobile. There is a sense of dramatic unity about the whole work, particularly as the narrative is arranged in three parts: Genesis to Noah, a Gospel harmony or amalgamation, and the Last Things together with Judgement. It is a lavish production and it is thought that it was intended for a wealthy urban readership, but it is early enough for the text to be still in Anglo-Norman, and it was composed by a Dominican.[2] The book raises the important matter of the interaction between the visual arts and the drama. There must have been a degree of cross-influence: it may not always be possible to show which influenced which, but the one does allow us to appreciate the other.

The critical problem which therefore arises is how to separate or iden-tify the aspects of worship and instruction from elements which might be considered entertainment. The last is more clearly identifiable in the twentieth century as the role of drama, but even here it is not exclusively so. We still go to drama to be entertained, but at the same time to con-template or share perceived truths or patterns of behaviour which we identify as images of life and conduct in a sense which is quasi-religious. And it is clear too that some drama has the function of celebration of qualities and virtues which are held in esteem. We should not overlook that a good deal of the medieval drama also contains condemnation of evil behaviour and a graphic presentation of its consequences; and again such a sense of outrage, sometimes debased to mere sensationalism, is also part of the modern experience of drama. Perhaps the chief difference for the medieval drama was that there was less scope for a variety of inter-pretations of existence, and that orthodoxy was an ever-present feature.

Nevertheless each of the characteristic aspects of the religious drama – its didacticism, its worship and its narrative – were expressed in a wide range of dramatic techniques. Although there was some resistance to drama in clerical circles, it was perceived by many that drama could be very successful as a means of promoting these elements. Hence its tech-niques were developed to a high level of sophistication. We therefore find that in the plays there is much effort expended upon plot, character-isation, satire and emotion, and that techniques were evolved for the extensive use of these whatever the religious objectives. Beyond this there is also the question of how such things as language and gesture, space and time are enlisted to make effective the encounter between text and audi-ence which we designate as performance.

It is convenient to consider plot in two broad categories: those which take on a narrative based upon the Bible or upon a legend which can be taken to be broadly 'true', and those which have a plot which is especially constructed or adapted to bring out a special point of doctrine, usually a moral or political theme. This broad distinction enables us to consider mystery plays and saints plays on the one hand and the allegorical drama of the morality plays on the other. It is true, though, that in these two broad types there is also a need to include characters of particular type to fit in with the kinds of plot here envisaged.

The English mystery cycles present the Christian story from the Creation to Judgement Day, and there is no doubt that the overall design which this narrative implies was highly popular, especially inasmuch as it centred on the Passion of Christ. There is a strong analogue here with the presentation of narrative in visual terms, as can be seen in various picture cycles and in paintings and stained glass which depict on the same canvas the events in the narrative in separate scenes. But the Bible was not the only or the most direct source for the actual narrative; very often it has been discovered that the dramatists used well-known summaries or versions of the traditional narratives, such as the *Stanzaic Life of Christ*, which was influential in the formation of the Chester cycle. At the same time there were individual sections of narrative which could only be found in specific versions which were not scriptural, especially where they involved plots which were not in the Bible but were elaborations built up apocryphally by later writers. Such a work is *The Gospel of Nicodemus*, which contains many details and episodes used in the cycles, such as the restoration of the sight of Longinus, the blind soldier in Crucifixion plays. The significance of this is that the narratives tended to come to the authors with a particular interpretation embedded in them. This can be seen most markedly in such sequences as the plays about the life of Mary in the *N Town* cycle, where the influence is not only in narrative but also in the attitude of worship conveyed, partly by liturgical means.

In characterisation there is also a striking mix of entertainment and instruction, as well as praise. The narrative drama contains many evil characters which often follow a pattern of character developed outside the drama and imported into it, or at least paralleled by iconography. Thus Herod in his rage over failing to kill the infant Christ and being deceived by the Magi rages in the plays to such an extent that his behaviour is a 'performance' and he becomes self-destructive, while in roof bosses he is frequently shown contorted with rage, his legs grotesquely crossed. Here also lies the mockery of evil characters whose language and gestures in the plays are overwhelmingly exaggerated, and whose actions sometimes reveal the frantic over-activity of the damned.

Admiration for good characters portrays them as long-suffering and devoted, responding to the demands of their faith with courage, but also in the cases of Noah and Abraham overcoming some pangs of suffering. The range of virtuous characters is surprisingly large since it includes the prophetic figures of the Old Testament, and those who supported Christ during his ministry and witnessed their faith during his life and after it. Many of these characters are linked in terms of the symbolic qualities which they represent. This typology was established in theological writing outside the drama and incorporated on a large scale. Thus Adam and Isaac are both made to anticipate Christ, the man who suffered. Such figuration pre-dates the plays and is not confined to characters only: it also occurs with events. The saving of the Jews from Pharaoh prefigures the release of souls by Christ in the Harrowing of Hell. These links really form a matrix of experiences which act poetically in the cycle plays, and it seems likely that they formed one of its most engaging features in the recognition and appreciation of what was familiar and reassuring even though threatened.

A pleasure of a different kind arises with the devils who appear in a number of traditional episodes. At a narrative level they are there to be defeated, even though the process includes the fall of man and the various attempts to seduce Christ, and belatedly to prevent the Crucifixion when Satan realises that it will be a defeat for him. Modern productions of the cycles have shown that the devils are much enjoyed by audiences young and old, even though for some there is still a frisson of fear. It is intriguing that the devils would have been considered 'real' in the Middle Ages and yet they were frequently seen in humorous terms.

Liturgical drama

This form of drama has a place in this chapter because it fits in with what has been said about worship, and because it derives largely from the same complex of religious ideas and doctrines. However, its usefulness for our purposes is that it shows an illuminating parallel dramatic mode to the main stream of vernacular drama. It presents several of the episodes found in the cycles, such as the visit of the Marys and the Apostles to the empty tomb; and it often links episodes into a long sequence. It used to be thought that liturgical drama was the origin of the mystery plays, but except for a few possible similarities, this cannot now be accepted. For one thing, it continued throughout the period, and indeed the texts which survive are often fuller after the years when we may suppose that the mystery cycles began.[3] Moreover, the liturgical drama is largely in Latin, chiefly because its function is to represent part of the biblical narrative which is embedded in the services of the Church. The Mass itself has also been held to have certain dramatic elements in processions, showing the sacrament and also in its structure, but the centrality of worship remains critical.

It appears that this kind of drama was always performed in church by clerics or members of an order. Thus it is fitting for three clerics, suitably vested, to pretend to be the three Marys approaching the empty tomb of Christ, and when the Angel asks whom they seek (*Quem quaeritis*), to say that they have come to find Jesus of Nazareth, and to be told that he is not here but has risen, according to his own prediction (*non est hic, surrexit sicut ipse dixit*). This episode is inserted at the appropriate moment in the Mass. Such a context was, of course, international, and as it happens most of the texts of the liturgical drama that have survived are demonstrably from overseas. We can be reasonably sure, however, that liturgical drama was performed in England. The Winchester *Quem quaeritis* is one of the earliest texts to survive (tenth century). There are known to have been performances of various episodes at Salisbury, Hereford, Barking, Lincoln and Chester, some of them stretching into the sixteenth century, until they were suppressed in 1548 under the Protestant regime of Edward VI. The most popular topics besides the Visit to the Tomb were the Prophets, the Shepherds, Herod, Lazarus, the Journey to Emmaus, Ascension and Pentecost. The Visit to the Tomb remained a central feature, perhaps because it concentrated upon the Resurrection as celebrated in the services on Easter morning. As this form of drama grew, some of the plays comprised several episodes and it is thought that the *Passion Play* (*c.* 1180) from the monastery of Benediktbeuern in Bavaria may have taken two hours to perform.[4] It covers events from Christ's appearance before Pilate through the Crucifixion to the point where Pilate agrees to the burial. The Visit to the Stable may have developed as an imitation of the Visit to the Tomb, and it certainly proved itself capable of more extensive development. It is clear that in some places liturgical plays became divorced from the exact place in the services for which they were developed, but the intention and the place of performance remained essentially ecclesiastical.

One characteristic which marks off the liturgical drama is that it is sung, not spoken. This means that the musical form is an important contributor to the overall effect, even where what is portrayed is an exchange of 'dialogue' between characters. Most of the words are taken directly from the Vulgate, and there must inevitably have been a recognition of this origin among those who heard them. The performances of these dramas did contain dramatic elements. Very explicit stage directions embodied movement in imitation of real life (such as seeking cautiously, or kneeling), dress, and even smell in the form of incense, which was used in the episode where Mary Magdalene buys ointment, and in the approach of the Marys to the tomb. The costumes, however, were limited to ecclesiastical garments, especially copes and albs, even for the women's parts.

The greatest objection to considering these plays as drama is that the role of the audience was markedly different – assuming that there actually was one. The performance as part of the service must have forced those present to be more of a congregation of worshippers than a theatre audience. There is no doubt that some of this drama was done in closed communities when there might be very few spectators, and those who were there could well have been members of the order. The performance, in other words, was not directed at the spectators. Like all religious ceremony, the liturgical drama is directed towards God. There is also the question of the layout of the church. It is possible to envisage that performances may have taken place in or near the sanctuary, really quite remote from a congregation, even though the music might have been audible. In spite of the complexity of some texts which have close inter-action of character and mood, there is a strong sense that the drama of these plays was subordinate to the purpose of worship which was the main intention of the participants.

On the dramatic side of the argument, however, it is clear that the music, the movement and the words were arranged in order to excite emo-tion. At times such episodes are put into lyric forms so that the dramatic effect is nearer to an operatic aria than a dramatic speech. The ritualistic element would be a means of controlling the action and the response to it. Many of the plays have processions as part of their action, and in these one of the chief functions, the celebration of Christ's acts, is made very plain.

There were some interesting developments of the liturgical drama where the emphasis shifted. In the Anglo-Norman *Adam* the performance has moved outside the church, and the action has become more clearly a per-formance with human characters and a closely written spoken dialogue, though there are still quotations from the liturgy. The *Shrewsbury Fragments* are somewhat later. They consist of the English parts of one actor in three separate plays: Shepherds, Visit to the Tomb, and the Journey to Emmaus. The manuscript (early fifteenth century) also preserves Latin hymns of a liturgical nature, which makes it clear that these plays were intended for an ecclesiastical setting. The Shepherds fragment is very like parts of the Shepherds play in the *York* cycle.[5] Things took a more comic turn with the *Feast of Fools* or the *Feast of the Asses* at which, in the Christmas season, the actions and words of the official liturgy were parodied by the least important members of the ecclesiastical community. Sausages played a comic part in these rites; asses were brought into the church, and anthems such as the *Gloria* begun normally in plainsong were made to end with the sound of braying. These parodies earned much condemnation from the authorities, but they clearly went on inside church communities for many years.[6] Such items illustrate the strength and diversity of this form of drama, and an awareness of it may have had some influence upon the development of the vernacular forms, but it is a sophisticated activity with its own norms and conventions.

Notes

1. *Biblia Pauperum*, A facsimile and edition by Avril Henry (Aldershot, 1987): the information which follows is derived from the introduction.

2. W.O. Hassall (ed.) *The Holkham Bible Picture Book* (London, 1954), pp. 31–45.

3. The main attack upon the older theory of continuity is by O.B. Hardison, Jr, *Christian Rite and Christian Drama in the Middle Ages* (Baltimore, 1965), pp. 1–34.

4. P. Dronke (ed. and trans.) *Nine Medieval Latin Plays* (Cambridge, 1994), p. 185.

5. See N. Davis (ed.) *Non-Cycle Plays and Fragments* EETS SS1 (Oxford, 1970), for text pp. 1–7, and commentary pp. xiv–xix.

6. *MS* 1.275–300.

Chapter 4

Texts of Mystery Plays and Moralities

I

In the light of the common features underlying all the medieval drama explored in Chapter 3 we consider in this chapter the five extant mystery cycles which share many episodes. In spite of all objections, it does seem that the Creation to Doomsday configuration was widely appreciated in England. However, the surviving texts have many individual features, and in order to interpret them we shall discuss the purpose for which each manuscript was made. The differences are remarkable enough to make it always necessary to be cautious about assuming that things were uniform in those cities where a cycle was at some time performed.

The first problem is unity and coherence. The medieval view of authorship was less individualised than it is today. Often the process was an accumulation of material from other writers, and the skill of the 'compiler' lay in the re-arrangement of it so as to construct meaning. In such circumstances, it was usually convenient to rely upon conventional features as a framework. Medieval works of great size did not necessarily have the kind of unity we have come to expect from post-Renaissance works such as *Paradise Lost*. The analogy of the way medieval cathedrals have grown up over many years, without the original architects having a clear concept of how they would eventually be developed has frequently been evoked. Even though there may be a degree of uniformity over the scribes' handwriting in the manuscripts, this actually may conceal the fact that the texts consist of sections composed at different times by different authors. Indeed, one can see attempts being made to give some of the cycle manuscripts the appearance of unity in spite of the extensive revision and re-writing which is a feature of most of them. In considering the manuscripts, it is also useful to try to establish not only why they were made, but also what use was made of them once they were in being. To make a manuscript for a large play was a considerable task and one that it would not necessarily be convenient to repeat too often.

There is very little sign of the existence of the vernacular cycles before 1375. Their evolution was probably associated with the establishment of the feast of Corpus Christi by Pope Clement V in 1311, to be celebrated on the first Thursday after Trinity Sunday. Depending on the date of Easter, it could occur from 23 May to 24 June. From this flowed Corpus Christi processions and eventually, by a process which is neither clearly established nor uniform, came the plays presented in processional form on pageant wagons at Coventry, York and Chester and a number of other places. Large cycle plays also appeared on the Continent at about the same time, but there is little evidence that they were close to the English model as far as processional performance on pageant wagons was concerned, nor is it apparent that the establishment of Corpus Christi played a significant role in their development. In contrast to the English cycles, most continental ones concentrate markedly and exclusively upon the Passion. What is in common, however, is that the resources of some towns and cities were used by the local authorities in England, Germany, the Netherlands and France to finance or facilitate the performances on a large scale out of a mixture of devotion and civic pride: this intention was frequently declared in prologues and in documents related to the production.

Once the authorities were thus engaged we find a clue as to why written texts were necessitated, but it should first be noted that the mystery plays existed primarily as an oral form. Though they may have been written down as individual plays by an unknown variety of authors at various times from late in the fourteenth century onwards, they were not initially written down for the purpose of being books to read so much as adjuncts to performance in some way. This means that originally the texts of individual plays were acting scripts rather than anything which we would now describe as 'literature' (the earliest use of this word in the modern sense is no earlier than 1812 in *OED* 3). It should be added that some help in establishing how the cycles were evolved can also be found in civic records over a long period, though records were usually made by authorities for such purposes as to record expenditure, to enact settlements of disputes, to keep the peace, and to stabilise contracts. Civic records were not created to tell us specifically about the nature of the drama or how successful it was.

We have most certainty about the nature of the text of the York cycle, and it also happens that the York records can on occasions be dovetailed in to show much about its development.[1] The first mention of any element is the storage of three pageant wagons in 1376, but the first detailed list of pageants as they were distributed for performance and paid for by the craft guilds of the city does not appear until the Ordo Paginarum made by Roger Burton, the Clerk, in 1415. Another list made at about the same time names fifty-six plays. From about this time there seems to have been an annual performance upon Corpus Christi, but the only text we have is the manuscript which was probably written as late as 1463 to 1477 when the plays may have been about a hundred years old.[2] The contents show that considerable changes had been made since the list of 1415, changes which depended upon a variety of causes, not least the variable economic fortunes of the guilds themselves. It does not seem likely that there was any previous central version of the play, and the creation of the manuscript was almost certainly the result of a decision by the authorities to establish an official text. Once it was set up, the manuscript became an official Register which was apparently used in the sixteenth century on the day of the performance at the first station of the procession as some kind of check on the proceedings. Moreover, it was monitored so that additions and corrections, some of them quite small, such as music cues or individual word changes, were entered into it.[3] Under the impact of the Reformation some plays were not performed in the sixteenth century, particularly three relating to Mary which still stand but are marked for omission. However, this implies that the manuscript had a very long life after its inception, and it suggests that some of the individual pageants remained fairly stable over a long period. There is no incontrovertible evidence that the whole cycle as recorded in the Register was ever actually performed on one occasion. Indeed there is some possibility that there might have been a variable selection from year to year.

There may have been an equally early start at Chester, but the first extant evidence for the existence of plays is a dispute between the Ironmongers and Fletchers in 1422 over who should have responsibility for the play of the *Flagellation*.[4] This indicates that a cycle was in existence and that there was a central text, the 'Original'. There was a period of expansion after 1521 when the date of performance was shifted from Corpus Christi to the Monday, Tuesday and Wednesday of Whitsun week. From about 1531 the cycle was known as the Whitsun plays. Like the arrangement at York, the plays were performed processionally by craft guilds, but it appears that the performances were never on the annual basis which was usually the case at York. There were only twenty-four plays at Chester, though each tends to be longer, and they were performed at fewer stations.

In other ways the Chester text is markedly different from those at York. We know it in its cyclic form from five manuscripts which all date from the years 1591 to 1607. They probably derive from the (now lost) Original, but in this case this was a kind of catalogue from which the guilds copied their plays, in return for a fee, and they were instructed which play to perform by the central authority. With the rarer performances and the fact that it is quite likely that the successive performances did not necessarily contain the same elements, it emerges that the whole cycle, as in any of the manuscripts, may never have been performed and therefore the integrity of the cycle becomes somewhat notional. The late date of the manuscripts also means that in some senses they are Elizabethan rather than medieval, even though they are the work of what was primarily an antiquarian or even a political interest, and this may give rise to some uneasiness about what exactly went on during the many years of performance. It has been felt that the genesis of the Chester text lies more firmly in spectacle than in the words for their own sake.[5] By contrast, there may be more variety in the York cycle, which suggests the work of a number of poets who were able to integrate their writing into a more explicitly verbal whole. Such a feature at Chester is all the more surprising since it implies an intention to interrelate plays in an aural sequence, and a supposition that listeners would be able to make the sort of connections we now make with written texts.

The last performance at Chester was in 1575. As at York, and indeed at other places, the cycles were suppressed because the Corpus Christi plays had come to be seen by the authorities as part of the Old Religion.

With the texts of the other two cycles in English we come a little nearer to the modern notion of a book, but the relationship of these two texts to processional performance by craft guilds is more remote. We cannot be sure that either of these cycles was ever performed in the form in which it appears in the manuscript: or perhaps we should say that if there are doubts about what actually happened at York and Chester, the doubts about *N Town* and *Towneley* are even greater. However, the discussion about staging in the next chapter will be concerned with the unquestionable performance qualities of all four cycles.

In the case of *N Town*[6] which originates in East Anglia near the Norfolk/Suffolk border, it is evident from stage directions that this cycle was not performed processionally on wagons, and there is absolutely nothing in the manuscript to associate the plays with craft guilds. Moreover, it has not proved possible to associate this manuscript with any town or city likely to have the resources to mount a performance of such an ambitious cycle.[7] The text itself is chiefly the work of one scribe who also is the compiler, and it has been carefully arranged to appear a continuous whole as though it were necessary or desirable for the work to have the appearance of unity. Prefixed to the plays is a set of Banns or a Proclamation detailing the contents of the individual plays. These are not accurate, however, and the inconsistencies between them and the individual plays mark the insecure coherence of the cycle as a whole. When it comes to the way the manuscript was made up, however, it is remarkable that some parts of it – notably, what is labelled Passion Play I – actually had a separate physical existence presumably before the codex was assembled in its present form, and this in spite of the fact that this section is in the hand of the same scribe as that of the rest of the manuscript. Thus one interpretation of the state of this text is that it was assembled from different sources, with sections requiring different forms of staging, and put together as a catalogue or perhaps as an anthology from which those interested in producing a play might choose suitable parts. In short, there are some features of this manuscript which suggest that its *raison d'être* was somewhat similar to that assumed for the lost Original at Chester: to be a source for decisions and choices about performance. It is particularly striking if the cycle was compiled in this way that it was made to conform to the idea of a cycle quite like York and Chester even though there are some variations and omissions.

As a manuscript of a play cycle this is possibly the oldest English language version. It bears the date 1468 in one place, but as this is not at the beginning it may refer only to a smaller segment. But since we have little evidence for its provenance or context, and since the manuscript shows signs of being assembled according to a plan, it is substantially a text with a different purpose from the others. Its compilation appears to depend upon the *idea* of cycle plays already in existence and famous as at York and Coventry. However, we shall see that embedded in it are many stage directions, suggesting that some of the compiler's sources may have been tested on stage, presumably somewhere in East Anglia.

The *Towneley* cycle, named after the Catholic family who owned the text for many years, is associated with Wakefield in Yorkshire, and it is the most impressive of all to look at since it is ornamented with red ink and with highly decorated capitals for each play. The name 'Wakefield' appears twice in the manuscript and four plays are attributed to guilds, by an admittedly later hand than the original scribe who wrote most of the text around the year 1500. There are external scraps of evidence which suggest that Wakefield did have a Corpus Christi play before 1557, but the manuscript itself gives no indication of a processional performance. The text itself is uneven dramatically. Five of the plays also appear in the York cycle, corresponding word for word in places, but there are also revisions and expansions within these borrowed texts. A few others also contain York material, and it is of interest that some of the borrowed elements may pre-date the versions copied into the York Register. The cycle contains five plays, which are substantially the work of the gifted dramatist who has subsequently come to be known as the Wakefield Master. He is also thought to have contributed to eight other plays. The extent to which he revised the whole cycle, however, has become a matter of controversy. Much of his work is written in a thirteen-line stanza which has come to be regarded as his signature. The copy has little in it to suggest that it was ever in close relationship with actual performance. If it is therefore a compilation for some other purpose, as the splendid appearance suggests, it seems that the compiler may have been following the example of other cycles, particularly York, which is but a few miles away, and sought to manufacture a cycle out of some local elements. It is possible that the compilation was an attempt to promote performance of the cycle as a whole by drawing together plays from different situations, possibly some from local parishes. There are some unusual omissions from the traditional sequence, and some plays were physically cut out of the manuscript in the interests of the Reformation.

To all this we need to add that there were certainly other (lost) cycles of plays at Coventry and Beverley, so that it remains a puzzle where the English cycle plays were first conceived, and when that would have been. There are a number of extant individual plays which were certainly part of a lost cycle such as the two Coventry Pageants, and some which may have been, such as the Newcastle *Noah* play, the Northampton *Abraham and Isaac* and the Norwich Grocers' *Adam and Eve*, which was performed on a cart. Some of these exist only in late copies. The *Abraham and Isaac* from Brome, a small village in Suffolk, is written in a hand not later than 1454. It is apparently a single play, though it has many lines in common with the Chester play on the same subject, and it is thought that the latter derives either from the Brome play or from a lost earlier version of it. The existence of these separate or separated episodes argues that the concept of a cycle was widespread whether or not attempts to achieve it were successful. Moreover, the fragmentary evidence we have of developments and enlargements later than the fourteenth century suggests that copying or deriving from other cycles went on for a long period. But in any case the life of the full cycles appears to be about 200 years from 1375 until they were suppressed by the Elizabethan authorities. The texts we have – immensely impressive as they are – give us incomplete glimpses into the full range of what actually went on.

The fifth cycle of plays based upon a narrative of the history of the world is the Cornish *Ordinalia*, which was written in Middle Cornish in the first half of the fifteenth century. If this ascription is correct, it is the earliest of the extant texts. It follows the cyclic pattern somewhat loosely, being divided into three roughly equal sections: *Origo Mundi* (The Beginning of the World), *Passio Christi* (The Passion of Christ) and *Resurrexio Domini* (The Resurrection of the Lord). Many of the episodes are in common with those in the other cycles, though it does not extend to Judgement. There is special emphasis upon some aspects reminiscent of the French *Passions*, especially the story of Adam's son, Seth, and also the narrative of Christ's death (there is no Nativity sequence). However, investigation of the sources has shown that the cycle draws upon material common to other cycles such as *The Gospel of Nicodemus* and *The Northern Passion*. The text originates from near Penryn, possibly from the Collegiate Church at Glasney. There is a good deal of internal information about staging; for example, there are staging diagrams, and plenty of stage directions about preparation of properties and movement. At one dramatic moment after Adam and Eve have left Paradise the stage direction reads, 'And he shall dig and the earth cries out, and again he shall dig and the earth cries out' (Norris I.28: translated).[8] The performance, which lasted three days, was not processional but took place in a *plen an gwary* ('playing place'), one of the Cornish rounds with a large central open space and scaffolds for the leading characters. There is no suggestion that the play was performed by guilds, or indeed that its context was a large town or city, like some of the English cycles.

From Cornwall there also survives *The Creacion of the World* (also known as *Gwreans an Bys*), which was copied in 1611 probably from a mid-sixteenth-century manuscript in late Middle Cornish. The original circumstances of its composition are not clear, but the text is remarkably rich in information about staging. Nothing is known about how much is lost to complete this play. As it stands, it takes the biblical narrative only as far as the end of the Noah episode. At the end, however, there is an invitation to 'Come tomorrow on time' when, among other matters, the Redemption would be shown: possibly there might have been several other days of performance, as in the French *Passions*, since this text deals with the events in a detailed manner. Though there are some echoes from the *Ordinalia*, the *Creacion* is considered to be an independent work.

The Cornish *Beunans Meriasek* (St Meriasek), which survives in a manuscript dated 1504, is one of the few survivals of the Saint plays which were undoubtedly very common in England and in France. Many texts seem to have disappeared at the Reformation. This Cornish play has its sources in Brittany, where Meriasek reputedly lived, but the material is essentially legendary. The dramatic purpose is to show the miraculous events of the hero's life, such as curing a blind man and a cripple, and taming a wolf, as well as showing events in the life of St Sylvester.[9] The play deals with Meriasek's life from childhood, and it was written for performance over two days.

The two surviving Saint plays in English, *Mary Magdalene* and *The Conversion of Saint Paul*, are found in the Digby MS 133 in the Bodleian Library. The former has a very large scope, combining apocryphal legendary adventures, including a journey to Marseilles, and her ultimate apotheosis from her life in the desert, with the limited events related in the Bible. It was written for performance on a large scale though its auspices are not apparent. It requires a place and scaffold type of production and it may have been divided for performance on two days. By contrast, *The Conversion of Saint Paul* draws chiefly upon scriptural details and presents a terse but effective account of Paul's conversion and subsequent miraculous deeds. The staging demands are relatively simple, though it does need two locations. One scene showing the despair of Belial and other devils is an interpolation by a different hand.

II

The morality plays present different problems with regard to text and provenance. Because there are so few of them it is also difficult to generalise
about what went on. Not only has the REED project shown that there
are few 'new' mystery plays, it has also shown, so far, that there is no
evidence to suppose that a large number of moralities have disappeared, or
that they were *commonly* performed in towns and villages up and down the
country as part of the staple of drama. Moralities are distinguished by the
opportunity for their authors to make up a plot for their own objectives.
In the process they may make use of well-known structures, such as fall
and rise, and also patterns of ideas and images such as the Coming of Death,
or the siege of a Castle of Virtue which can be widely found in theological literature. Indeed it is the recognition of the universality of these kinds
of symbol which may give them their particular force. Because they use
characters which represent types or abstractions, another opportunity for
invention or for following well-known conventions, they are commonly
known as allegorical, though this term will be discussed in Chapter 6.

The main purpose with regard to the five surviving moralities in this
chapter is to establish the nature and provenance of the texts, and the
position is much simpler than for the mystery cycles because there are so
few to consider. The earliest, given the title *The Pride of Life* by James
Mills who edited the play in 1891, was preserved as a fragment of some
502 lines. It was copied in Ireland by two scribes, one of whom was
probably working from dictation. Both scribes used some Irish ortho-
graphy, but it is thought, from place-names and from some linguistic
forms, that the exemplar (or original) may have been English, originating
in the south-west Midlands. The play may have been composed as early
as the middle of the fourteenth century, which makes it the earliest extant
example of drama in English, apart from some much smaller fragments
which may be earlier.

Though the second half of the play is lost, there is fortunately a Prologue which summarises the plot. The theme of the morality is the
Coming of Death, who is to appear as a King towards the end of the play,
with disastrous results. The action we have shows the King of Life, the
hero, boasting of his power in spite of warnings by his wife and the
Bishop, and it breaks off as his Messenger issues a challenge to the King of
Death. The threat is given in the Prologue:

Deth comith, he dremith a dredfful dreme –
Welle aȝte al carye;   *should all be anxious*
And slow fader and moder and þen heme: *slew,   uncle*
He ne wold none sparye.   *spare*

(81–4)

Apparently the King of Life was to be rescued by the intercession of Mary. There is sufficient here to show that the play exemplifies orthodox doctrine about preparation for death, a theme which appears in at least two of the other surviving moralities, as well as widely in many other artistic forms, including the Dance of Death.

Three of the other moralities, *The Castle of Perseverance*, *Mankind* and *Wisdom*, appear in one manuscript, which is known as the Macro plays after its eighteenth-century owner, who may have been responsible for having them bound together. It is apparent that they all are associated with East Anglia. Although the last two had the same owners during the Tudor period, and although the work of the same scribe appears in both, the three plays were written out separately, and by means of the watermarks they can be shown to be independent. The survival of these plays, along with the East Anglian aspects of the *N Town* cycle and the Digby *Mary Magdalene*, *The Croxton Play of the Sacrament* and a number of other plays and fragments, has led to a realisation that this area must be recognised as one of the most important in the development of the early drama. Possibly the relative prosperity of the medieval wool trade, and indeed other links with the Low Countries, led to a willingness to encourage drama. Certainly the staging of these dramas suggests that plays were performed in a variety of ways and in a variety of locations, some urban, some rural. Only Norwich and Ipswich are likely to have provided a developed urban context.

Perseverance is the most substantial of the three, having 3,649 lines. The text is the work of one scribe, and though some attempt has been made to suggest that the Banns at the beginning and the Debate of the Four Daughters of God with which the play ends could have been written by separate authors, it seems most likely that the work was written by one poet. Certainly the language and what may be called its dramatic style – the ways in which performance is implied in the text as in the use of scaffolds in relation to the lower playing area – suggest that it is the result of one imaginative act.

The play is remarkable for its inclusion of a number of devices and figures which are common to medieval preaching and which encapsulate religious attitudes: these include the Seven Deadly Sins and the corresponding Seven Virtues, the World, the Flesh and the Devil, the Four Daughters of God. The action shows the fall and rise configuration associated with falling into sin and being redeemed, the chief adversary of man being Avarice. It also contains the Coming of Death. Most of these set pieces are realised in allegorical mode which sets out to show the force of the ideas concerned. Central to the action is the siege of the Castle defended by the Virtues, and attacked by the Sins in an attempt to force Mankind out. The play is a remarkable translation into dramatic terms – involving visual elements, movement, a sense of place centred on the scaffolds of principal characters, and overall structure of great simplicity and force which in the end shows that God's mercy extends to Mankind because he asked for it at the moment of his death. The staging will be dealt with more fully in the next chapter, but it is clear that this author at least envisaged a production in much detail, and the manuscript as it stands is one of the most important in the whole corpus of medieval drama for the way it envisages dramatic activity. The Banns seem to suggest that this text was used by a travelling company, though in truth it is difficult to imagine that so large a play requiring the complex staging demanded by the accompanying diagram could really be itinerant. However, there are some similarities with the large-scale French *moralités*, and there is evidence that these were done in more than one city in the fifteenth century. The *Perseverance* diagram is an invaluable survival. It shows the Castle in the central space, and around the circumference are the scaffolds of World (west), Flesh (south), God (east), Avarice (north-east), and Belial the Devil (north).

Mankind (1465–70) is a much shorter play and almost certainly would lend itself to itinerant production. The manuscript refers to a number of towns and villages in Cambridgeshire, Suffolk and Norfolk, and the play requires virtually nothing for its set. The action is intimate, informal and impertinent. Its author was keenly aware of the vitality of language both as a means of persuasion towards virtue, and as a way of showing depravity, particularly idleness, which is a leading theme of the play. Thus there is an impressive sermon in the text, as well as some outspoken mockery of it. Such a theme may be appropriate to Shrovetide when the play is thought to have been performed.

Like all moralities in which the objective is to prove or demonstrate a moral point, the success of the play is in part linked to the skill in devising a plot. In outline it is about fall and redemption, which is perhaps the commonest configuration of events, but here we are shown in great detail the means by which Mankind is led into evil ways, which include neglecting the religious duties enjoined upon him by the priestlike Mercy. The villains, Newguise, Nowadays and Nought, are given much lively stage business and they are also required to build up a close relationship with the audience, who are in some sense their victims. But the most successful evil character, the one who produces results, is the devil Titivillus who appears with a grotesque mask and a net. He has a close link traditionally with the abuse and misappropriation of language. The linguistic sophistication suggests a learned author, perhaps from the university, even though the performance might have been rural.

The scribe who made the manuscript of *Wisdom*, the third of these Macro plays (c. 1460) was also responsible for most of the manuscript of *Mankind*, and there is good reason to suppose that he was Thomas Hyngham, a monk of Bury St Edmunds. The play's highly symbolic nature, and its elaborate language, is accompanied by some emblematic action, including dancing. The nature of this sophistication has led to suggestions that it was associated with lawyers, or with a religious house, but this has been given greater point by the recent suggestion that the play is at least in part a satire upon the political and economic activity of John de la Pole, Duke of Suffolk, and his relatives, and that its creation was an attempt to intervene in local politics. This view is partly connected with livery and heraldic devices, especially the lion, which was one of Suffolk's devices.[10]

The status of *Everyman* is anomalous. It has been shown to be Dutch in origin, having been composed for a Rhetoricians' Chamber where it was customary to present plays on themes, like a debate, or a competition. Though the original proposition is not known for certain, it may very well have been the problem of what is of most use to a human at the coming of death, a theme which we have noted elsewhere. The value of the play as an insight into medieval drama has perhaps been made problematic since it was the first such play to be revived in modern times, and the insight it gave has been taken as axiomatic, even though it is more typical of the Dutch than of the English. The play survives only in printed form: there were four editions in the early sixteenth century. None of them shows much evidence of performance.

The geographical distribution of the medieval drama available to us is such that we may conclude that in the fifteenth and sixteenth centuries there was vigorous activity in Cornwall, in towns and cities of the Midlands and the North, and in East Anglia. In other parts of England the absence of surviving texts does not, however, argue that there was no such drama: indeed, there are indications to the contrary.

The surviving texts of medieval drama are nearly all manuscripts. We need always to bear in mind that scribes would have different objectives in mind, and these are not necessarily close to the process of printing and duplicating a book for wide distribution among readers. Sometimes the manuscripts were made to record what had happened in performance. Sometimes they were an attempt to stabilise text or to prevent change. Sometimes they may have been written before a performance as a means of creating it, or even as a means of offering opportunities for selection. Sometimes the manuscripts have the appearance of being generated for study or presentation rather than performance. Similarly we need to look very carefully at stage directions as it is not always possible to tell whether they are records or proposals. This doubt will persist into the later period when we encounter printed texts more commonly.

Notes

1. The REED project (Records of Early English Drama based at Toronto) is surveying and printing dramatic and musical records up to 1642. Volumes for

York, Coventry and Chester are most relevant to this discussion. For details of these and of the drama texts used, see Abbreviations.

2. British Library MS Additional 35290, originally containing 46 pageants.

3. P. Meredith, 'John Clerke's Hand in the York Register', *Leeds Studies in English* 12 (1981), 59–73.

4. For a transcription of the relevant document, see R.M. Lumiansky and D. Mills, *The Chester Mystery Cycle: Facts and Documents* (Chapel Hill, NC, 1983), pp. 204–5.

5. A.F. Johnston, *Editing Early English Drama* (New York, 1987), p. 127.

6. British Library MS Cotton Vespasian D VIII. The name derives from the Banns or Proclamation which promise that the plays will be performed at 'N Town', an unspecified and still unidentified location. This cycle has also been called *Ludus Coventriae* (though it has nothing to do with Coventry), and the *Hegge Plays* from a name on the manuscript.

7. The most convincing ascription so far is to Thetford in Norfolk: see A.J. Fletcher, 'The N-Town Plays', in *Companion*, 163–88 (166–7).

8. Quoted by J.A. Bakere, *The Cornish Ordinalia* (Cardiff, 1980), p. 156. See 'Staging', pp. 151–69.

9. See *Beunans Meriasek*, edited and translated by W. Stokes (London, 1972), ll. 534–58, and 1103–1127.

10. J. Marshall, 'The satirizing of the Suffolks in *Wisdom*', *METh* 14 (1992), 37–66.

Chapter 5
Staging

In this chapter we shall be concerned with some practical aspects of staging the medieval drama, especially in the light of the previous discussion about the nature of the surviving texts. Not all of them provide explicit details of even the simplest aspects of staging, and there is usually much room for conjecture. But it is possible to see that the dramatists had or developed sophisticated devices for establishing contact with audiences. This implies a sense of a relationship between audience and play, even to the point of considering what the physical nature of the contacts between actor and audience might have been. Underlying this there may also have been matters of social class in that some forms of medieval drama had distinctive social functions, being addressed to all classes or perhaps only to selected groups.

Even though most medieval actors were amateurs this does not seem to have prevented the evolution of very demanding roles, suggesting a high degree of acting skills, though this could be eased to some extent by stylisation of roles or characters. Alongside this goes some remarkable expectation about what could be achieved by complex staging effects. Both these aspects are present whether the performance was indoors or in the open air. However, staging was often determined not by realistic criteria so much as by the method of how to exploit acting spaces, large or small – and we had better not speak of stages since that can be rather misleading as to the physical nature of the acting space – and often by a symbolic use of the space or spaces available. Stage space could and did carry a meaning in itself whatever the action which was to take place upon it.

Consideration of staging should not be confined to the actors, to the space in which they performed, and to the audience. There are also important aspects of performance such as costume, properties, music, as well as variations in dramatic speech and the groupings or configurations of characters as they appear in the action. All these features emphasise that the plays were by no means simply a matter of text: there was – as there always is – an interpretative process in staging which was presumably of equal importance in the effectiveness of the performance, and one cannot judge the success of medieval plays simply by regarding them as though they were books for reading rather than as scripts which needed perform- ance to realise their full potential. After all, in any theatre some of the most important theatrical effects are achieved by an absence of words when a host of other staging considerations come into effect. Even in a theatrical culture where there were powerful overriding moral, religious or even political requirements which had to be met, it is still true that a judgement about what could be achieved on stage had to be made. The success of this depended upon a great deal of experience of stage condi- tions even though the creators and performers might technically have been amateurs. And it is true that we can only perceive somewhat vaguely the role of director which now seems so important in imagining and bringing about a performance.[1] Probably performers were highly depend- ent upon traditions and practices which had been built up over genera- tions. This would especially appear to be the case in the circumstances controlling the guilds' preparation of the cycles at such places as York, Chester and Coventry: handing on skills and practices within a guild from father to son seems a distinct possibility.

Broadly speaking we need to consider four types of staging: perform- ances on pageant wagons which can be substantiated in some detail at York, Chester, Coventry and Norwich; open-air performances with some fixed locations with some kind of construction and a useful largish space between for action and movements (often known as *place and scaffold* staging); the halls of great houses, and colleges which had roughly the same configuration; and the unlocalised, even impromptu staging which could be set up by itinerant actors who really required very little beyond a space with the audience around to watch them. For all these we shall need to consider the layout of the stage, the placing of the audience, the conduct of the actors, and some special effects. One of the most challeng- ing aspects in considering the staging of medieval and Tudor plays is to bear in mind that these different forms were in use more or less through- out the period.

I

The use of pageant wagons may have arisen from the Corpus Christi procession which allowed various bodies such as guilds to present them- selves throughout the streets of a city to a large number of spectators. The route itself might be significant, especially where it started and where it ended, and for the spectators it allowed a large number to see and to be seen in the perennial way of audiences in terms of public esteem and civic honour. The increasing importance of processional entries to cities by kings and rulers enabled a large variety of artistic effects to be presented to the eminent visitor, often with reference to local myths and legends. (For further details, see Chapter 10.) Processional staging shared with such enterprises the necessity or indeed the desirability of spending large sums of money to embellish such important civic events.

Though we do not have any reliable pictures of English wagons, it is likely that they did not follow a standard pattern. The most important controlling requirements would be that they should be large enough to contain a significant number of actors and small enough to be man-oeuvred through the narrow streets of medieval cities like York. They would also have to be high enough to be seen over the heads of spectators, some of whom would be standing at street level. Some descriptions of the wagons at Chester make it likely that they could have two storeys, or perhaps even more, so that the lower level of action was high enough to be seen by people standing in the street, and there could a higher level for parts of the performance as required. The actual shape of the wagons could vary considerably, though once again we should here recollect that the performances went on over a period of about 200 years and many variations were no doubt made to meet different requirements, and as technology evolved. The illustration from Brussels of the Triumphs of Isabella in 1615 shows that on that occasion wagons were made in the form of a ship, or a tree of Jesse, or a stable with a roof on top: so the idea of a two-level box on four wheels found in some antiquarian reconstruc-tions does seem unnecessarily restrictive.[2]

The staging of the cycles at York, Chester and Coventry required that the wagons moved round a set route, stopping at fixed locations called stations, for the performance of each play in turn. As there are known to have been up to fifty-two pageants at York, it has caused some concern that even if, as is attested, a start was made by the first play at the first station, Holy Trinity Priory, Mickelgate, at 4.30 a.m., it would be well after midnight before the last play, Doomsday, was completed at the last station on the Pavement. Nevertheless, it may have been so: but two ways of minimising the difficulties may have been that some plays such as the Shepherds and the Nativity could be done in tandem, and also it may not have been found expedient or desirable to do all the plays every year.[3] Whatever was the solution at York, the difficulty was not so apparent at Chester, where the number of plays was smaller, there were fewer stations, and, eventually, as we have noted, the performance was transferred to three days at Whitsuntide. The information about the wagons does not come from the plays themselves: it has to be reconstructed and re-interpreted mostly from records at the cities concerned. This has one important disadvantage since many of the records are not directly concerned with describing the appearance of the pageants: the concern is more likely to be about materials, cost, and with what to do about difficulties arising in specific guilds. However, at York the Mercers' inventory for their pageant has come to light, and it shows that there was a lifting device to be incorporated into the construction: such a device strengthens the belief that performances on the pageant wagons could be on two levels.

Once the wagon was in position at the station the performance could take place on its various levels, or down on the street level. For the Doomsday play there was a separate place designated for the souls and there may have been a hell mouth separate from the main wagon. The famous stage direction in the Coventry *Shearmen and Tailors Play* indicates that Herod at least descended to extend the performing of his spectacular rage 'in the street also' (783 s.d.). (The manuscript, now lost, was copied in 1534.) In the Mason's play of the Magi at York horses were used. However, apart from such striking incidents there was a great variety of events in the plays which did take place upon the wagons: conversations, exhortations, interrogations, adorations, blessings. There was often a throne on the wagon from which Pilate, or Herod or Pharaoh could conduct business. The initial impression of each pageant would be crucial in establishing a mood, and similarly the plays may end with blessings, threats, liturgical music, and a sense of going away to the next event. The Mercers' contract indicated that there was also decoration of the wagons, so that one of the possible ways in which the plays on pageants made their impact was a visual or pictorial one. This could have been intensified because the pageants may have played 'end-on' in the narrow streets rather than across their broader sides. As each event arrived on its wagon, the audience would have to adjust to a new configuration, and sometimes to widely differing number of performers: all the disciples on stage for the Last Supper, or just Mary Magdalene and Christ in the garden. No doubt the Harrowing of Hell would be based upon some kind of battlement from which the Devil could first taunt Christ, and from which after Christ's assault the souls could be released from Purgatory.

Turning more specifically to the audience, some of them could be very close indeed to the actors and therefore a deep sense of being near to wondrous events would be generated. However, some evidence suggests that at York eminent citizens would pay to have a station at their houses so that they and their guests could look down on the action of each play from an upper level. Possibly some such citizens might also be entrepreneurs with a scaffold of seats at the station which could be hired out. It is important, once again, not to assume that there was uniformity at the individual stations, especially as the lie of the streets and corners differed. Quite possibly each station was out of sight of the previous one, but nevertheless there would arise a sense of the goings-on at adjacent stations, and we may suspect that this sense of the whole city being involved in a festive way on the day of the performance was an overriding one.

This peripheral or even subliminal awareness has proved to be quite striking in the modern revivals of processional performance of the Chester and York cycles. The impression might be intensified as some events were enacted, narrated or recalled in successive pageants.

There were so many stations that the audience would naturally be able to choose which one to watch at, and there appears to be no reason why the spectators should not move about from one station to another. Because the streets were so narrow, and even the crossroads such as Minster gates at York were fairly small, the size of an audience at each pageant was probably not more that 200 or so. This would have dividends in visibility and audibility.

The actors were presumably all guild members, and at York it was the responsibility of the guilds to ensure that a good enough standard was achieved – fines were imposed if not. There was a spirit of competition between the guilds,[4] and from year to year some continuity would develop as to who played each part. Indeed the individual guilds would probably evolve ways in which they thought it fit to present their play from time to time. Usually there is one or perhaps two larger parts, and also opportunities for lesser roles for less distinguished or less experienced actors. However, in the York Conspiracy there is a well-developed contrast between Annas and Caiaphas in the dialogue. At Chester, but not at York, there are sometimes Expositor roles in individual plays whose responsibility it is to bring out doctrinal implications of the actions: they point to biblical or even patristic aspects.

It is a matter of great interest with regard to the *Towneley* and the *N Town* cycles that we cannot apply many of these characteristics to them because there is no evidence for guild involvement at the latter, and, as we have seen, very little for the former. Nor is there anything positively to suggest wagons in *Towneley*, and there are such slight indications for *N Town* that render them highly improbable. This may be revealed in the *Towneley* text where sometimes the work of the Wakefield Master seems to imply a different kind of stage from the wagons: the *Second Shepherds' Play* is a case in point, requiring two locations, and virtually simultaneous action. But it must of course be admitted that wagon–based performance remains a possibility. For *N Town* there are clear indications that the staging of some parts of the collection at least were performed in the *place and scaffold* format to be considered below.

Modern experimentation, which admittedly has had to be based on many conjectures upon all sorts of data, including such basic matters as the actual size of the wagons, has shown that even with amateur actors on wagons audibility can be good. This is partly because the walls of the surrounding buildings act as sounding boards, and it may also owe something to the support which the highly organised nature of the verse gives to the spoken voice, particularly by means of stanzaic form, alliteration and rhyme. There is also a good deal of repetition in the texts of words or ideas, or of structures which reiterate, giving helpful support for audibility. It is now widely felt in the light of experience that versification of the text is a great help in the open air.

It has been found that the particular configuration of a wagon, with two levels placed in a street, gives many opportunities for grouping actors in many different ways on or around the wagon. This includes an important vertical dimension which has implications for dominance and submission. Further dramatic contrasts can also be made by silence and noise, the most notable example of which is the silence of Christ under the savage mockery of his tormentors mental and physical.

As each pageant arrived at its station the actors could make a strong impact, perhaps in contrast to the play which had just departed, and there seems little doubt that this would be enhanced by the striking visual impacts such as the design in the Mercers' wagon:

> ij [2] peces of rede cloudes & sternes [stars] of gold langing [belonging] to heven; two peces of blue cloudes payntid on both sydes; iij [3] peces of rede cloudes With sunne bemes of golde & sternes for the hiest of heven, With a lang small border of the same Wurke.[5]

This play is the last of the cycle and when it was played at the last station the sky must have been dark. There would have been an iconic effect from candles or torches on these dazzling surfaces, accompanied by the melody of the angels (melodia angelorum).

For the supernatural characters, including devils and angels, it was the custom to wear masks, God and Christ usually in gold, and the devils with a variety of deformity, including two faces. This might be a further help to amateur actors, but there is perhaps another advantage. During the whole cycle the part of Christ, and indeed of a number of other characters, would be played by a succession of different actors, not necessarily similar to one another physically. The presence of such recurring features as masks, or haloes, or perhaps the characteristic headdress of a high priest or a king would help to identify the persisting nature of the role without requiring a specific 'character' to be suggested.

As regards special effects, beyond matters of costume already noted, even on a long June day there must have torches needed at morning and evening – of particular interest in the last play of Judgement when the Bad Souls are dragged off to hell, no doubt with screams and groans. Fireworks were also a feature which could have a strong effect outdoors. There is a great deal of music in the cycles. It seems certain that for some of the Shepherds, for instance, the singing had to be very accomplished, perhaps even to the standard of professional musicians.[6] In addition to this there are strong effects of liturgical music of a nature likely to be generally known and singable. We should also find that the performances had plenty of musical effects: sweet and harmonious for heaven, but cacophanous for the devils. Indeed it seems likely that hell mouth, and what went on in and around it, would have been sensational. In the French tradition this included not only cacophany, but also a stink so great that adjacent seats had to be sold more cheaply.

II

In spite of all the deficiencies in our knowledge of wagon staging we can conceive of the staging at York and Chester in many specific ways, not least because this kind of staging can be related to the topography of these particular cities. When we come to *place and scaffold* it is much more difficult to be specific, except perhaps in the staging of the Cornish cycles in the *plen-an-gwaries*, though we do not actually know whether the texts we have were done in such 'rounds' as now exist at Perran and St Just in Penwith. However this kind of staging was widespread in England and in France.

Judging from the texts of the *Castle of Perseverance*, the Digby *Mary Magdalene*, and the Passion Play I in the *N Town* cycle, performance depended upon having both fixed locations which could be identified with individual characters, or the significance of a particular location, as well as a largish space between, sometimes called the 'place'. These fixtures presumably took the form of scaffolds, as they are named in *Perseverance*, though, as with the wagons, it is probably unwise to assume that they were similar in appearance. In this play, for example there are the scaffolds of Deus and of the Devil. In the former the Four Daughters plead for Mankind and thus seem to require a throne, and furniture appropriate for a court. Mankind is dragged off to the latter by the Bad Angel to suffer torment and has to be rescued. In both cases it seems likely that the scaffolds would be given an appearance in some respects not unlike the wagons for hell and heaven.

The status and provenance of the *Perseverance* manuscript leaves us in some doubt about whether we can certainly conclude that it was ever performed, and we do not know in what circumstances this might have happened or how many times. Nevertheless it is clear that performance was at least envisaged in some detail, and this can be seen most evidently in the way the other important element of staging is used: the space between the scaffolds. This is dominated by the Castle of Perseverance, itself a structure big enough to contain seven Virtues and Mankind, and to be the object of a siege by the attacking evils. It is also high enough to require ladders. The stage diagram asks for a ditch or a barrier around it, but there is a caveat that the sight lines must not be obscured. Thus the space in the middle of the playing area must be big enough to allow for movement to and fro, the arrival of the besiegers being achieved by warlike processions, with trumpets and drums, from three scaffolds of the World, the Flesh and the Devil which are situated on the edge of the arena. But the space is not only for movement: it exists for things to happen in it. The most notable of these is the death of the protagonist, which takes place in the central space at the foot of the Castle.

Thus the dramatic action of this play can operate over a variety of physical features. Some of them are intimate, as within the scaffolds, and some of a much more ambitious nature on a large scale, employing a large number of actors in various capacities. Moreover, since the scaffolds have some height, there are dramatic effects to be gained by ascending and descending. For example, when Belial is outraged by the incompetence of his servant Vices he descends to beat them in the place. At the same time there is great importance to be attached to the symbolic nature of the scaffolds and the Castle, so that we are not dealing with a realistic enactment so much as with circumstances which are to some extent real, but which contain within them transcendental significance.

Probably the same broad principles of staging were employed for the Digby *Mary Magdalene*, which is also from East Anglia. Here there are some nineteen named locations (similar large numbers of places are found in the French *Passions*). One practical solution is that some of these are more important than others and may act as composite scaffolds. From the action and dialogue it appears that the most important are Heaven and Hell, the House of Simon, the Palace of the King of Marcylle, and the Castle of Magdala in which Mary is besieged by the Seven Deadly Sins, reminiscent of *Perseverance*. Some of these are actually called 'towers', suggesting height and more than one level. Within them, action of some complexity takes place, and there is a good deal of business in coming and going from them. There is no evidence, however to suggest that the layout of the whole area for performance was circular, and the most plausible arrangement may well be a semi-circular one with Hell at one end and Heaven at the other.[7]

The narrative of the play is very complex, but it is grouped so that some places which are used early on do not re-appear, while new ones are required later. This may suggest that some of the scaffolds were given different designations as required, a practice which can also be paralleled in the French tradition. There are many spectacular effects, including music and fireworks, thunder and lightning, a burning house, clouds which open, and, most appealing, a ship: 'Here xall entyre a shyp wyth a mery song' (394 s.d.: a sea shanty?). This ship is used twice, and on the second occasion, the sail having been raised, the direction is '*Et tunc navis venit ad circa placeam*' (1878 s.d.: 'And then the ship comes around the place'), thus making use of the central space as a sea. During this voyage several important actions take place on board, and the Boy has to climb into the shrouds from where he spies the castle (1719–20). It is also apparent that there is cutting from one location to another so that the audience is aware of more than one centre of interest at the same time.

In Passion Play I of the *N Town* cycle it is apparent that the staging depends upon having a number of locations identified with specific persons or places, and again there is extensive movement between; movement which has independent dramatic significance and is not just a convenient way of moving characters about, or of creating a sense of different locations for the purpose of verisimilitude. This particular set of episodes is internally consistent in its staging. In the unlikely event that the whole cycle in the manuscript were ever performed, there might have been a fixed and complex heaven present all the time. The descent of the Angel with a chalice to Christ may suggest this.

The stage directions are elaborate, concentrating upon costume for some characters, and upon making clear on which parts of the acting area the individual episodes occur, including movement between. Five principal places are used. On a '*stage*' for Annas and a '*scaffold*' for Caiaphas the two 'bishops' conduct their business, the beginning of their conspiracy. Having communicated by a Messenger who goes back and forth across the place, they themselves move into the place where they meet and go into '*a little oratory*' for an extensive 'convocation'. Jesus appears in the place and acquires an ass from a castle, which is not a major site. He travels to the *House of Simon the Leper* where he celebrates the paschal lamb, is worshipped by Mary Magdalene, and establishes the sacrament. It is from this House Judas goes to negotiate his sale with the 'bishops' (the High Priests) in their oratory. Jesus leaves the House and goes to the *Mount of Olivet* where the arrest takes place. In the place Judas meets the Devil, and the bishops' men process in military style towards making the arrest. The location of Jerusalem is probably managed in the central area, without a specific scaffold. The action required is that the citizens prepare the way, Jesus proceeds along it, and he weeps for Jerusalem: but as there is no sign that he actually enters the city, it seems likely that it did not exist as a scaffold. The bishops' convocation and the extended action at the House of Simon go on simultaneously, and the attention of the audience is apparently controlled by opening and closing curtains on these two places. Initially Annas and Caiaphas are required to 'show' themselves on their respective scaffolds. Thus there are mechanisms for controlling and directing the attention of the audience, and for ensuring that there is a sense of different activities going on as part of the spectacle.

III

The plays discussed so far can yield considerable amounts of information about the staging for which they were written, but there are plenty of others where it is much more difficult to deduce it. In broad terms, however, we know from records assembled by the REED project that from the fifteenth century onwards, and perhaps before, there were many companies of players, usually under the patronage of the nobility, which travelled about and were paid by corporations, colleges, monastic houses and individual magnates. The most likely and convenient place for performance was the so-called great hall of palaces, castles, great houses, abbeys, Inns of Court, colleges at Oxford and Cambridge or, more simply, the local lord's home. Such halls followed a common pattern, and as indoor theatre they make an important contribution to the history of staging. There would be a raised dais at one end for the lord, who, accompanied by his principal guests, sat with a table in front, the social circumstances being usually a meal and the play an entertainment to complement it, before, during or afterwards. Normally other tables ran down the long sides of the hall for the many guests at the meal who constituted the bulk of the audience. The fourth side had two openings which led to the kitchens, through which the audience, and eventually the actors, could enter. Above this was a gallery which was commonly used for musicians, though it might have been difficult to keep actors out of it if they thought it could be useful. This end was usually masked by screens which became the backing for any fixed item of staging such as a throne, though scenery in a modern sense was still a long way off. As we shall see, there was great flexibility in these open arrangements, and within the main area of the hall actors could carve out spaces for themselves and direct the attention of the spectators in various ways. Indeed the flexibility was such that in some places the centre of attention was changed completely by building an acting stage across the middle of the hall dividing the audience into two sections.[8] There are practically no definite ascriptions of particular plays to specific halls, though we do know that a version of Sir David Lindsay's *Ane Satire of the Thrie Estaitis* was done at Linlithgow Palace on 6 January 1540, and the hall there, now a ruin, is the obvious place for an indoor winter performance. (Much later we can identify specific court locations for John Lyly's plays: see Chapter 11.)

Sometimes the texts of the plays show unmistakable signs that the dramatist was working with the configuration of the hall in mind, as in the case of Henry Medwall's *Fulgens and Lucres*, but there are others like *Mankind* where the play could certainly work successfully in such a setting, but which could actually be done almost anywhere, indoors or in the open air. By the same token it is quite hard to find plays which were certainly done outside, though there is a prayer for good weather in *Pride of Life*, and John Bale states that he performed some of his scriptural plays at the Market Cross in Kilkenny on 2 August 1553. In addition to the occasion in Linlithgow Palace, *Thrie Estaitis* had outdoor performances at Cupar in 1552, and at the Greenside in Edinburgh in 1554.

The evidence that *Fulgens and Lucres* was performed in a hall is unmistakable, but in considering it we should note the extent to which Medwall makes the most of the setting, interweaving it with the substance of his play to make a remarkable entertainment. The setting is the hall arranged for a meal, with people having eaten (I.3), and also with a division before the second part of the play accompanies a later sitting. This is supported by a series of references to the meal (I.1416, 1422, II.11). The action of the play works on two levels: the main plot being the dispute between Gaius Flaminius and Publius Cornelius for the hand of Lucres, daughter of Fulgens, a senator of Rome; while there is also a competition between two servants A and B for the hand of Jone, the maid. But A and B also have an existence as members of the audience who are present at the entertainment. Though at a certain point they cross over into the fictional world, they retain a special function in communicating directly with the audience both about the real world of the hall where the feast and performance are taking place, and also about various aspects of the fictional world as wooers themselves, and servants of Flaminius and Cornelius. In other words, their entry into the play world is deliberately equivocal, and is a means of making the audience aware of the illusion it entails.[9]

The specific evidence for the place where the play is given includes the reference to 'These folke that sitt here in the halle' (I.1413), and A's remark, 'Whan I entred the halle' (II.50). Near the beginning of the second part there is a good deal of business about B's knocking at the door: A responds with 'One of you go loke who it is' (II.75), presumably sending someone nearby (actor, diner, or both?). There is a lord present referred to as 'the master of the feast' (I.1426), whose sanction is required for the playing of the second part (I.1431–2). Several times the actors come through the audience. Though Medwall is interested in the 'make room' convention, he varies it so that one actor calls for room for another:

> Geve rome there, syrs, for God avowe!
> Thei wold cum in if thei myght for you.   *if you were not in*
> *the way*
> (I.193–4)

Such managing lines are spoken by A and B, and not by the main characters. They are also used to name the principals:

> *A:*   And wher is feyr doughter Lucrece?
> *B:*   She comyth anon. I say, hold thy pece!
>
> (I.200–1)

The nature of what is going on is clarified by references to entertainment as 'sport' (I.40), and 'myrth and game' (II.890). The action includes a number of decorative features which align the proceedings with festivities: thus there is wrestling, music on a tamboryne (*pipe and drum*, l. 389), singing and dancing. Notable is the knockabout duel between A and B referred to as 'fart, pryke in cule', which entails them fighting while tied up in a crouching position so difficult to manage that they have to get Jone to help each of them to get into it (I.1169–1214), and Gaius to extricate them (I.1244–50).

The main action of the play is a dispute in two parts as to whether Lucres should marry Cornelius on the grounds of his noble family, or Flaminius on the grounds of what he has achieved, though of common background. The role of A and B is to set this up, to echo some of the chief ideas, and to manage the audience's response by direct address to them and also by the complications of their own dispute over Jone. But it is apparent that the festive element is an important part of the proceedings, in terms of theatricality, quite as significant as the debate.

The various kinds of attention to the audience may well be related. Apart from references to their comfort as diners, they are called upon as witnesses (I.1017, II.846–7), and as possible commentators (II.218). Player A comments upon their divided taste for comic and serious:

> For some there be that lokis and gapys   *look*
> Only for suche tryfles and japys   *jokes*
>   And some there be amonge
> That forceth lytyll of suche madnes,   *value*
> But delytyth them in matter of sadnes   *seriousness*
>   Be it never so longe.
>
> (II.30–5)

After the argument for the hand of Lucres has been completed, A asks the 'gode women' for their opinion (II.848), and B warns the men about marriage (II.860). Both thus sustain the sense that the debate is open ended, without authorial judgement.

One of the most striking things about the staging of *Mankind* is that the dramatist has a very strong sense of an offstage area which he could exploit. This is really to say that he builds up for the audience a kind of imagined space which they cannot see but which is essential to the understanding and enjoyment of what is presented before their eyes. There is a great deal of coming and going, and entrances are often pointed by lines like Mercy's 'Out of this place I wolde ye went' (148), and Mankind's angry rejection of the villains, 'Hye yow forth lyvely, for hens I wyll yow dryffe!' [drive] (380). But in the course of the plot when it is necessary to bring on Titivillus, the devil, he is made to speak from offstage and will not enter until the villains Newguise, Nowadays and Nought have exacted a collection from the audience. When this is completed, Nowadays announces him with Latin, as though conjuring a spirit:

> Ita, vere, magister. Cumme forth now yowr   *So indeed, Master*
>   gatus!   *. . . on your way*
> He ys a goodly man, sers; make space and
>   be ware!
>
> (473–4)

Later in the play there is a game in which Mankind's coat is cut down to a more fashionable size. For this purpose Newguise takes it out of sight first (675) and brings it on again, thrusting his way through the audience:

> Out of my wey, sers, for drede of fyghtynge!
> Lo, here ys a feet tayll, lyght to leepe abowte!   *a fine cut suitable*
>   *for leaping about*
> (696–7)

But Nought thinks it still has too much cloth, so off he goes:

> I xall goo and mende yt, ellys I wyll lose my hede.
> Make space sers, lett me go owte.
>
> (700–1)

When he comes back with the 'joly jakett', it is short enough to fence in (719–20). While all this is going on Mankind is being induced by Mischief to swear to carry out a variety of sins, including Lechery. Thus the business which is visible, laughable and exploits movement offstage, is cleverly integrated into the moral decline of Mankind.

It is clear too from the quotations given here that the idea of making one's way through the audience – sometimes impolitely – is part of the sense of space, and also that the villains frequently address the audience. This is especially true of Titivillus, the star turn, who is invisible to Mankind but not to the audience, whom he involves closely in the steps by which he undermines him:

> I promes yow I have no lede on my helys . . .   *lead   heels*
> I xall go to hys ere and tytyll therin.   *ear   whisper*
>   *Macro plays:*
>   *Mankind*, II
>   (555 and 557)

A few moments later when Mankind falls asleep Titivillus says to the audience:

> Ande ever ye dyde, for me kepe now yowr sylence.
> Not a worde, I charge yow, peyn of forty pens
>
> (589–90)

When his plan has worked he takes his leave:

> Farwell, everychon, for I have don my game   *everyone*
> For I have brought Mankynde to myscheff and to
>   schame.
>
> (605–6)

There are some indications that the play might be performed in a hall, including a reference to those who sit and those who stand (29), and Nought goes off at one point saying goodnight (161), but these are not conclusive, and it is clear from what we have noted about space that the business could perfectly well be conducted in the open air.[10] This is true for practically all the other details which form part of the entertainment and are integral to the plot, such as the mock court, and the sequence of event in which Titivillus destroys Mankind's resolution by putting a board under the earth to be dug, and by removing his spade.

One may add, in conclusion, that the discussion offered here has a positive result: however difficult the interpretation of the nature and status of medieval texts may be, there is plenty of information available about the complexities of performance and many indications that dramatists had insight into how performance might be arranged.

Notes

1. One of the most useful accounts of a sixteenth-century director is found in J.E. Tailby, 'The Role of the Director in the Lucerne Passion Play', *METh* 9 (1987), 80–92.

2. This procession shows many medieval items in spite of its late date: St George and the Dragon, the Nativity, Michael fighting with the Devil, Christ and the Doctors, the Annunciation. See Denis van Alsloot, *Isabella's Triumph (May 31st 1615)*, ed. J.W. Laver (London, 1947).

3. R. Beadle, 'The York Cycle', in *Companion*, 97–8.

4. Competition also developed during the plays at Lille, and among the many Rhetoricians' Chambers in the Netherlands.

5. York REED, I.55–6, where the Inventory is given in full. It is dated 1433, by which time the idea of the cycle must have been well established and a good deal of experience would have been accumulated as to what was desirable or effective.

6. The musical requirements for the Shepherds vary, but it is most likely that in some cycles they were professional singers, especially in *Towneley* 13; see R. Rastall, *The Heaven Singing* (Cambridge, 1997), 356–8, and 364.

7. J. McKinnell, 'Staging the Digby *Mary Magdalen*', *METh* 6 (1984), 125–52.

8. See A.H. Nelson, *Early Cambridge Theatres* (Cambridge, 1994), 31 (Fig. 19), and 109.

9. It could well be that the ambivalence is the theatrical manifestation of the *exploratory* nature of the debate over nobility noted by J.B. Altham, *The Tudor Play of Mind* (Berkeley and Los Angeles, 1978), pp. 24–5.

10. A door is mentioned by Nought at the same exit (158), but the phrase is apparently proverbial and hence it is not necessarily to be taken literally.

Chapter 6
Dramatic Values

It is of course artificial to try to separate dramatic values from content as though the one could be added to the other as an 'x' factor. We may have difficulty too in being sure exactly what Tudor audiences expected from their drama, and we are inclined to make assumptions that they expected something similar to what we seek and enjoy today. It is not clear, for example, how much a sense of (civic) duty might have been important for participants as actors or spectators. There are unmistakable signs that religious worship, including the rehearsal of parts of the liturgy, played a part in the dramatic experience. The presence of many aspects of spectacle, some of it closely associated with procession and civic entry, is another characteristic of early drama which it is difficult (though not impossible) to evoke today. Though there were probably very few professional actors, it seems likely, to judge from the ambitious nature of some stage effects, and not least the concentration of some dialogue, that actors were nevertheless very competent, and probably handed on their skills to their successors even though these were usually amateurs. Expectations about technical staging devices were also high.

In considering dramatic values it will be convenient first to discuss the mystery cycles and then the morality plays. However, it should become clear that in spite of enormous differences between these two genres there are some common factors. At their fullest extent in the cycles at York and Chester, and in the large-scale morality *The Castle of Perseverance*, we find that medieval dramatists were capable of sustaining dramatic interest over a very long period of acting time, in the open air, using an extensive amount of physical space in various theatrical and symbolic ways, and managing very large audiences: and the practices of French *mystères* and *moralités* in the fifteenth and sixteenth centuries support this suggestion emphatically. This is partly a matter of having very large resources available – both financial and human – but it also argues that writers and directors were interested in making an impact on audiences by sustaining their attention over a long period. Frequency of performance may have had considerable impact upon how the plays or pageants were seen. The plays at York were done almost annually over many years, and a good proportion of the individual plays may have survived with little change for long periods. With the other cycles the evidence for continuity is much harder to come by: Chester appears to have gone through a major change in the early sixteenth century and it was performed at irregular intervals; it is difficult to establish a consistent base for the Towneley plays, while *N Town* may never have had a complete performance at all.

I

In assessing the dramatic values of the cycles we must also take into account the didactic element. This may not be congenial to modern taste, yet it is an integral part of the plays, for they were preoccupied with a wide range of teaching functions. At one level there was a concern to increase the familiarity with the narrative from Creation to Doomsday. This would be of benefit not only to those who needed teaching because of ignorance, but also as a means of reinforcing the experience of the well-informed by the repetition of known and loved stories.

The presence of known local people, members of the guilds, performing the play suggests the interaction of the here and now of the streets of York with its no doubt familiar configuration of buildings, as against the longer perspectives of history and the intersection of eternity into the historical narrative of tradition. One of the strongest effects of the York and Chester cycles as we have them is the sense that God wished not only to create human history but also to intervene in it in emphatic ways, at the Creation, the Nativity, the Crucifixion and Resurrection especially. There are also very striking smaller-scale events such as Christ's triumph against the Devil at the Temptation, marked by approval from on high, and also at the re-alignment of history implied in the harrowing of Hell and the defeat of the Devil for ever.

In broad terms the choice of subject matter for cycles varied: there are plenty of examples of saints' lives in visual forms, and some dramatic ones such as St Remy at Rheims.[1] The cycle form is common in France, though it does not always follow a comparable structure to the four extant English cycles, which, as it happens, were more or less the same even though the individual episodes were differently distributed, expanded or compressed. The Cornish cycle is closer to some French versions in the selection of incidents. Beyond this it appears that the lost Beverley cycle also told the story from the Fall of Lucifer to Doomsday,[2] but the evidence is that, although fragments of cycles have survived, Coventry, Norwich and Newcastle did not present the whole.

The concept of some characters is intimately related to didactic ends, as in the role of John the Baptist as a forerunner who brings out the humility and humanity of Christ, or in the case of Mary Magdalene whose love and devotion outweighs her former obloquy. On the other hand, some personages have no historical place: their role is to explicate the significance of the events portrayed in the narrative, as with the Chester Doctor who brings out the significance of the three temptations faced by Christ by reference to a sermon of Pope Gregory the Great (12.169–216). In N Town there is an elaborate development of the Contemplatio figure in parts of the cycle whose role is partly explicatory and partly a matter of worship. Even some of the most striking episodes in the cycles may be given overt didactic importance. This would apply to episodes warning about death and the best way to prepare for it, as in the N Town Death of Herod, where the figure of Death, God's Messenger, makes an appearance, or in the lyric passage in Towneley spoken by Lazarus from the tomb which has the intermittent refrain reminiscent of penitential lyrics, 'amende the whils thou may' (31.194, 201, 202, 209, 217). The didactic nature of such material ensures its place also in morality plays, such as The Castle of Perseverance and Everyman.

Some characters depend firmly upon well-established types, which may indeed be found outside the plays themselves in patristic writings, or in non-dramatic poetry. There are also reflections of such conventions of character in iconographic works. An example would be Herod, noted for his rage in the cycles, and often portrayed visually with his legs crossed to show his fury, as in a roof boss at Norwich cathedral. Many other evil characters, such as Cain and Judas, both of whom wilfully oppose God, are also presented following such conventions. But the essential doctrine about humans is that they are there to be saved by means of Christ's Redemption. Thus, while the stereotypes of evil may be theatrically satisfying because they conform to what is expected, the possibility of grace extending to Lazarus, Mary Magdalene, Peter and others suggests that however corrupt people may become, the potential for salvation remains real and will continue so.

Such material lent itself to a cyclic presentation, and there were many examples in pictures where the narrative effect was deliberately pursued. Memling's Passion, for example (c. 1470, in the Sabauda Gallery in Turin), shows succeeding events in a simultaneous presentation, so that one can see Christ being mocked and beaten in the centre of the picture, the carrying of the cross in the lower right corner, Peter's cutting off the ear of Malchus in the lower left, and the Crucifixion on a distant hill at the top centre.

The popularity of cyclic form in the Middle Ages shows itself in many such iconographical items.[3] They present in visual form a narrative 'told' by separating out individual scenes for particular attention and illustrating them in some detail, which may be realistic or symbolic. In the visual arts there is the specific relationship between one scene and another, as well as the possibilities of contrast and difference. Conventional images depict the way Christ at the Resurrection puts his foot out of the open tomb on to the body of one of the sleeping guards, or the way as a boy he is placed upon a throne when he disputes with the Doctors. Such images may have been so well known that they could affect how such scenes were dramatised, but the point of greater importance is that there was a consciousness of cyclic narrative which could be exploited.

Among the advantages of the cyclic form is the possibility of diversity in unity. There could be an overall intention to which the individual plays would contribute in different ways. Individual characters, scenes or even visual gestures could anticipate later items in the cycle, or they could be used for recall. In both visual and dramatic cycles there is the important judgement to be made as to actually what is selected for illustration. In the dramatic form there is also the advantage of being able to carry through systematically words and symbols, doctrinal or didactic elements essential to the main purpose.

It may be that this was an effective form of teaching, but perhaps the excitement of different emotions at the same time was an integral part of the experience, and it is not such a great step to suppose that the experience of being present at a processional performance may have been similar, even if there was an acknowledged didactic function. The presentation of such scenes may also be informed by other objectives, especially in terms of the interrelated biblical typology, as when the coming of the flood in the Noah plays pre-figures the Last Judgement, and the intimate cross-referencing between Adam, the first man who fell, and Christ the God-man who came to redeem him and all his kin. Sometimes the thematic links are more directly didactic, as in the significance attached in the Chester play of Abraham (4) to the importance of the priesthood by means of Melchizedek.

The presence of extensive comic episodes also makes for two-sided dramatic effects, some potentially damnable, some worthy of grace. On the one hand, laughter may separate characters from God, as when Cain in Towneley, hearing the voice of God, mockingly asks whether God is out of his wit. The comedy of the Shepherds is a recurrent practice as we shall see, but the presence of comedy makes for a more beneficent view of them to be generated. Alongside this we may consider the extensive comedy associated with the Devil and his various manifestations and followers. Though he be crafty and threatening to humans and to Christ, and though the possibility of damnation should and could not be taken lightly, his ultimate fate was disaster and this could be anticipated by making him ridiculous and incompetent. Even the fall of Lucifer could be seen as comic in that, after his vain boasts, the change in his appearance was made clear by stage action. But it is a matter for interpretation as to how ridiculous the Devil should appear. His inability to counter the power of Christ inevitably puts him at a disadvantage, and the dramatic conceptions place him in an inferior position in such episodes as the Temptation and the Harrowing of Hell. It is perhaps this circumscription of his activities by the divine power which has led to a view of the mystery cycles as parallel to Dante's *Divine Comedy* in their finally beneficent outcome.[4]

The discussion in Chapter 4 of the nature of the mystery cycle texts leaves us with a particular problem about dramatic values. Since the practice of authorship for the cycles is more than a little incoherent, and our insight into the comprehensive nature of the individual cycles can only be through somewhat distorting and no doubt rather limited windows, the role of the individual pageants or plays against their place in the context of an overall design for the cycle must remain somewhat problematic but also deeply intriguing. This is especially so where an identity for a reviser can be established, as in the case of the Wakefield Master. Some whole plays, especially the two Shepherds' plays, for example, can be firmly attributed to him on stylistic grounds, but we also find that he probably had only a small part in revising some of the other texts which have come down to us, such as the Peregrini (play 27). There are strong variations in weight and depth between individual pageants, and though we can describe the dramaturgy as varied, differences in dramatic mode are often such as to suggest that the cycles may be at best eclectic. It is certainly difficult to envisage the work of one author as the creator of each cycle.

With the York cycle we should regard the rich variety of dramatic material as a particular strength. There are marked contrasts between the savage and brutal comedy of nailing the silent Christ to the cross by the four aggressive and voluble torturers and the tender scene between the risen Christ and the Mary Magdalene in the garden where there are only two characters present. Moreover, if the production was processional on pageant carts, such contrasts would be emphatic in that each new play would have to impose its own particular mood on the waiting audience on arrival at each station. This could be done partly by musical effects if the players arrived singing, and there seems little doubt that the spectacle of the characters processing in their differing costumes would also have a notable effect.

We can now turn to a more detailed consideration of some of these issues by examining the Shepherds' plays in the English cycles (they are absent from the Cornish), and by looking at the *N Town* cycle which, as we have seen, does bear distinct signs of being arranged and perhaps written to a plan.

II

The Shepherds' plays

There are six Shepherds' plays extant: a section of the Coventry Shearmen and Tailors' play, one complete play each from York (play 15), Chester (7), and N Town (16), and two from the *Towneley* cycle attributed to the Wakefield Master (12 and 13). Though the Shepherds are to be found in the scriptural account (Luke 2:8–20), it is generally felt that they were not much elaborated in the theological commentaries, and it becomes interesting to ask why all the versions adopted such a degree of similarity in narrative and in treatment. One of the attractions of Shepherds for the vernacular dramatists might have been that they could be made to speak in common language, and no doubt to appear in common costume, so that it would be possible to see in them much of contemporary life. It is for this reason too they remain of abiding interest for us in later years. Their speech may at times be a matter of local dialect; they may refer to local places; and what they eat, and what they talk about – the weather, hard times, sickness, wives – are all rich in local colour. The Towneley plays are especially close to local dialect, and their author (the Wakefield Master) is deeply interested in the vitality of local speech, exploiting its rhythms and its vocabulary for distinctive dramatic effects. He even has the villain, Mak, accused of speaking with a 'Southern tooth' as part of the process by which he is differentiated from the other characters.

The similarities between the plays include the convention of having three Shepherds (perhaps a parallel to the three Magi), a prophecy of the birth of Christ, the response to the message of the angel(s) and their song, and a disposition to sing themselves. Guided by the scriptural narrative, the dramatists show them at Bethlehem, having followed the star, where they worship Christ and give him simple presents which accord with their lowly status, and yet in some ways foreshadow the forthcoming power of Christ. (The N Town Shepherds, however, do not make gifts.)

The extent of the similarities suggests that a common view of them had emerged in spite of the absence of extensive theological exegesis. In dramatic terms it would seem that their presence was particularly desirable or useful because by their prophecy, and by their links with the contemporary English world as distinct from that of historical Bethlehem they could be seen to mark an important turning point in the structure of the cycles. This is underlined because in most of the plays the visit to the stable involves worship, usually in a stanzaic form which begins with the word 'Hail' as each Shepherd brings out particular attributes of the coming life and ministry of Christ. It is very convenient doctrinally to have an opportunity at the point of Christ's birth to create an interpretative framework and to anticipate details of what is to come. The purpose of such activity is probably to give emphasis to the idea of peace, and to stress that Christ in his redemptive role was come to heal the sin originated by Adam. There is a repeated theme also about the harm done to the Devil by the Nativity, one which foreshadows the harm done to him at the Crucifixion. They are valued as examples of vigilance and faith vital at this point of Christian history.[5]

Turning to the individual plays, we find that the York version proceeds with a special devotional intensity which is typified by the forthright way in which the Shepherds' prophecy is introduced in the first stanza.

Oure forme-fadres, faythfull in fere,	*forefathers*
Bothe Osye and Isaye,	*Hosea Isaiah*
Preved þat a prins with-outen pere	*prophesied*
Shulde descende doune in a lady,	
And to make mankynde clerly,	
To leche þam þat are lorne.	*heal lost*
	(15.5–10)

The dramatist keeps up the devotional atmosphere by making the Shepherds react to what they see, by references to 'heele' (*health*) and to 'wirshippe', and by the touchingly simple gifts – a brooch with a bell, cobnuts on a ribbon, and a spoon big enough for forty peas. However, the dramatisation is especially interesting since it obviously places great emphasis upon the visual. We cannot now be sure what the Shepherds actually saw, since the moment of revelation is treated obliquely in the text, but it cannot be doubted that the audience would also have seen it. Details emerge piecemeal in the subsequent dialogue: 'right as the angel saide', but the text does not actually give his words. It is notable that the dramatic purpose of their singing is actually said to be to record, make memorable what the Angel has told them.

The *N Town* play shares this last feature with the *York* for the transition from receiving the Angel's message to Bethlehem is very abrupt, and one has a sense that much of what might have been visible is lost. But before they go the Shepherds sing the antiphon *Stella celi extirpavit* ('The star of heaven has driven out [the plague of Death]') as the stage direction (16.89) makes clear. However, they discuss the Angel's song which they have apparently heard, but which is not cued, and seek to remember it closely. As they differ in their memories we have here, in little, one of the frequent themes and indeed actions of the plays: the quarrels between the Shepherds.

Primus Pastor	Ey, Ey, þis was a wondyr note
	Þat was now songyn above þe sky:

	I haue þat voys ful wele I wote – Þei songe 'gle, glo, glory'.	
Secundus Pastor	Nay so moty the so was it nowth	*as I hope to thrive, it* *was not so understood*
	I haue þat songe ful wel invm In my wytt weyl it is wrought. It was 'Glo, glo, glas, glum'.	
Tertius Pastor	The songe me thought it was 'Glory' . . .	

(16.62–70)

Though this is thus done very briefly here, and the comic effect is somewhat problematic, this one small piece of business is a type for other disputes over this topic and over others in the plays from *Chester* and the *Towneley* cycles. Another feature of this play is the elaborate recital of prophecies by all three Shepherds, which has led some critics to see them as possible representations of the clergy, exercising perhaps a pastoral role.

Even though the *Chester* and *Towneley* plays follow most of the characteristics noted so far, it is plain that they are the work of authors who give themselves much more scope for invention with regard to structure, and also a much more varied approach to enactment. Their achievement raises (again) the problem of the relationship between teaching and entertainment. Both authors are strictly mindful of the scriptural source, and in general present this material in terms which are defined by a conventional approach to the interpretation of it; but they show themselves able to expand and innovate in remarkable ways. The *Chester* author enlarges the feast of the Shepherds (also found in *Coventry* and *Towneley* 12) to grotesque proportions, both in terms of the vast number of items, and of the kinds of items they consume. One has to presume that all the nineteen or so items (green cheese, a sheep's head, a pig's foot, ham, tongue, pudding, cake . . .) are real stage properties which are produced from pockets and bags, though of course there would be scope for comic effect in miming the whole process of assembling the feast and consuming it. Here and elsewhere with the Shepherds there is a strong farcical element, but it is strictly limited by an overriding devotional purpose.

Earlier in the play there was a similar example of accumulation in the remedies for the sheep ailments, the scab, the rot and the cough, which Hankin, the First Shepherd, assembles. The writer's interest in action is furthered by the wrestling match which follows the feast: the Shepherds' boy Trowle challenges his three masters and throws each of them in turn. These performance items work very well on stage, but it is also very intriguing that recent interpreters have sought with some success to suggest that they are partly determined by theological objectives. For example, the feast may be related to the fast customary at Advent, which was

broken by the feasting at Christmas lasting twelve days; the role of Hankin
as leech for his flock has been seen as a parallel for Christ come to heal
the wounds of humanity; and the success of Trowle, who apparently does
all the work, has been taken as a representation of exalting the humble,
thematically significant for the Nativity.[6] Though they need to be treated
with caution, such interpretations are valuable because they bring out the
underlying sense of celebration for the coming of Christ which is essential
to the overall structure of the cycles.

But if these are comic innovations, there are also more serious ones, for
when the Shepherds come to make their offerings (a ball, a flask and
spoon, and a cap – with some old hose from Trowle 'for other jewells,
my sonne, / have I none thee for to give' [593–4]) they are parallelled by
four Boys who also make offerings (bottle, hood, pipe and nuthook). The
greetings which accompany these offerings draw attention to Christ's
roles 'kinge of heavon so hye . . . the maker of the stare / that stoode us
beforne' (552, 567–8). Beyond this it emerges that Hankin will become a
hermit, and Trowle will also go to a hermitage. Perhaps these brief
quotations also give an inkling of the simple beauty of much of the
language of the adoration passage.

At times the language of the Shepherds invented by the Wakefield
Master is much harsher:

Primus Pastor	Is none in this ryke	*kingdom*
	A shepard, farys wars.	
Secundus Pastor	Poore men ar in the dyke	
	And oft-tyme mars.	*suffer*
	The warld is slyke;	*such*
	Also helpars	
	Is none here.	
		(12.133–9)

This note of complaint is common to both his plays, and he exercises
himself to give a harsh picture of the lot of Shepherds, who seem to give
a sense of the corruption of humanity and cruelty of its predicament.
They themselves are harsh men in a harsh world, and the author turns a
bleak eye upon circumstances as well as people.

In writing two plays he was probably merely trying to develop the
achievement of the first. The title of the second in the manuscript is
Incipit Alia eorundem, best translated as 'Here begins another of the same
(shepherds)', and, as we shall see, the Second Shepherds' Play takes up and
extends many of the characteristics of the first. To bear this in mind is some
defence against treating the former in isolation as a unique achievement,
when really it can be integrated with the rest of what its author contributed to the *Towneley* cycle.

His invention in presenting the Shepherds is notable for its incorporation of narrative material from elsewhere, especially from folkloric sources, but he has a very positive attitude to performance which helps to integrate the material effectively. In the first play he demonstrates the folly of the Shepherds by adapting the folk tale of the wise men of Gotham. Two of the Shepherds engage in a vigorous quarrel about whether the First shall drive his sheep past the Second, the point being that the sheep are imaginary. They enact, with deep commitment and mounting anger, the details of the confrontation, addressing each other and the sheep by turns:

Secundus Pastor	Not oone shepe-tayll	
	Shall thou bryng hedyr.	
Primus Pastor	I shall bryng, no fayll,	
	A hundreth togedyr.	
Secundus Pastor	What, art thou in ayll?	*ale*
	Longys thou oght-whedir?	*Do you belong anywhere?*
Primus Pastor	Thay shall go, saunce fayll.	*without*
	Go now, bell-weder!	
Secundus Pastor	I say, tyr!	
Primus Pastor	I say, tyr, now agane!	
	I say skyp ouer the plane.	
Secundus Pastor	Wold thou neuer so fane,	
	Tup, I say, whyr!	

(12.157–69)

At the heat of the row the Third Shepherd arrives and, perceiving their folly – 'Where ar youre shepe, lo?' (12.195) – he sets about demonstrating it. Following the precedent in the folk tale, he shows them that their wits are barren, pointing to a sack which he empties by pouring away the meal it holds. As he loses his corn by doing so, it rests with the Shepherds' rebellious boy, Jak Garcio, to point up the folly of teacher and taught. Although the author has made the most of the tale in dramatic terms, it is clear that his handling of the Shepherds falls closely within the conventions found in the other plays. Later, with this quarrel made up, they still argue over the 'holsom' ale as Primus drinks first:

Tertius Pastor	Ye hold long the skayll:	*cup*
	Now lett me go to.	
Secundus Pastor	I shrew those lyppys	
	Bot thou leyff me som parte.	

(12.359–62)

The vitality of such exchanges is not to be missed: the author was very skilled in writing dialogue in which the concerns of the speakers are made to play off one another. Perhaps there is still an intriguing difficulty in deciding upon the extent to which these Shepherds should appear ridiculous: their future contains a whole-hearted welcome for the Child at Bethlehem, mixing the homely with the eternal:

> Hayll, lytyll tyn[e] mop   *tiny, moppet*
> Rewarder of mede!
> Hayll! bot oone drop
> Of grace at my nede!
> Hayll, lytyll mylksop!
> Hayll, David sede!
> Of oure crede thou art crop:
> Hayll in Godhede!
>
> (12.673–80)

In the Second Shepherds' Play we encounter the same skilled handling of dramatic speech, with a strong flavour of proverbs, exclamations, oaths, and of local dialect which all increase our sense of the immediacy of the suffering of the Shepherds. Again they share with those in other plays crucial metaphors of scriptural learning and healing, and their prophecies again occur – 'Of David and Isay'. These Shepherds sing even more than the others, and they analyse learnedly (perhaps pompously?) the musicality of the Angel's song – 'Was no crochett wrong, / Nor nothyng that lakt it', (13.950–1): an approbation which is apparently followed by an imitation done so badly by Primus, that Secundus asks, 'Can ye barke at the mone?' (*moon*, 13.956).

But the dramatic impact of this play is chiefly carried by the character of Mak, the sheep stealer whose theft of a sheep and subsequent hiding of it in a cradle as though it were a new baby is a folk tale with many versions.[7] The author's linking of this tale by means of the discovery of the lost sheep with the worship of the Child in Bethlehem appears to be an innovation. Whether it is or not, the dramatic exploitation of the parallel has commanded great attention in the twentieth century. There are echoes from the passage about the sheep baby in the worship of Christ (as in 'lytyll day-starne' [*day-star*] at ll. 834 and 1049), and the author is also able to depend upon the configuration of three Shepherds for both episodes, thus opening up a range of religious imagery of great complexity which includes the Trinity. Mak himself is made something of a necromancer, and he is repeatedly linked with the devil, explicitly by his own words and behaviour, and implicitly by his treatment.

With a subject which is, like that noted in the first play, concerned with making a fool of the Shepherds, and ultimately of Mak himself, the play owes a good deal to the techniques of farce. Mak nearly gets away with his cradle trick. It is only when Primus asks on departing, 'Gaf ye the chyld any thyng?' that Tertius rushes back eager to give sixpence so that the final reversal comes with great speed and delicious suspense upon Mak and his wife. In a strange way the generosity of these hard and suspicious Shepherds breaks through Mak's evil device, and morally and psychologically the way for the Adoration of the real baby is prepared. If this is so, then the sense that in spite of everything these ordinary Shepherds are a means of grace of peculiar appropriateness is confirmed.

But in this the play gives us a problem which has excited much critical endeavour: it is the question whether the Mak episode, which lasts for 732 lines out of 1088, and the much shorter Adoration are adequately linked. Because no other Shepherds' play does this, the Second Shepherds' Play has been seen as somewhat eccentric. Its defenders have striven to show how close the links are between these two elements, and it must be added that in performance there is usually no sense of unease because the Mak episode is written with such dramatic economy in spite of its apparent length on the page. The farce really works and the proof of this pudding is in the playing.

This discussion of the Shepherds' plays shows that different authors make successful use of common material, drawing upon their sense of dramatic effect to arrange it. It remains to look now at a cycle which, in spite of the difficulties over coherence, may illustrate the particular effectiveness of a cyclic play.

III

The N Town cycle

The existence of the cyclic tradition discussed earlier means that the compiler of N Town had at least one established model for the assembling of his text, which presumably occurred towards the end of the fifteenth century. Manuscript studies have shown that he did not add much that was new to his various exemplars: the main exceptions to this are the stage directions. But the selection of incidents and episodes is a creative process in itself, and it is clear from what we have considered earlier about the manuscript that to a large extent he was incorporating material in his own hand, whether he was the author or not. The evidence of the Proclamation and its relationship with what is actually present in the codex suggests that in part at least there was some kind of comprehensive authorship, however much the process of compilation may have modified it. In broad terms, if he was assembling at some point after 1468, there would have been the famous and popular cycles of York, Chester, and Coventry to offer some guidance.

One of the discernible intentions in parts of this cycle was undoubtedly to bring doctrinal elements to the fore. As it happens, this can be illustrated by the activities of the speaker Contemplacio who appears in two sequences, the series of plays about Mary (plays 8, 9, 10, 11 and 13), and in Passion Play II (plays 29–31 and parts of 32 and 34). In the first he shows some polite concern for the audience, and is rather apologetic about the performance. He also gives details of the narrative in advance, emphasising its function. These aspects can be exemplified in his second stanza:

> This matere here mad is of þe modyr of mercy;
> > How be Joachym and Anne was here concepcyon   *by*
> Sythe offered into þe temple, compiled breffly: *Then*
> > Than maryed to Joseph, and so, folwyng þe salutacyon
> > Metyng with Elyzabeth, and þerwith a conclusyon
> > > In fewe wurdys talkyd þat it xulde not be tedyous
> > To lerned nyn to lewd, nyn to no man of reson.   *nor*
> > > Þis is þe procese; now preserve yow, Jhesus.
>
> > > > > > > > > > > (8.9–16)

Though the idea of Mary as the mother of mercy is a commonplace, it is also a leading theme in many of the *N Town* pageants, and notably it is one of the key issues in play 11, *The Parliament of Heaven*, an episode which does not appear in the other cycle plays. For this play, Contemplacio is given a Prologue of 48 lines which takes the form of a prayer that God would 'com down here in to erth' (11.10). Significantly this request is based upon an insistent call for mercy:

> Good lord, haue on man pyte . . .
> Lete mercy meke þin hyest mageste.   *temper*
>
> > > > > > > > > (11.6, 8)

At the end of the Visit to Elizabeth, the last episode in the Mary play, his epilogue has a special function in the presentation of the story of Mary in that he explains how the *Ave Maria* came about through the Angel's greeting, and he also comments that her family was remarkable in generating also the *Benedictus* and the *Magnificat*.

Contemplacio's appearance in Passion Play II is a direct address to the audience: it is much simpler than in the Mary play, drawing them into the idea of grace, love and charity, but principally concerned with managing the narrative. For some unexplained reason he speaks of the previous year's play having shown the story up to the Betrayal, clearly a conscious summary of Passion Play I. He then briefly proceeds to the subject of the present play and urges the audience to take good heed of it.

His presence taken as a whole reveals the compiler's concern for the audience and its instruction.

Besides these direct addresses this cycle is notably rich in other examples. Passion Play I has prologues by the Demon, and John the Baptist; there is the prologue of Den, the Summoner, for *The Trial of Joseph and Mary*, play 14. The Demon's speech should perhaps be seen in the light of his unusually developed presence in *N Town*: he appears here and in other places for which there is no parallel in the other cycles. His role is partly a challenge to Christ's identification with mercy, and it is made more interesting in a number of places because he finds it very difficult to establish whether the man Christ is also divine. This issue, which has been dubbed the 'abuse-of-power theory', appears in all the cycles.[8] It suggests that Christ deliberately concealed his divinity in order to tempt Satan to overstep his allowed sphere of influence by attempting to kill Christ who is God, while mistaking him for a human being.

In the *N Town* version the opposition is presented in its most coherent form, and it is linked with a persistent interest in the activity of the Devils. *The Temptation of Christ* (play 23) begins with a conference of Devils. Satan sees Christ as a threat:

> If þat he be Goddys childe
> And born of a mayd mylde
> Than be we rygh sore begylde
> And short xal ben oure spede!
>
> (23.23–6)

Belyal and Beelzabub help to persuade Satan to try the temptations 'in synnys thre' (50). When the first two temptations fail, Satan becomes more desperate, and decides he must begin 'a newe travayl'. His list of places shown to Christ from the mountain is the most elaborate of all the cycles – 'All þis longyth to me' (23.178). But Christ will not yield, and Satan, admitting that he is baffled, goes off to hell letting 'a crakke' (23.195).

Perhaps his most striking speech, unique to the cycle, is the long Prologue to Passion Play I, most of which is directly addressed to the audience:

> I am 3oure lord, Lucifer, þat out of helle cam,
>   Prince of þis Werd and gret Duke of Helle!
> Wherefore my name is clepyd Sere Satan
>   Whech aperyth among 3ow a matere to spelle.   *explain*
>
> (26.1–3)

In a cycle which is rich in sermons, as for example in the *Woman Taken in Adultery*,[9] this speech features as an anti-sermon in which he promises reward for sinners, and makes an appeal to the emotions of his listeners:

> Gyff me ȝoure love, grawnt me myn affeccyon
> > And I wyl vnclose the tresour of lovys alyawns *alliance*
> And gyff ȝow ȝoure desyrys afftere ȝoure intencyon.
>
> > > > > > (26.61–3)

The speech offers much detail of the Demon's view of history, which plays its part in the cycle by showing that there are overall considerations and themes, even though in one respect one has to see the speech as the introduction to the once separate Passion Play I. But even at this stage the Demon does not accept Christ's divinity:

> Goddys son he pretendyth, and to be borne of a mayde, *claims*
> > And seyth he xal dey for mannys saluacyon. *die*
> Þan wxl þe trewth be tryed, and no ferdere be delayd,
> > Whan þe soule fro the body xal make separacyon.
>
> > > > > > (26.41–4)

It is followed by another sermon by John the Baptist which rebuts much of what Demon says, but the real reply is to be found in the installation of the Eucharist dramatised at *The Last Supper* (play 27). Here the place and scaffold configuration we have noted is used to remarkable effect. The action is a slow build-up of tension between the conspirators on one side and Christ on the other, with Judas moving between the two. Cayphas, informed by him, gives his instructions:

> No lenger þan make we teryeng, *delays*
> > But eche man to his place hym dyth. *prepare*
> And ordeyn preuely for þis thyng,
> > Þat it be don þis same nyth.

The stage direction follows immediately in the text:

> *Here the buschopys partyn in þe place, and eche of hem takyn here leve be contenawns* [by gestures], *resortyng eche man to his place with here meny* [their followers], *to make redy to take Cryst. And þan xal þe place þer* [where] *Cryst is in sodeynly vnclose rownd abowtyn shewyng Cryst syttyng at þe table and hese dyscypulis ech in ere degré: Cryst þus seyng:*

Jesu Brederyn, þis lambe þat was set us beforn
> Þat we alle have etyn in þis nyth: *night*
> It was comawndyd be my fadyr to Moyses and Aaron.
>
> > > > > > (27.345–51)

And, as they all stand (cf. l. 357), he goes on to explain the sacrifice of the
new lamb, linking his own Passion with the Eucharist, and showing the
strength of his love as a counter to the Demon's deception:

> And with fervent desyre of hertys affeccyon
>   I have enterly desyryd to kepe my Mawnde   *Last Supper*
> Among ȝow or þan I suffre my Passyon.   *before*
>   (27.365–7)

The verbal echo from the Demon's speech quoted above should not be
missed. It forms a prelude to the highly imagistic and rhythmic language,
based on the scripture, but having independent poetic qualities of its own
which is used about the Eucharist:

> With no byttyr bred þis bred ete xal be:
>   Þat is to say, with no byttyrnesse of hate
>   and envye,
> But with þe suete bred of love and charyte
>   Weche fortefyet þe soule gretlye.   *fortifies*
>   (27.397–400)

Significantly at this high point of religious emotion, Christ is given a line
about the Devil:

> So to dystroy ȝoure gostly enmye þis xal be kepte
> For ȝoure paschal lombe into þe wordys ende.
>   (27.387–8)

    Laughter plays a significant role at times in this cycle, though one
might suggest that like much of the characterisation, it is controlled by
the complex of didacticism and spirituality we have been considering.
Two examples may illustrate this. Firstly, the discovery by Joseph of
Mary's pregnancy is handled by means of a comic presentation of him as
a foolish old man. The language is in marked contrast to that just discussed and it suggests more the comedy of cuckoldry – 'Ow, dame, what
þinge menyth this?' . . . 'ȝa, ȝa, all olde men to me take tent' (*notice*) (12.34,
49). The underlying motif is possibly the marriage of May and January.
But this folly is contained, perhaps because the audience knew from the
Annunciation – not to mention other common assumptions – what had
really happened, and also because in the development of this particular
play he is put right by the Angel (sent direct from Deus), who treats him
very gently, as does Mary. His contrition is complete.

In the *Woman Taken in Adultery* the action as well as the dialogue is comic. Though the sardonic descriptions by the accusers have a grim truth, there is comedy in the moment of action when they bang upon the door and the young man emerges with his shoes untied and his breeches in his hand (Latin s.d. at 24.124). He makes a good deal of noise and goes off cursing them all. The accusations against the woman, now desperate, rise to a crescendo as they bring her before Christ, who, scripture prompting, silently writes in the sand. Thus the comedy of the outburst works successfully by turning attention towards the silent wisdom of Christ, and we should note too that this is the play which begins with a sermon from Christ on the desirability for mercy for sinners who repent – which the adulteress wholeheartedly does.

By contrast with these comic episodes which end within the divine embrace, play 20 contains the episode of the death of Herod. Though this appears in other cycles, the treatment is unique here in that Death himself appears on the stage, presumably in horrific guise. He has a soliloquy while Herod is already set at table in celebration of the slaughter of the Innocents: from the dialogue before and after Death's speech it is clear that Herod does not hear him, and so the warning of Death is directed pointedly at the audience. Death speaks of his inexorable power, hinting at the dance of Death, and he has a spear to bring down human pride. He strikes just as Herod in triumph calls for trumpets, and the Devil carries off the victims – This catell [*property*] is myn!', exulting in his own 'myrthe' and 'sportys'. Once again the compiler ensures the presence of the Devil at a critical moment. Death concludes the episode with a grim self-description based upon the theme that he comes suddenly, and people should be aware.

Structurally, this sequence is of interest because it shows the needless death of the children, and the bleak consequences of Herod's designs as a warning: it is followed by the play of Christ and the Doctors (play 21) which embodies the emergence of divine wisdom in the humanity of a young child, in a play significantly more sophisticated in argument than its counterpart in the other cycles. In turn this leads to the plays of the ministry which embody so much of Christ's doctrine. Here we may perceive that whatever the piecemeal nature of the composition of the original episodes, the assembly of the components by the compilator carries a good deal of the most profound objectives of the cycle within it. At times, as we have seen, there are specific pointers which relate the significance of one part of the narrative to another, but there are also long sequences where the simple juxtaposition of incidents makes them reflect upon one another. It is more difficult to know how deliberate this may have been, but it is undeniably a successful feature of the *N Town* cycle.

IV

Morality plays

The term 'morality play' is not really medieval, though some plays were referred to as 'moral plays' quite early on. For the historian of drama it has become a convenient term for those plays which are not structured on scriptural or mythological narratives, but which have at the centre some doctrine to impart. Whether simple or complex, the doctrine controls the choice of incidents, the plot, the characterisation and the staging. It gives to the author of these plays a power of initiation, enabling the design to be constructed by a process of invention and imagination even though the doctrines upon which it is based may be orthodox and conventional. Equally, the same process of 'compilation' noted earlier may still obtain. This process is not so different for the authors of interludes, and the distinction between the two types is not clear-cut. By convention, however, interludes are thought of as being shorter, and the term is usually applied to sixteenth-century plays.

There are only six extant moralities from before 1500, and because they are so few, some of them at least have been subjected to more scrutiny than most other medieval plays. Hence there are some dangers in generalising about these plays as though they formed a distinctive genre. The moralities to be considered are the *Macro plays* (*The Castle of Perseverance, Mankind* and *Wisdom*, all from East Anglia), *The Pride of Life*, *Everyman*, and Henry Medwall's *Nature*. It is apparent from what we have already said about the staging, as well from what follows, that they are very different in scope.

The moralities rely upon systems of allegory. For practical purposes this means that most of the characters are abstractions whose main task is to carry a representational or symbolic function. They may stand for vices or virtues, or they may represent social classes. Centrally, there may be generalised human figures like Humanum Genus, which stand for human beings in different circumstances of life and age. Alongside this, in the drama, goes the dynamic thrust of the plot whereby events are made to refer to underlying truths, judgements or observations. Thus the key to both plot and character is not realism, probability or verisimilitude but the relationship to something which lies behind the external phenomena. As Northrop Frye put it, 'We have allegory when the events of a narrative obviously and continuously refer to another simultaneous structure of events or ideas.'[10]

The characters in an allegory are usually programmed to stay the same: Pride is always Pride whatever happens to him. A fundamental change in the discourse can be signalled by bringing in another character representing the new state. As identification is crucial, there have to be effective signals in movement, in appearance, in gestures and in action. For example, in a sixteenth-century manuscript of a Majorca *Last Judgement* the following instructions are given:

> Avarice [shall walk] in a long robe, an ink container at his waist, a purse in his hand with objects inside to make a sound like money jingling when he wishes, and a book under his arm. On the other side of him shall walk Sloth in a short jacket, in sagging breeches, with a pillow under his arm for having a rest when he feels like it.[11]

The pleasures to be derived from this may explain why allegory had such a long run, for allegory was an extensively used form of explication, and presumably entertainment, for nearly a thousand years. It offered, especially in the drama, the chance to present realistic details of pleasing suitability (like's Sloth's pillow), the technique of self-explanation, the strong sense of justice in the narrative whereby rewards are appropriate to action and character, and the pleasure of decoding the sense of the allegory which can at times be like that for a detective story. We shall find that this last type of allegory becomes more prevalent in the sixteenth century when allegory turned more specifically to political objectives.

One of the characteristics of allegory is that it offers a schematisation of experience, and certain generalised patterns became commonplace. Among these are:

- The Coming of Death;
- The Pilgrimage of Life;
- The World, the Flesh and the Devil;
- The Dispute between Good and Bad Angels;
- The Siege of a Castle;
- The Battle between Seven Deadly Sins and Corresponding Virtues (Sometimes called *Psychomachia* [Battle in the Soul] after a poem by Prudentius);
- The Debate of the Four Daughters of God (also called The Parliament of Heaven);
- The triumph of Avarice, often seen as the chief Sin;
- Fall and Salvation of the sinner.

Though the last is the most common overall structure, and one which persisted into sixteenth-century interludes, these patterns could be interwoven and there was no particular need for them to be continuous or comprehensive. This can be illustrated from *Perseverance*, where the overall structure is Fall and Salvation, which occurs twice. The siege takes up a long section in the middle of the play, after the first fall and rise, and it involves the conflict of Vices and Virtues. The two Angels watching closely over the hero intervene from time to time to try to influence his actions and decisions. The last sequence of this play is the debate of the Four Daughters responding to a cry for mercy by Man as he dies. Avarice is responsible for twice breaking his resolve. With the intermittent use of these allegorical devices the play has enormous scope for a variety of dramatic situations and individual sequences.

One of the most remarkable is the death of the hero, who has fallen for the wiles of Avarice:

> 'More and more', þis my steuene.   *cry*
> If I myth alwey dwellyn in prosperyte,   *might*
> Lord God, þane wel were me
> I wolde, þe medes, forsake þe   *as recompense*
>   And neuere to comyn in heuene.
>
> (2773–7)

Immediately Mors appears and quickly identifies himself to the audience:

> ȝe schul me drede euerychone
> Whanne I com ȝe schul grone;
> My name in londe is lefte alone:
>   I hatte drery Dethe.   *am called*
>
> (2787–90)

Death, no doubt fearful to behold, strikes Humanum Genus with a spear, whereupon Mundus sends his boy to grab all the possessions of the victim. The horror is that when the boy is asked for his name he gives it as I-Wot-Neuere-Whoo (I-Don't-Know-Who), and Man's precious possessions pass away into the hands of an unknown and unfathomable recipient. Physically, he registers the coming of death:

> I bolne and bleyke in blody ble   *swell, turn pale, state*
> And as a floure fadyth my face.
>
> (2999–3000)

But if *Perseverance* is planned on a grand scale the same is not true of *Mankind*. Though there is still a good deal of doctrine coming from the priest-like Mercy, the main dramatic effects turn upon the at first foolish mockery of Mankind by the fashionable villains Newguise, Nowadays and Nought. They almost literally tie Mankind up in knots, and bring him great sorrow by inducing him to give up his holy practices and duties and to come near to despair as he thinks he no longer has any hope. But this play, like *Perseverance,* does give scope for a devil in the form of Titivillus, who succeeds in breaking Mankind's devotion to honest labour – a keen allegorical point in a play which has idleness as a key theme.[12] The devil appears as a character in several morality plays and is sometimes presented comically, but here Titivillus is very clever and he contributes to the drama by making the protagonist commit a fatal error. In this play, which may have been meant for Shrovetide, he appears to be more in the nature of a folk monster than a comic character, and the players make a collection from the audience before he shows himself. Once the breach is made, the other villains come to take over Mankind. The process here is worked by an intensive use of comedy, verbal and physical. These two aspects play an essential part in the working of this play because there are many verbal jokes and much abuse, but there are always physical ones to be seen as where the villains attempt to bring Mankind's coat up to fashionable requirements by shortening it. Although there is no large-scale spectacle as in *Perseverance,* there is plenty of detailed stage business in the mockery and conspiracy against both Mankind himself and against Mercy. There is also a strong sense that the audience is there to be used and managed as the play progresses.

If the theatrical vitality of *Mankind* is readily apparent, as indeed a number of twentieth-century productions have shown, the case of *Wisdom, Who is Christ* has proved more difficult. Modern audiences quickly respond to the ingenious comedy of the villains in *Mankind,* and from these they may be induced by skilled playing to perceive the persuasive balance given by the virtuous Mercy. But *Wisdom* has no comic sequence, and its plot is not really much beyond a rather simple Fall and Salvation. The key, however, may lie in the allegory, supported by a very extensive system of onstage symbols. The real needs in performing this play are to exploit the very rich descriptions of costume, and to allow full scope for movement and dancing since in dramatic type this play anticipates the coming of the masque in the seventeenth century. These can be seen as complementing the sophisticated verbal imagery.

The essential allegory is twofold: that Christ is an embodiment of true Wisdom, and that Anima, the human soul, may find salvation by accepting a role as the Bride of Christ. Much of the material of the play seems to associate it with the monastic life, but there are strong arguments for seeing it also as a vindication of more secular aspects. Though there is some mystical imagery relating to the union with Christ, it seems that much of this is commonplace, and the play may have been intended for a fairly mixed audience. But the action of the play also involves some striking detail. Anima's fall is not caused by her own fault, but by the way the Devil perverts the three constituent parts of the soul – Mind, Will and Understanding – inducing each to embrace a Deadly Sin. As a character she merely shows forth the results of the failings of her constituent Mights. The presentation of Lucifer is well managed because, for once, the arguments he puts have some truth in them. He claims that a purely sheltered conventual life is not real service, and that true faith should be shown by living a mixed life (*vita mixta*): one of his chief arguments in support of this is that Christ himself did not live a protected life but entered into the world. Anima's fall is presented dramatically by her disfigurement: '*Here Anima apperythe in þe most horrybull wyse, fowlere þan a fende*' (902 s.d.). This is amplified a few moments later by: '*Here rennyt* [*runneth*] *owt from wndyr þe horrybyll mantyll of the Soull seven small boyes in þe lyknes of dewyllys*' [*devils*] (912 s.d.).

As in *Perseverance*, there are moments here when the visual aspects of the performance similarly carry much of the allegorical force, as for example when the Virtues defeat the Deadly Sins by pelting them with roses, and it should be seen as one of the achievements of the morality plays that they exploit the visual extensively. This may be because it was felt that one could learn as much with the eyes as with ears (a proposition not entirely foreign to modern advertising). The development of the drama in the Middle Ages, while it may have had a theoretical background in terms of theology, also benefited by a disposition to exploit onstage nonverbal techniques. We have seen a similar tendency in the iconographical aspects of the mystery plays.

In all three morality plays so far discussed there are strong emotional and spiritual elements. To some extent that may be a reflection of late medieval piety in which fear as well as intense love played a great part. Hence perhaps the exploitation of the idea of Christ as the bridegroom and the use of imagery from the Song of Songs in *Wisdom*. Devotion had such strong emotional elements in it that it might lead to people changing their lives radically. Thus the fear and horror felt over the debasement of the beautiful Anima would have its effect, as would the excitement of confrontation in the long and powerful battle scenes of *Perseverance* (which are of course largely unscripted), and the pathos of the dying cry for mercy. It would be wrong to see the experience of the morality play on stage as a purely intellectual exercise or as one simply concerned with the confirmation of dogma; there is every evidence that the plays worked through the emotions, and one of the chief means of doing that is by allowing the plot to isolate emotional moments. Several of these plays bear a close relationship to sermons, which often added to the formal intellectual structures a strong emotional appeal.

The case of *Everyman* is significant here. It is a translation from a Dutch original, originating in a Rhetoricians' play, presumably based on a theme which asks what is most likely to be of help in the preparation for Death. It is difficult to underestimate the importance of this theme in medieval society as a great deal of time and resources were expended upon it.[13]

It is remarkable that the English version was printed at least four times between 1510 and 1530, though there is no direct evidence for its having been performed. Perhaps it was more important then as a book of devotion than as a text for playing, but we have no way of checking this.

But instead of a witty debate supported by comic material, *Everyman* comprises a rigorous and remorseful examination of all the different possibilities of support in the hour of death, and the pathos of the protagonist's isolation and loneliness continues to grow throughout the action. Even today this predicament is still found to be moving in performance:

> O, all thynge fayleth, save God alone –
> Beaute, Strength, and Dyscrecyon;
> For whan Deth bloweth his blast,
> They all renne fro me full fast.   *run*
>
> (841–4)

The play is a remarkable example of dramatic imagination even though there is very little information about possible staging. This may be because it is a translation out of its native environment. It is not broadly typical of the other English plays in structure, and there is no concentration on particular Sins as often happens in the others, yet the Coming of Death is, as noted, a configuration of some frequency, and the play answers to the emotions involved very acutely. In spite of the absence of direct conflict or confrontation between good and evil, this text reveals that there is a dynamism within its structure which produces dramatic development of great power as the urgency to find an escape from the intensifying predicament increases.

The two other early moralities bear some relation to what has been discussed here. In *Nature* Medwall, the author, may in some respects anticipate devices we shall encounter in the sixteenth-century interlude, especially the extensive use of aliases by the evil characters. It is also clearly designed to be played in a hall.[14] However, the play follows the characteristic morality allegory of the pilgrimage of life in which Man has to engage with Worldly Affeccyon. It is an allegory which suggests that humans must live in the world, and gives a strong impulse towards the necessity of Penance when things turn out badly. Like *Wisdom*, this play gives importance to the conflict between Reason and Sensuality who work here as essential components to life. The Seven Deadly Sins are presented without the more formal structures in other plays like *Perseverance*. Indeed Medwall, along with the manipulation of aliases, gives to the Sins a mutually destructive behaviour which undoubtedly exposes their corruption. Entrances and exits are cleverly used to show the development of allegorical points. The dialogue is particularly vigorous, often reflecting a topicality which is acute and closely observed. Man under the influence of Sensuality comes in dressed as a gallant, and the surprise of Glotony is very neatly handled, but it is clear that the main function of this very crisp exchange is to underline the allegory:

Man	Trouth, as ye say I know yt well.	
Glotony	What gentylman ys thys? Can ye tell?	
Bodyly Lust	Wotyst thou never?	*Don't you know?*
Glotony	No, by the bell, I saw hym never byfore.	
Bodyly Lust	Is yt our mayster?	
Glotony	Nay, by the rood, It ys not he – woldyst thou make me wood?	*mad*
Man	Yes, I am the same!	
Glotony	I cry you mercy! I se yt well now! Byfore I knew you not, I make God a vow, In ernest nor in game.	
Man	Why? Bycause I have chaunged myne aray?	
Glotony	For that cause, trow ye? Nay, nay, That ys not the thyng That can dysceyve me, be ye sure!	

(2.564–77)

This dialogue in stanzaic verse has its precedents in some of the speech in *Mankind*, but in this play it is developed in a far more complex manner as these characters become involved in a very close exchange.

Unfortunately, *The Pride of Life* now exists only as an imperfect photograph of a fragment, though some of the missing latter part may be conjectured from the Prologue. The extant speech reads like a poem, but the text of the play itself is highly dramatic both in its concept of how to use the stage and in the vigour of the dialogue, including the ways in which the characters talk directly to one another. The protagonist, the King of Life, speaks boastingly of his power and looks forward to a conflict with Death. The play is strong on allegory in that it demonstrates clearly what each character stands for, and there is a remarkable sense in the play of the clarity of the allegorical method. This is perhaps aided by direct and simple language which goes straight to the point, beautifully controlled by the tight versification, as in the Bishop's sermon:

Paraventur men halt me a fol	*hold*
To sig þat sot tal;	*tell that foolish tale*
Þai farit as ficis in a pol –	*fare as fish in a pool*
The gret eteit the smal.	*eat*

Ricmen spart for no þing   *spare*
  To do þe por wrong;
Þai þingit not on hir ending   *think*
  Ne on Det þat is so strong.

(359–66)

One large ingredient is the coming of Death, but the use of Mirth, the King's Messenger, is a way of extending the King's boast, and he also suggests that he will help to destroy the King by encouraging his indulgence through flattery. In spite of his two Knights, Health and Strength, Death overcomes the King of Life in battle, as the Prologue explains:

With him driuith adoun to grounde
  He dredith nothing his kniʒtis;
And delith him depe depis wounde
  And kith on him his miʒtis.   *showed his power over him*

(89–9)

That this, possibly the earliest dramatic text in English (*c.* 1350?), should show such competence in allegory and in dramatic language must give rise to questions about what is now lost. There are a few clues suggesting a number of different threads in the previous centuries, but almost nothing survives in the vernacular. There are also a few Continental texts which may argue for a wider dramatic tradition: particularly Hildegard of Bingen's *Ordo Virtutum*, and the *Antichrist* play from Tegernsee (both twelfth century) in some respects share allegorical techniques with morality plays. In France the earliest *moralités* such as the late-fifteenth-century *Lomme pecheur* do not significantly pre-date their English counterparts, though they do exhibit some similar stage techniques. Moreover, the countless references now emerging in the Records of Early English Drama to various kinds of entertainer in the Middles Ages, whether they be singers, mimers or tumblers as well, makes one think that there was a great deal going on, but apparently very few people thought it necessary or desirable to write anything down.[15]

The expanding data from the written records have not revealed the existence of many previously unsuspected moralities. We are left with the paradox that the plays discussed do show a variety of rich dramatic features which can be made available to modern critics and performers to enjoy and develop, but that the perceivable quantity is small. On the other hand, it is perhaps the moralities rather than the mystery cycles which had greatest potential for development because of the flexibility of the genre. It may be that because their authors, and those of the interludes indeed, had the opportunity of inventing plots and situations, albeit initially controlled by allegorical structures, there would be scope for new material to be implanted, whether from other polemical discourses, or from mythological, chronicle, humanist or classical origins. The fall and rise structure particularly provided a popular framework until the re-emergence of tragedy as a dramatic form. The moralities had also evolved comic techniques, particularly in the conduct of evil characters, which proved valuable.

Notes

1. See J. Koopmans (ed.) *Le Mystère de Saint Remi* (Geneva, 1997).

2. *MS* 2.340–1.

3. See, for example, *The Holkham Bible Picture Book*, edited by W.O. Hassall (London, 1954), *The Biblia Pauperum*, edited by Avril Henry (Aldershot, 1987), and the altar carving at the cathedral in Odense in Denmark by Claus Berg, *c.* 1470–1532.

4. R.D.S. Jack, *Patterns of Divine Comedy: A Study of Medieval English Drama* (Cambridge, 1989).

5. G.D. Smidt, '*Vides Festinare Pastores*: The Medieval Artistic Vision of Shepherding and Manipulation of Cultural Expectation in the *Secunda Pastorum*', *Neophilologus* 76 (1992), 290–304.

6. Kolve, 156–66.

7. R.C. Cosbey, 'The Mak Story and its Folklore Analogues', *Speculum* 20 (1945), 310–17.

8. T. Fry, 'The Unity of the *Ludus Coventriae*', *Studies in Philology* 48 (1951), 527–70.

9. Peter Meredith has shown that this play is a dramatisation of a sermon which appeals on strong emotional grounds in favour of mercy: '"Nolo mortem" and the Ludus Coventriae Play of the Woman Taken in Adultery', *Medium Aevum* 38 (1969), 38–54.

10. *Encyclopaedia of Poetry and Poetics.*

11. P. Meredith and J.E. Tailby (eds) *The Staging of Religious Drama in Europe in the Later Middle Ages* (Kalamazoo, 1983), p. 89.

12. Paula Neuss, 'Active and Idle Language: Dramatic Images in *Mankind*', in N. Denny (ed.) *Medieval Drama*, Stratford-upon-Avon Studies 16 (London, 1973), pp. 41–68.

13. Eamon Duffy, *The Stripping of the Altars* (New Haven and London, 1992), pp. 310–27.

14. Meg Twycross, 'The Theatricality of Medieval English Plays', in *Companion* 71.

15. The texts relevant to these traits, and information about possible performances, are discussed by Richard Axton, *European Drama of the Early Middle Ages* (London, 1974), *passim.* Vernacular fragments are found in items VIII to XIII of Norman Davis (ed.) *Non-Cycle Plays and Fragments*, EETS SS1 (Oxford, 1970).

Part II

Humanism, Renaissance and Reformation

Chapter 7
Education and Polemic: Classical Comedy and Tragedy

This chapter is concerned first with some of the changes which affected the development of drama in the sixteenth century, and then with tracing the particular lines of classical comedy and tragedy up to the opening of the public theatres in 1576.

In discussing the medieval drama in Part I we have already crossed into the sixteenth century because many well-established ideas were naturally carried forward. But the shifts of emphasis in English, or indeed British, national life were very great after the turn of the century and they tended to accumulate round two nuclei, the Renaissance and the Reformation. Neither of these can be regarded as entirely independent, but the effect upon the development of drama which they created or enabled was enormous. In brief, they ushered in a much greater variety of dramatic structures, many experimentations in form and in performance, and many changes in the way drama could be used, or even exploited. By the end of the sixteenth century these changes had also ensured the development of a professional theatre in which people could make their livelihood from the making and performing of plays.

With the Renaissance we find a disposition to rediscover and revalue classical writings, especially, in the drama, the plays of Seneca, Plautus and Terence, and to a lesser extent the Greek dramatists. But the changes were made more complex because contemporary interpretations in Italy, France and Burgundy played a large part in framing the re-appraisal of this classical material. Moreover, new political authorities, even before the Reformation had fuelled them with extremist attitudes and passionate ideologies, had come to see the arts as a means of expressing and indeed controlling political authority. Thus the arrival of Henry VII, at the beginning of the Tudor dynasty, saw a great influx of Burgundian ideas, as in the King's collection of books, and the scholars such as Bernard André and Quentin Poulet whom he gathered around him to establish a new royal image.[1] In broad terms, they were complemented by architects, designers and craftsmen, and the combination of all these arts manifested itself in great public shows like the quasi–dramatic reception in 1501 for the Lady Katherine of Spain, consort of Arthur, Prince of Wales, and more portentously of Henry VIII. A fuller account of this and other similar public ceremonial in the streets will be found in Chapter 10, but here we note that there was a long tradition in London and in other cities of welcoming important foreign visitors as well as of celebrating or displaying important national items such as coronations or royal births. This was much developed under the Tudors, who grasped its propaganda value, and also at times became involved personally in organising and responding to performances. Henry VIII particularly had strong international ambitions extending to invasions of France and Scotland and to support for a grandeur in royal entertainment which came to be expected. Personal involvement of monarchs in such entertainments led to an increase of status, and a consequent increase in the resources which could be made available. The urge for display was manifested at the meeting with Francis I of France at the Field of the Cloth of Gold in 1520.

There are links here with the more formal kinds of civic drama such as the Corpus Christi plays, in that the contents of civic processions and entries were often jealously guarded by the corporations as their own privilege and had strong local associations. At the same time we have more and more evidence of public drama at a much lower level of society, especially in the parishes, which were an influential part of local government. This is discussed in more detail under 'Parish drama' in Chapter 10. The many kinds of entertainment here produced had a widespread provenance. We can go some way towards describing them, but we are rather short of texts, or detailed accounts of performances. There is no doubt, however, that such local entertainments were a staple of the dramatic life in the Tudor period, and they undoubtedly preserved survivals from much earlier celebrations and entertainments.

The concept of humanism leads us also to a changed sense of the value of the arts, including drama, and it shows itself in two ways which were influential upon the theatre. On the one hand, it helped with the introduction of secular ideas, and indeed, with the development of secular plots or stories (not solely from classical sources but also from romance and chivalry). In this way the actual material of plays became part of new concepts of human activity both in public and personal spheres. On the other hand, humanism placed great emphasis upon education as a means of developing the individual and preparing him for both private and public roles. The most important humanist figure was Desiderius Erasmus (?1466–1536), the Dutch scholar whose writings were enormously important in both secular and religious dimensions. In the latter, especially his critique of the Church from within, spearheaded by his edition of the Bible, he sharpened attitudes towards the Church.

This was a period of intense religious devotion among the faithful, indeed the first years of the sixteenth century saw some of the greatest manifestations of late medieval piety, and England was conspicuous for its devotion both in practice and in the amount of resources given to religion.[2] This showed itself in such things as the cults of the Virgin and the Saints, and the extensive resources which were expended upon good works of charity, and upon instituting chantries where priests were to sing masses for the dead in perpetuity. It is perhaps no accident that in the history of drama it is the period when the cycle plays were at their most vigorous. Yet there was still much that was wrong, corrupt and even ridiculous in religious life. Erasmus was one of those who drew attention to it, especially in his *Colloquies* (1522) where, for example, he questioned the value of pilgrimages, one of the chief manifestations of piety. Such critical attitudes, it transpired, could not be contained inside the Church, and heretical or Protestant ideas gradually made it impossible for some people to remain within. In the sixteenth century the drama embodied criticism from within in the plays of John Heywood, and from without in those of John Bale. The work of these dramatists makes for an extraordinary polarity in the drama of the 1520s and 1530s, and there are others like Sir David Lindsay, the Scottish courtier-dramatist, whose work reflects the intensity of religious controversy in the 1540s and 1550s. Instead of being primarily concerned with devotion, religious drama moved significantly towards politics. At times it became convenient for the monarch to restrain dramatic activity through licensing; but it also became expedient to use it in support of the complex changes in state policy associated with the Reformation. One result of this is that a significant proportion, perhaps a majority of extant sixteenth-century plays, are manifestly in support of the Protestant government.

Printing has a growing role in the history of drama. Early in the sixteenth century it became possible to disseminate texts more widely by the multiplicity of copies. This must have meant that playwrights could be more aware of one another's work, and that gradually a market for play texts developed having specific requirements and characteristics. It is particularly interesting, as noted in Chapter 8, that the publication of plays by Medwall and Skelton was significantly delayed. The essence of this is that the timing of publication can become a public and indeed political act which may be differentiated from the moments of composition and of performance. Moreover plays could be revised for publication as required by external forces.

Along with the religious dimension we also find changes in the material basis of society, especially the growing importance of the secular middle class. This was a natural development of medieval phenomena such as the way the merchants of York, aldermen and masters of their crafts, promoted drama as a means of glorifying their city, a process which continued in the sixteenth century, or the increasing prosperity of the wool industry in East Anglia. But now the increases in foreign trade and commitments made possible a more ambitious programme for an educated middle class.

The mercantile structure of English city life continued to expand and the guilds and their entertainment – not only mystery cycles and the like – were among the pacemakers. The livery companies in London developed a strong interest in their own entertainment.

The changes also generated an increased interest in training for professions. For the churchman this might lead to the need for patronage from the nobility, but for lawyers the objectives in public life could be much wider. Through the century there is increasing evidence for the interest of lawyers in plays, usually for performances at one of the Inns of Court, but also showing itself in the legal aspects which emerge in some texts such as Norton and Sackville's *Gorboduc* (1562) and Thomas Garter's *The Virtuous and Godly Susanna* (1569). Lawyers depend upon a sophistication in the use of language and the lawyers' plays evidence this.

Classical comedy

A new emphasis upon classical literature is one of the keynotes to the early sixteenth century. It follows the popularity of classical subjects and literary techniques in Italy, and it was significantly advanced by the invention of printing which led to the appearance of Greek and Latin texts in western Europe from the late fifteenth century onwards. This is not to say that in the case of comedy Latin authors like Terence were not known in medieval times, as the Christian adaptations by Hrotswitha in twelfth-century Germany make plain, and there is some limited evidence for performances in medieval times. It is not so much a completely new beginning as a re-emphasis which rapidly grew in importance. This was stimulated by changes in educational practice which gave much greater emphasis to the study of classical plays, especially comedies, in schools.

Erasmus is a key figure in this. His own theological and biblical scholarship led him to be critical of many aspects of the Roman Catholic Church. Even though he never left it, he gained much respect from reformers like Martin Luther and John Bale who followed some of his teaching, especially about the Bible, and accepted many of his criticisms of Church practices, such as pilgrimages and the worshipping of images, taking them to the point of schism. Erasmus's revaluation of belief included a re-translation of the New Testament and extended to a perception that educational curricula needed to be changed in order to promote the ideals of Christian living which were the centre of his life and teaching.

In comedy he particularly centred attention on the Roman playwright Terence (*c.* 190–*c.* 159 BC). The concern Erasmus felt for high standards was tempered by his obvious enjoyment of comedy, and his perception that the young could share in this. This proved true over the next hundred years or so, though there were no doubt plenty of young scholars whose first experience of Terence was physically painful. He thought highly of what he considered to be the purity of Terence's language, and, in his advice to Colet who was setting up his new school at St Paul's in London in 1514, he discusses how to study a comedy using Terence as a model. He recommended learning by heart, and remarked that, as 'Terence is the best model of diction, you should be always turning the pages'. He thought the style was 'pure, concise and closest to everyday speech'.[3] Considering decorum, he shows a keen interest in the variety of the types of Terence's characters:

> [A teacher] should show that decorum especially is studied,
> not only in its universal aspect, I mean that youths should
> fall in love, that pimps should perjure themselves, that the
> prostitute should allure, the old man scold, the slave
> deceive, the soldier boast, and so on, but also in the
> particular delineation of different characters as developed by
> the poet. For example in the *Andria* Terence introduces
> two old men of widely different temperament [Simo and
> Chremes]. . . . Likewise he introduces two young men of
> divergent natures [Pamphilus and Charinus].[4]

Erasmus's approach was determined by Christian principles which placed great emphasis upon rationality. Whatever else his advocacy offered, this concern for persuasiveness was of great value to the succeeding generations of scholars, lawyers and artists who sought to extend the study of classical comedy. It could be justified as a means of moral education, and in the detail of the plays of Terence, and of various imitators which will be discussed shortly, there could be presented and perceived a moral value. Erasmus himself was much exercised to defend Terence from the charge that he promoted immorality by his portrayal of wickedness. The answer lies in rational discrimination: 'These characters are depicted for us in plays . . . so that we may first see what is seemly or unseemly in human behaviour and then distribute affection or rebuke accordingly.'[5] The mention in the previous quotation about the differentiation between characters of similar type supports this rationalisation. However, in spite of this defence, the doubt about immorality in drama, and in comedy in particular, would not go away and the need to combat it appears again and again in prologues throughout the sixteenth century.

In addition to his theoretical support for the teaching of Terence in schools and universities, Erasmus's work may have helped in other ways. His *Colloquies* were dialogues about a variety of subjects, some of which touched upon ecclesiastical abuse. Partly based upon some of the *Dialogues* of the fourth-century Greek poet Lucian, they were widely read, not least because of the high reputation Erasmus could command through much of Europe. 'Reading' might also mean reading in different parts or voices, a practice of great psychological interest in the Renaissance since it offered ways of juxtaposing opposite viewpoints. His close relationship with Sir Thomas More, who was himself actively interested in drama, extended to the co-operative translation of Lucian. Through More he may have influenced John Heywood, More's relative by marriage, whose successful and influential work will be considered below. Erasmus himself edited the works of Terence in 1532.

Erasmus's theoretical position was supported in a number of ways. For one, the critical writings of Donatus, the fourth-century grammarian, were used in close connection with the printed editions of Terence as instructional manuals. Donatus showed the fourfold construction of comedy which became a standard of criticism for generations. The division comprised the *prologue*, the *protasis* in which the characters were introduced, the *epitasis* in which the plot was complicated, usually on the basis of errors, 'perturbations' or misunderstandings, and the *catastrophe* in which there was a resolution of the errors and a happy ending. Like Erasmus, Donatus had used Terence as an example and model in his exposition.

Not all the subsequent commentators on Terence held the same views as Erasmus, but there is no doubting that even more critical comments fed the strength of this dramatist's reputation. For example, Philip Melancthon, the German reformer (1497–1530) who edited Terence's plays in 1527, echoed Erasmus in advocating learning by heart because of the value of moral instruction, and approved even a 'superstitious diligence' in explanation. Sir Thomas Elyot defended Terence in his influential treatise *The Governour* (1531), which addressed the education of gentlemen, and echoed the moral defence by Erasmus, making use of a popular image: 'Comedies . . . be undoubtedly a picture or as it were a mirror of man's life, wherein evil is not taught but discovered [revealed].' Following his own rhetorical principles he turns defence into an attack upon moralistic opponents:

> If the vices in [the comedies] expressed should be the cause
> that minds of the readers should be corrupted, then by the
> same argument not only interludes in English, but also
> sermons, wherein some vice is declared [made plain], should
> be to the beholders and hearers like occasions to increase
> sinners.[6]

Terence became part of the intellectual background. Among those who were less impressed on moral grounds, Martin Bucer (1491–1551) thought the Bible was more profitable for instruction, but acknowledged the charm of Terence. Even Juan Luis Vives (1492–1540), who was not so sure about the correctness of Terence's Latin as praised by Erasmus, and who supported the condemnation of his 'immorality', published the *Linguae Latina exercitatio* (1532). This was a series of dialogues about the life of schoolboys and it became a school-book vying with the *Colloquies* in popularity. Sir Thomas More refers to characters of Terence in his attack upon Luther, and compared his opponent to Thraso, Phormio and Parmeno, unsavoury characters from the comedies who became 'types' in the sixteenth century.

In the light of this intense and persisting debate we may consider the practical questions of performance and the generation of new texts in a Terentian idiom. Though records are inevitably patchy, we can be certain that performances of Terence and Plautus went on from time to time in Cambridge from 1510–11 through to 1585–86 and beyond, principally at King's, Queens' and Trinity Colleges. At least twenty-five performances can still be dated in this period. In some colleges attendance was apparently compulsory, which inevitably led to a certain amount of unrest. There is evidence of a play by Plautus performed for Henry VIII at Greenwich in 1519, and the same author's *Phormio* was done for Wolsey in 1528.

At the production at Queens' College in Cambridge in 1522–23 there are some staging notes which help to fill in some details of the mechanics of performance.[7] The original classical comedies were done in the open air before large audiences of all social types, but at the Renaissance the theatrical ambience changed. For one thing the audience became more select, usually drawn, as the above references show, from educational or courtly circles. The very strong English tradition of using the great hall of colleges and secular houses for performances could easily be adapted to the primary requirement of the staging of classical comedy. This was that the action should take place in a street on to which a series of doors opened from the houses of the principal characters. This convention was strong enough in classical times for Terence himself to ridicule it; but it could allow the two entrances at the kitchen end of English halls to be used as a rough approximation.

This interrelationship between identifiable classical elements, and more specifically English ones, shows itself in some texts which have survived, but the balance between the extremes of direct imitation and concealed and often ingenious cross-reference varies enormously. Of the texts which will be mentioned here, the anonymous translation of Terence's *Andria*, called *Terens in Englysh* (*c.* ?1530), is faithful to the original. Consequently, it offered two important dramatic characteristics which were much imitated. One is the way the plot moves through a series of intrigues which are occasioned by the motif of the long-lost child. This gave scope for all sorts of recognitions and reunions essential to the construction of classical comedy which paid so much attention to the resolution of difficulties and mistakes. A second lies in the preoccupation in the prologue about the capacity of the English language to cope adequately with classical material and expression. Here the expectation is optimistic because the author thinks that English has adapted itself:

> . . . we keep our English continually
> And of other tongues many words we borrow
> Which now for English we use and occupy.
>
> (ll. 23–5)

As a result, readers may learn by this translation.

The substance of this relatively pure Terentian text reveals that kind of dialogue which was commonplace. For example:

Simo: Oh, Good! what hear I? If this true be
That she saith, all is dashed.

Lesbia: Thou showest a kind mind
Of the young man.

Mysis: Very good. Come in, follow me,
That we tarry not too long behind.

Lesbia: I will.

Davus: What remedy to this ill shall I now find?

Simo: What, doteth he on the strange wench so sore?
Ah, now I know all! I was so blind
That till now I could scant perceive it before.

(III.i.8–15)

Here the characters are summing up what has just happened and revealing their intentions either in monologue or in exchange with others. This self-revelation most likely fitted in well with a similar process in allegorical plays. There is a tendency to bring out universal truths whatever the context, and the purpose of much of the dialogue is to present conflicting points of view and the reasoning that underlies them. Even in this rather commonplace sample the concentration of Terentian dialogue is apparent.

In most of the plays in question the amount of anglicisation is extensive. *Thersites* and *Jack Juggler* (both printed *c.* 1562, but composed earlier) apparently take over some classical material. In the former the hero follows the type of the *miles gloriosus*, a soldier engaging in ridiculous boasting, though some of the substance of the play, including the delightful cure for worms, is invented. The classical element in *Jack Juggler* comprises some highly effective dialogue which is based upon the assumption of disguise in Plautus's *Amphitruo* (Titus Maccius Plautus, Roman comic poet, *c.* 254– *c.* 191 BC). Jankin Careaway's sense of his own identity is comically challenged when he meets Juggler who will not admit to being anyone else other than Jankin. The rest of the Plautine plot concerning the adultery of Jupiter for which the disguise was initially adopted is rejected, perhaps because the auspices were a school production. In his cunning, his determination to score off Careaway, and perhaps in his very name, Juggler shows some similarity with the Vice, a conventional and purely English stage character whom we shall consider in dealing with the interludes.

As it happens, both these plays have been tentatively attributed to Nicholas Udall, the undoubted author of *Roister Doister* (written and performed by January 1553 and printed in 1566). There is no doubt that he was at times a schoolmaster, holding posts at Eton and Westminster, and he wrote *Floures for Latine Spekynge* (1534), a highly influential textbook using Terentian texts as models for speaking and for appreciating style.

In *Roister Doister* the links with classical comedy are strongest in characterisation and in the structure of the plot, but not in its actual subject matter. Ralph Roister Doister is modelled upon the convention of the boastful soldier, though in his case his sheer stupidity and self-deception are much emphasised. These weaknesses are exploited by Matthew Merrygreek, his companion, acting like the classical parasite, who appears to want to further Ralph's courtship of the virtuous Christian Custance, but actually exposes him repeatedly to mockery and failure. The plot does not deal with the characteristic amorous intrigues, deceptions and mistakes of the classics, but the events which it contains are marshalled and arranged in such a way that both the bold outline of each episode and the increasing complication necessitating a fifth-act resolution are palpable. The play is arranged in five Acts, a characteristic of the sixteenth-century classical revival even though the texts of Terence are not marked in this way. The turns of events are also given a mock-heroic tone, which may suggest a classical origin, especially in Ralph's outrageous expectation that all women must love him, and in the battle which he eventually fights and loses against Custance's women, he wearing a kitchen pail on his head for armour.

Other smaller touches also suggest the classical models, such as the elaborate play on 'husband', and on the occasions when Matthew, apparently Ralph's ally, actually beats him, as in the battle in Act IV. One famous joke, Matthew's deliberate misreading of Ralph's love letter, also found its way into Thomas Wilson's *The Rule of Reason* (1553) as an example of mispunctuation leading to 'Ambiguity'.

On the other hand, the play is remarkable for some departures from the classical precedents which argue either an independent English tradition, or a felicitous combination or confluence of classical and native. For the former, the strongest example is the frequency of songs as the various failures of Ralph's wooings are pointed by elaborate ditties. At one point he is so downhearted that Matthew organises a dirge, and his final reconciliation with Custance and her true husband is also celebrated with a song (l. 2000 s.d.). Possibly the frequency of songs is a reflection of the musical skill of the boys for whom the play was written.

The English origins are likely for items such as the foolish knight who is found in the romances, and once again the parasite seems to share some characteristics of the Vice, especially in that he deceives the hero he is supposed to help. The burlesque wooing might be a motif from folk drama and ceremonial. In the character of Christian Custance, Udall also follows a more 'English' line as she is not a Greek prostitute or a silent aristocrat, but an upright and forthright young woman who compares herself to Mary Magdalene, Susanna and Hester, all found in Christian sources.

The unknown author of *Gammer Gurton's Needle* (1553), a 'Mr S.', M.A. of Christ's College, Cambridge, constructed a play which has generally been acknowledged as close in structure to Terentian comedy, but at the same time he has put it into a dramatic context heavily suggestive of rural England, complete with 'mummerset' diction. Though his identity has not been determined, there seems every probability that, being of an academic background, he deliberately set out to avoid any suggestion of typical classical subject matter: unlike *Roister Doister* and *Jack Juggler* there is no direct reference. Instead he has a mock conjuration of the Devil, a brawl between Gammer Gurton and Dame Chat, and at least one character, Hodge, who is near to being a fool.

The plot, however, is tightly constructed, though even here the idea that all this strife and comic misunderstanding should result from something as trivial as the loss of a needle seems partly a mockery of classical plots, especially as the resolution depends upon the chance rediscovery of the needle as though it were some long-lost child. The five-act structure clarifies the development of the intrigue of Diccon, who, though an English 'Bedlem' (a 'simple' fool), skilfully plays off the conflicting interests of Gammer Gurton and Dame Chat, and of Hodge and Dr Rat. He is like the classical parasite in that he achieves the desired confusion by telling different stories to the other characters, by lying indeed. This plays to the audience's superior knowledge of events.

At the beginning of the fifth Act, the Bailey has the unenviable task of sorting out the complex muddle Diccon's mischief has constructed, details of which are thoroughly known to the audience by means of the Terentian device of Diccon's telling what is projected. They have also been given a summary of the plot in the Prologue; a speech remarkable, incidentally, for the absence of any outline of moral objectives such as was commonplace in interludes. There is a perverse streak in Diccon's character, but significantly, and in spite of the Erasmian defence of the ethical value of Terentian comedy, the author avoids a moral interpretation – again, one suspects, by design. The text is also characterised by a variety of word games and extravagant linguistic devices, such as Hodge's 24-line narrative speech which has every line end in 'see now':

My Gammer Gurton heare, see now,
Sat downe at this doore, see now . . .

(ll. 753–76)

But these are designed to promote the objective of mirth noted in the
penultimate line of the play: 'at our last ending thus mery we bee' (l. 1279).
These things being so, it seems apparent that the theoretical notions of
Terentian comedy are present in this play almost by default and that its
peculiar nature is a testimony to the strength of the conventions of classical
comedy discussed here.

Classical tragedy

The development of classical tragedy in western Europe bears some re-
semblance to what has been described for comedy, but there are significant differences in the pace of its rediscovery as well as substantial divergence
in its impact. The development of printing and the place tragedy came to
hold in the educational system are critical factors. Lucius Annaeus Seneca
(5 or 4 BC–AD 65), who was widely known as a tragedian and moralist in
medieval times, was the first to be printed, in 1474, at Ferrara, and there
were further editions in 1491 and 1493. Sophocles (496–406 BC) was
brought out in Greek by the Aldine press at Venice in 1502, followed by
Euripides (485–406 BC) a year later, and Aeschylus (525–456 BC) in 1518.
The knowledge of Greek was not common and there was a distinct wave
of translation of Sophocles and Euripides into Latin, including versions of
the latter's *Hecuba* and *Iphigeneia in Aulis* by Erasmus in 1524.

In spite of this, the influence of Seneca remained the strongest of the
classical tragedians throughout the century. The question of performance
remains a thorny one. Whatever their dramatic, or indeed theatrical qualities,
classical scholars are still in dispute as to whether his works were actually
performed in ancient times.[8] There is no doubt that they were done in
the Renaissance on the Continent, but from the English records this
begins somewhat later than performances of classical comedy: probably
not before 1551–52 at Cambridge, for example.[9] There is, however, an
extensive series of productions of plays by Seneca, and of original tragedies
modelled on his plays, in Italy somewhat earlier.

Nevertheless, the development of ideas about Seneca, an increased
familiarity with his plays and his aesthetic and moral characteristics are
features of the English dramatic environment in the sixteenth century.
This was aided by a good deal of critical or theoretical discussion, some of
which emanated from neoclassical Italian critics. These developed and

extended theories dependent upon Aristotle's *Poetics*, which in part discussed some characteristics of Greek (but not Roman) tragedy. But the
study of classical tragedy does not seem to have been a matter for schools.
For example, Elyot thought that they were appropriate for students of
more mature years.[10]

There has been a vigorous critical debate in recent years about whether
the influence of Seneca was exaggerated by the Elizabethans themselves
and whether this has misled literary critics into overemphasising what
may be perceived as a rather minor ingredient.[11] There is, however, no
doubting that many educated men and women attributed importance to
his work, particularly on moral grounds, that there were imitators of his
work on academic stages, and that ideas and techniques from his plays
were eventually fed on to the popular and professional stage, most notably
by Thomas Kyd's *Spanish Tragedy* (1587). The difficulty in distinguishing
the direct influence is made greater because in some respects his work has
parallels with some features of what is clearly native English drama, as
represented particularly by the morality plays and their successors, the
interludes. In this section I shall deal with what may be regarded as strictly
Senecan aspects and return to the question of interaction in Chapter 9
after considering the developments of these latter types of play.

The phenomenon of Seneca's influence must turn upon why his writings, and behind them his personal circumstances, might have appealed
to Tudor writers. His tragedies portray a universe which is embroiled in
unresolvable conflict resulting in physical violence and death and in which
human passions are intense to breaking point. Seneca lived close to the
imperial court in the reigns of Claudius and Nero, and his plays reflect
the dangers of tyranny and the fears it engendered. In order to survive,
one had to be devious, and also one might find it wise to develop some
measure of stoicism or detachment: a way of expressing philosophically
one's individuality in the face of overwhelming circumstances. This latter
emerges strongly in Seneca's moral, non-dramatic writings, but the dramas
are potent because through dialogue they are particularly effective as a
means of juxtaposing oppositional forces, emotions and attitudes. If one
didn't know the circumstances of his times, Seneca's plays might seem over-
dramatic or sensational; but it is perhaps wiser to see them as a means of
coming to terms with a particularly horrific period of Roman history.

It must seem therefore that Seneca's plays gave to Tudor intellectuals a
means of expressing their response to their own times, and we may
support this suggestion by the extraordinary popularity of John Foxe's
Acts and Monuments (1563), commonly known as 'the Book of Martyrs',
which became one of the books most frequently owned by Englishmen:
a chronicle of the horrors of religious persecution which preceded, accompanied and followed Henry VIII's break with Rome. These included the
burning of Robert Barnes (1540), Anne Askew (1546) and Thomas Cranmer

(1556), all famous Protestant martyrs. The violence of public executions and the emotions they engendered, horrifically theatrical in themselves, may thus be linked with the increasing momentum of the popularity of Senecan tragedy in the second half of the sixteenth century.

In the light of this, however, it is interesting that Seneca avoided the presentation of violence as stage action. In this he may have followed Greek precedent, but he developed a most explicit and potent mode of description which conveyed the horrors of assassination and ritual slaughter. To begin with, his Tudor imitators followed this method, but in time the opportunity of onstage representation of physical violence was irresistible: indeed it may have been imposed upon Senecan restraint precisely because physical suffering was explicit in the native English drama, as in the Crucifixion in the mystery cycles.

Many of the characteristics of what may be called the first phase of the English Senecan interest are epitomised in *Gorboduc*, performed among lawyers by the Gentlemen of the Inner Temple before Queen Elizabeth on 18 January 1562. Its authors were distinguished public figures close to the heart of Elizabethan political life: Thomas Norton was a lawyer and diplomat, and Thomas Sackville, a relative of Anne Boleyn, became an ambassador and eventually Lord Treasurer in 1599, and was created Earl of Dorset in 1604. The political intentions are quite specific: to point out the dangers of changing the royal succession, and to urge the young, and so far unmarried Queen to make provision for an heir. The patriotic concern is perhaps furthered by the choice of a story from the mythical history of Britain popularised by Geoffrey of Monmouth, and by Grafton's *Chronicle* (1556).

For the authors, Senecan tragedy seems to have been a method of showing destruction. Using a five-act structure, in which they exercise a careful selection from many possible incidents in the sources, they show progressively the fall of King Gorboduc and his family, as though they were cursed like the families of Agamemnon or Oedipus. Gorboduc himself is guilty of an initial political error in making over his kingdom to divided rule by his two sons. This is presented as a recipe for disaster, since Ferrex, the elder, resents that he did not inherit the whole. His military activities are suspected by Porrex, the younger, who makes a pre-emptive invasion, killing his brother. Gorboduc summons Porrex to answer for his crime, but before he can make a judgement, Videna, his wife, kills Porrex in revenge for having murdered Ferrex, who was her favoured son. This brings us to the beginning of Act V, where it is reported very concisely that the people have rebelled and killed both Gorboduc and Videna (offstage). The substance of this last Act is the civil strife that then breaks out among the nobles.

Two issues dominate the characterisation of Gorboduc himself: whether he was guilty by his initial error and whether he was the victim of a curse.

Though the original plan was his, it was not agreed by all his advisers; indeed, the purpose of the debate between them seems to be to show their divergence. When the results become clear he exclaims:

> What cruel destiny,
> What froward fate hath sorted us this chance?
>
> (IV.ii.223–4)

Thus the management of the tragedy produces a tension over the king's responsibility, and it is likely that this is meant to be a part of the political message. Eubulus, the wisest of the advisers, is given the last moralising speech, in which he says:

> Hereto it comes when kings will not consent
> To grave advice but follow wilful will.
>
> (V.ii.396–7)

His last remarks, however, are in the spirit of despair characteristic of Seneca:

> But now, O happy man, whom speedy death
> Deprives of life, ne is enforced to see   *nor*
> These hugy mischiefs, and these miseries
> These civil wars, these murders and these wrongs.
>
> (V.ii.434–7)

The chief themes, political and tragic, are sustained in the play by means of dumb shows which precede each Act, and by Choruses which pick up the symbolism in each case. Act IV begins with

> *First, the music of hautboys began to play, during which there
> came forth from under the stage, as though out of hell, three furies,
> Alecto, Megaera, and Tisiphone, clad in black garments sprinkled
> with blood and flames, their bodies girt with snakes, their heads
> spread with serpents instead of hair . . . each driving before them a
> king and a queen. . . . Hereby was signified the unnatural murders
> to follow.*

The names of the Furies, and the later reference to them by the Chorus as being sent out by Jove for revenge, link this important piece of business with the classical precedents, increasing the sense of a hostile and inhuman universe.

The choice of the sensational story and the way it is handled suggests that the mode of Senecan tragedy could be made to serve political purposes, but also to gratify emotional needs. Feelings in the play are always strained and there is a strong tension between the growth of jealousy and fear exhibited by the plotting, and the argumentative or rhetorical forms of expression which are used. This latter aspect, not surprisingly, fits in with the educational objectives we have identified in comedy, but it became a feature of Senecan drama that it should could contain many pithy phrases or *sententiae*. These were often a form of wit, using wordplay and antithetical structures. Often holistic views of the action could be summed up in a single phrase, and this would be more prized if it could be seen to have a general application to human affairs. Such is the opinion expressed by Philander, who in the debate over Gorboduc's decision, takes the middle way:

> When fathers cease to know that they should rule
> The children cease to know they should obey.
>
> (I.ii.276–7)

It is perhaps because of many examples like this that Seneca came to be thought of as a highly moral dramatist, and in this we find a significant modification of his work by Elizabethan writers and commentators. Whereas for Seneca the universe was cruel and inhospitable, dominated by supernatural powers indifferent or hostile to human activity, in a Christian ethos it was necessary to see a divinely ordered universe in spite of the terrible events which pressed upon human beings. This in turn meant that a moral or indeed instructive purpose might be found in such events. Hence the conflict noted above between the possibility that what happened to Gorboduc was his own doing, and the notion that he was accursed. The conflict was never actually resolved, and this ambiguity may be one of the reasons why tragedy, not solely in the Senecan form, became such a significant feature of the Elizabethan stage. The position was perhaps sharpened by the impact of the Machiavellian villains who also are to be seen in Senecan drama, though less powerfully than we shall find them in Marlowe and Kyd.

In the wake of *Gorboduc* there followed a number of other classical tragedies, but it may be more illuminating to consider the *Tenne Tragedies* (of Seneca) edited by Thomas Newton in 1581. This was a collection of work by different translators starting with Jasper Heywood, who had published the *Troas* (1559), *Thyestes* (1560) and *Hercules Furens* (1561). The son of John Heywood whose work is considered in Chapter 8, Jasper was a young, distinguished Fellow of All Souls' College in Oxford, and this perhaps explains the academic nature of his work. However, there is something to be derived from the way he frames his translation and the ways in which he departs from the original. He saw his work as useful to younger scholars: in his Preface to *Troas* in spite of a declared ideal of fidelity he aspires to the 'grace and maiestye of style' appropriate to tragedy, and regrets that 'our English toong is far unable to comparre with the latten'. In fact, he pursues stylistic elegance persistently, though this has the interesting effect of frequently lengthening the concision of the original. Though today such an emphasis upon moral themes may seem unlikely to provide entertainment, such things were undoubtedly anticipated and enjoyed, especially when they were embodied in what was seen as desirable and fashionable poetic forms.

He makes a number of additions to the original *Troas*. Adding a Chorus after Act I, he shows his desire that tragedy may have political value, warning that all kings are subject to the tomb, and he brings out a warning note to all:

> In slipper joy let no man put his trust.
>
> (l. 553)

> a mirrour . . . to teach you what you are.
>
> (l. 571)

> Whom dawn of day hath seen in high estate
> before sonnes set, alas hath had his fall.
>
> (ll. 573–4)

These expressions exemplify his interest in *sententiae*.

The emotional aspect of Seneca's drama is enhanced by his addition of the Spirit of Achilles: for being trapped by the Trojan Paris,

> Vengeans and blood doth Orcus pit require
> to quench the furies of Achilles yre.
>
> (ll. 621–2)

The effect of this is to increase the terrible passions of the play, especially rage, for it is rage which supplies motivation for horrifying deaths. The style is decorated with frequent classical allusion, but there are attempts to use a plainer expression as well:

> Great is the raunsom ought of dewe to me
> Wherwith ye must the sprites, and hell appease,
> Polyxena shall sacrifised be,
> Upon my tomb, their yreful wrath to please
> and with her blood, ye shal asswage the sease.
>
> (ll. 558–602)

A similar though shorter interpolation of three stanzas intensifies the suffering of Andromache anticipating her son's slaughter. (Lines 1145–65 are specifically headed as translator's additions in the printed text.)

As a political theme there is also an addition about why Jove allows such disorder in human affairs. In an ancient style this is apparently attributed to chance, but the underlying significance is the way man's will perverts the true order of things,

> Regarding not the good mans case
>   nor caring how to hurte the ill
> Chaunce beareth rule in every place
>   and turneth mans estate at will.

(ll. 1972–5)

Thus the interpolations are concerned with the nature of tragic language, the role of kings, the image of the mirror, the motive of vengeance from ire, pity for victims and divine injustice. The choice of differing verse forms is another means by which the translator imposes his own emphasis upon the text. Jasper Heywood uses fourteeners, tetrameter couplets and rhyme royal, the last with some success on the subject of human impermanence:

> For as the fume, that from the fire doth pas
> With tourne of hande, doth vanishe out of sight
> And swifter then the northen boreas
> With whirling blaste and storme of raging might,
> Driuthe far away and puttes the cloudes to flyght,
> So fleeth the spright that rules our life away,
> And nothing taryeth after dying day.

(ll. 1122–8)

This discussion has dwelt upon some details of Jasper Heywood's translations, partly because they were among the first to be published, and partly because they can stand for the works of Alexander Newton, John Studley and of Thomas Newton himself. Together with the theoretical support for the value of Senecan tragedy and with those original works in the genre we have noticed, they exemplify an important and committed part of the Tudor dramatic scene.

Classical drama, especially in Latin, became an important imaginative resource through the century. It was institutionalised for a complex of cultural reasons into the education system. While there was initially a tendency to confine performance to school, universities and Inns of Court – all part of a private and amateur theatre – the plays became so much a part of the intellectual life of the time that it now seems inevitable that they were taken on to the public stage. The greatest impact was that of *The Spanish Tragedy*, one of the most popular plays of the century, and this public exposure depended upon the ingenuity of those who were prepared to bring performing and presentational skills to it.

Notes

1. Gordon Kipling, *The Triumph of Honour* (Leiden, 1977), pp. 16–38 and 79–93.

2. The strength and depth of late medieval piety is described in detail in Susan Brigden, *London and the Reformation* (Oxford, 1989), and E. Duffy, *The Stripping of the Altars* (New Haven, 1992).

3. Desiderius Erasmus, *Collected Works* (Toronto, 1974–), vol. 24, pp. 416.2–3; 669.9–11.

4. *Collected Works*, vol. 24, pp. 687.23–689.5.

5. *Collected Works*, vol. 1, p. 59.

6. Quoted by Howard Norland, *Drama in Early Tudor Britain, 1495–1558* (Lincoln, Nebraska, 1995), p. 136.

7. REED *Cambridge*, I, 93.

8. G. Braden, *Renaissance Tragedy and the Senecan Tradition: Anger's Privilege* (New Haven, 1985), pp. 230–1, n. 1.

9. Productions of comedies and tragedies are discussed by B.R. Smith, *Ancient Scripts and Modern Experience on the English Stage, 1500–1700* (Princeton, 1988).

10. Norland, p. 137.

11. For the debate, see G.K. Hunter, 'Seneca and the Elizabethans: A Case-Study in Influence', *Shakespeare Survey* 20 (1967), 17–26; and F. Kiefer, 'Senecan Influence: A Bibliographic Supplement', *RORD* 28 (1985), 129–42.

Chapter 8
Individual Dramatists up to 1555

In this chapter, which is chronological in outline, we shall find that for several dramatists a good deal is known about their personal lives and works, so that a private as well as a public dimension is often ascertainable for their achievements. We can deduce some of the motives and purposes of their writings, and go some way to showing why drama in particular was their chosen form of expression. This is even true of writers like Skelton and Bale whose dramatic output is only a part of a much larger corpus. In both written texts and performance an increasing variety of objectives and effects were pursued. In the first half of the sixteenth century the greatest contributions we can perceive were those by Henry Medwall, John Skelton, John Heywood, John Bale and Sir David Lindsay. There are also some significant but lesser figures in John Rastell, William Cornish, whose work is virtually all lost, and John Redford, together with some now anonymous writers whose works survive in *Youth*, *Hickscorner*, *Gentleness and Nobility*, and *Respublica*, a work whose attribution to Nicholas Udall is still problematic. As to possible models for this increasing volume of works, the classical examples discussed in Chapter 7 were influential in certain environments. The Corpus Christi plays remained a rather separate entity, with very few exceptions, but the morality play proved to be the most important native stock upon which the theatre of the new age was to be grafted. The essence of the morality play was that its purpose, the moral objective of each one of them, could be made anew, and this provided the means of development and innovation.

Henry Medwall (?1461–?1501)

The last record that Medwall, who was born on or about 8 September 1461, was still alive occurs in the year 1501, but his known plays were not published until *Fulgens and Lucres* was printed by John Rastell (?1475–1536) between 1512 and 1516, and *Nature* by his son, William Rastell

(1508–65), *c.* 1530.[1] *Fulgens* is thus the first known printed play, a tribute to John Rastell's enterprise which we shall note elsewhere; it is one of the earliest that can be attributed to a known author, and it is the first extant play on a secular subject. It is generally supposed to have been written originally for performance in the household of Cardinal Morton, Archbishop of Canterbury. However, there is now some evidence that the play may have been considerably enlarged, perhaps by Rastell himself, and aimed at a reconciliation between Mary Tudor and her brother Henry VIII, principally on the ground that it deals with the delicate matter of the woman's choice in marriage, a right which Mary took for herself in marrying Charles Brandon, Duke of Suffolk, in 1516.[2]

The play has been successfully produced in modern times, revealing that it is made up of a mixture of dramatic effects, of which there are three chief ingredients. One is the choice which Lucres is to make between two suitors, Publius Cornelius, a patrician, and Gaius Flaminius, a commoner. Apart from the woman's choice itself the discussion is largely about the nature of true nobility, a source of endless interest at this time. Though this is not apparently a school play, the dispute is conducted in a rhetorical manner likely to appeal to an educated audience. Secondly, there is the framework whereby two actors emerge from the audience to present the play and comment on it, as well as pursuing their own fortunes with reference to Jone, the maid of Lucres. Moreover, this part of the play, spread over a number of episodes, sets a remarkable contrast and is notable for many jibes at the expense of women, as well as plenty of coarse jokes and some obscene fooling. The two players, A and B, draw upon a repertoire which includes word-play, and also a vulgar game which they call 'farte pryke in cule' [*cule*: arse]: though the details of this game are rather obscure, the dialogue makes it clear that they have to be bound and to have a staff fixed 'thorow here' (1.1169–88). The third ingredient, almost lost to us in the text, is the dancing, which is presented with a flourish and must have made up a considerable amount of playing time in the great hall for which the play was designed. All three aspects suggest that Medwall was able to draw upon some well-established procedures, whether rhetoric, word-play, physical games or dancing, and the play is striking for the way it brings these various techniques together.

In *Nature*, his other surviving play, there is also a reliance upon established traditions, for it is one of the few surviving complete moralities, and it does not significantly depart from the characteristics of this genre that we have noted in Chapter 3; indeed it is a remarkably full example of it, and it bears resemblances to some of the French *moralités* as well. It presents phases in the life of Man, especially in his youth where innocence is important (signified by the character Innocencye, his nurse), and in his old age. Nature describes the order of the universe and explains that Man, given 'empryse' [*rule*] of the world, is guided, or misguided, by Reason and Sensuality. Although Reason claims to be the worthier, Sensuality will not accept this and asserts the orthodox point that Man has free will:

> And certaynly the fre choyce ys hys
> Wheder he wyll be governed by the or by me.
>
> (1.332–3)

Man encounters the Deadly Sins, of whom Pride is the most powerful here. The presentation of the Sins is managed with great variety and inventiveness in Part 2. The playing of these roles is enlivened by the ways in which the moral faults of the Sins are made plain, a feature which is perhaps one of the chief attractions of allegory for the author, and also for the receiver. Envy says at one point, 'Ye gave hyme better clothyng / Than ye dyd me, / And better wagys and fees also!' (2.718–20); and a stage direction has 'Then cometh in Glotony wyth a chese and a botell' (2.757 s.d.). This process of signification and recognition is very close to satire, and yet it seems to be an indispensable part of the way allegory works and it is one of its chief attractions. To begin with, Man gives some precedence to Reason, but when he is introduced to World, who clothes him, he gradually falls under the sway of Worldly Affection, and it is said that Sensuality will have control of his life for the first 40 years (1.325–6): it is he who introduces Man to Pride, and the traditional episodes in tavern and brothel show his decline. However, the Sins are matched with Virtues who gradually bring Man to repentance.

Both of Medwall's plays are undemanding as regards settings, but they are full of devices of language and movement which show them to be the work of one accustomed to stage effects. They are both written in two parts to allow for a meal in the middle, and this feature suggests that the great hall might have been the intended venue. In the case of Nature, it looks as though the end of Part 1 has been managed so as to give Man a temporary respite from sin by means of Shamfastnes (1.1371–89).

To return to the printing of the two plays, it appears that this was due to the Rastells, and not to the author. It gives rise to an aspect of the drama of great significance throughout the sixteenth century and beyond. If John Rastell did produce his edition of *Fulgens* in order to comment upon or influence the marriage of Princess Mary and Charles Brandon, it shows that he was aware that drama when printed could be a politically significant action to be distinguished from both the writing and the performing of plays, which may, in their turn, also be separate political actions. Moreover, if *Nature*, which is so traditionally Catholic in its concepts, really was printed by William Rastell around 1530, its appearance may be taken as a part of the political/religious controversy surrounding Henry VIII's divorce and the Reformation in which his father was beginning to engage. It is particularly poignant that John Rastell was Catholic

in outlook until some point after 1530 when, as Bale claims, he was converted by *A Disputacion of Purgatorye* (1531), John Frith's response to the
publication of Rastell's own pro-Catholic work, *A New Book of Purgatory*,
in 1530.[3]

John Skelton (?1460–1529)

Skelton's extensive and varied work has been found to have strong political interests, but at the same time there is an acute sense of his own
personality in it. The political dimension may have arisen because of the
need to obtain and sustain the support of a patron throughout his life, and
it appears that he was not always successful at doing this. The point is a
reminder that writers of whatever genre at this time could hardly survive
on the income from their work: they needed the backing of someone
whose interests could be furthered by publication or performance. Recent
scholarship has revealed more and more about the political contexts of
drama in this period, and this is especially the case with *Magnyfycence*,
Skelton's one surviving play.

His career began well: he claims to have been laureated by both
Oxford and Cambridge, as well as by the University of Leuven, and for a
period he was tutor to Prince Henry, the future Henry VIII, at his father's
court, perhaps as early as 1494. But he was dismissed by 1504, and given
a living at Diss in Norfolk. Thereafter there are many signs that he
attempted to restore himself to the centre of affairs. From about 1511 he
appears to have lived in London. His poetic output was enormous: most
of it has a particular political context where he hoped to have an influence. For example, his elaborate and learned allegory *Speke, Parrot* was
written in 1521 on the largely false assumption that by attacking Wolsey
he might persuade the King to appreciate the mixture of satire and
scholarship which he himself could offer the court.[4] The poem was not
successful in terms of his own fortunes, but it is a highly potent mixture of
self-display – he himself is the multilingual parrot – and it shares one significant characteristic with *Magnyfycence*, his ability to manipulate allegory.

At its most abstract level, Skelton's play is about kingship, centring on
the quality of magnificence or fortitude, one of the four cardinal virtues
which many writers, ancient and medieval, had considered essential to a
successful king:

> Fortitudo
> Whame philosphres by theyre sentence
> Ar wonte to cleepe Magnyfycence.[5]

It implies a mixture of qualities, including courage in adversity, public display on a grand scale, and a strong but sympathetic justice towards subjects: that there is some vagueness as to specific meaning may have been useful. The play reveals how Magnyfycence, the princely hero, may be led by folly into accepting wicked and extravagant advisers who take from him his true judgement and incite him to demeaning indulgences. He can only be restored to his rightful position by the impact of Adversity and the influence of more circumspect councillors. Though the plot thus retains the fall and rise structure of earlier morality plays, it is apparent that this is no longer an allegory of the soul's eternal fate, but one in which the fortunes of this world are the main preoccupation.

In spite of the suspicion that Skelton did not write many plays – we know of only two lost ones, an interlude of *Virtue*, and a comedy *Achademios*, and have the possibility that the surviving fragment of *Good Order* is also his – *Magnyfycence* is a remarkably adept play in its overall structure, as outlined above, and in the invention of individual scenes and episodes. The structure, making the most of the particular advantages of the allegory of rise and fall, allows the sensational change of fortune in which Magnyfycence, after exercising good judgement initially, is seen to grow more and more foolish, until, in despair, he falls victim to his erstwhile supporters who now ridicule him.

This latter part of the play is grim with tragic reverberations, whereas the approach to disaster is made more pointed by the inventiveness of comic playing. It is likely that Skelton drew upon the French *sotties* for his portrayals of fools: he is indeed one of the earliest English dramatists to put fools on stage, and the French theatre at this time was rich with plays involving them, some with the entire cast consisting of *sots*. Folly, in the characters of Fansy and Foly, is the means by which Magnyfycence is undermined. After the introductory sequence in which Magnyfycence is in agreement with Felicity, Measure and Liberty, 'Convenient persons for any prince royal' (l. 173), it is Fansy who brings in a different kind of mocking language ('too large', says Magnyfycence), and he quickly initiates the stage game of disguises by giving his name as Largesse. The technique, however, is partly one of concealment here because the audience is not yet told Fansy's true name, and if he wears a fool's costume, as appears later, it is not yet revealed. To add to this, he presents a letter of introduction from the Prince's absent councillor, Sad Circumspection, which turns out to be a forgery by one of Fansy's associates. His demonstration in a narrative of the benefits of largesse convinces Magnyfycence and they depart together. This significant exit is cleverly entangled with the arrival of Counterfeit Countenance who nearly gives the game away by trying to talk to Fansy. The moral or allegorical risk here is nicely indicated by a stage direction:

Here [Magnyfycence] should act as though he were reading the
letters silently. Meanwhile let Counterfeit Countenance come in
singing; when he sees Magnyfycence let him withdraw on tiptoe
gradually; but after a short while let Counterfeit Countenance come
back looking and calling from a distance, and Fansy waves him to
silence with his hand.

(l. 324 s.d., translated)

Thus Skelton is exploiting conventional aspects of the morality play to
create an atmosphere of intrigue and conspiracy: the audience must be
guessing correctly, because some of this material is giving conventional
signals, and they could also be interestingly unsure of exactly what the
show signifies.

The next sequence is a series of soliloquies in which four villains explain
themselves: Countenance is followed by Crafty Conveyance, Cloaked Collusion, and Courtly Abusion. Their names, perhaps derived from Skelton's
earlier satirical poetry, are all vices of court, and their significance is
created in the soliloquies and in the by-play full of cunning words and
revealing gestures, aided and abetted by Fansy. Aliases are adopted, but
these are now manifest to the audience. As the intrigue intensifies, Skelton,
perhaps influenced by the *sotties*, brings in Foly, the second fool. The
meeting of the two fools is a set piece of comedy, with moral overtones.
They encounter one another like long-lost school mates; and become
involved in a bartering over Fansy's bird (it is not quite clear whether this
is really a hawk, or only a comic owl – perhaps a deliberate ambiguity?),
and Foly's mangy cur. Whereas Fansy has been the example of wild fantasy,
and is called 'brainsick', he has also been deeply involved in furthering the
activities of the courtier villain: he is probably an example of a 'natural',
or ignorant fool. Foly looks more like an emblem of folly: he wears the
fool's costume and carries a bauble, and he exploits his proximity to the
prince by offering him foolish language. Possibly he is an artificial or witty
fool. Such is the emphasis upon corruption that Magnyfycence himself is
absent for about 1000 lines while the two fools and the four courtly vices
display and conspire. On his return Magnyfycence rejects Measure, treating him to a performance of his rage, egged on by Collusion.

The crisis comes when Magnyfycence, who rejoices in Foly's speeches,
says his 'wordes hange togyder as fethers in the wynde' (l. 1818) and Foly's
tongue runs away from reality:

> I coude and I lyst garre you laughe at a game: *if I pleased make you*
> Howe a wodcocke wrastled with a larke
>   that was lame;
> The bytter sayd boldly that they were to   *bittern*
>   blame:

The feldfare wolde have fydled and it wolde   *fieldfare*
  not frame;
The crane and the curlewe therat gan to grame;   *fret*
The snyte snyveled in the snowte and smyled   *snipe*
  at the game.

(ll. 1835–40)

But it is Fansy who brings the news of disaster as he admits his own deception, and Adversity comes to test Magnyfycence with punishment and shame. The portrayal of the disaster is shared by Liberty who is now out of control, by Poverty, and by the mockery of Conveyance, Collusion and Countenance in such a way that Despair and Mischief bring Magnyfycence to the point of suicide. Thus the range of events in this play is extraordinarily wide, and the dramatic effects complex. At one point Magnyfycence speaks tragically of his downfall:

O feble Fortune, O doulfull Destiny!
O hatefull happe, O carefull cruelte!
O syghynge sorowe, O thoughtfull mysere!
O rydlesse rewthe, O paynfull poverte!   *hopeless pitifulness*

(ll. 2048–51)

The quotations given here may also illustrate Skelton's metrical resourcefulness. In their soliloquies the four courtly villains all speak a version of rhyme royal, the verse form which was commonly in use for serious and imposing speeches. In each case the verse debases the form, supporting their corruption by means of a want of decorum. However, the variety of use is no doubt part of the entertainment and the play poses in an intriguing way the tension between moral instruction and the sheer exploitation of theatrical effects, whether of movement, gesture or language.

The political dimension of the play has long been a matter of conjecture because the hero has been thought to represent Henry VIII. It now seems likely that the four courtly vices may be versions of the King's 'minions', a group of young men who were his close companions as he grew to manhood, who had access to his person and in whom he placed some political trust. By May 1519 their excesses were such that the Council requested the King to correct the matter, and according to Edward Hall, the chronicler, they were replaced in the King's chamber by 'foure sad and auncient knightes'.[6] Their behaviour, especially their Frenchified ways (l. 877) links with complaints about the 'minions'.

It follows that Skelton's portrayal of events is a retrospect, and any political impact will have been somewhat oblique. Moreover, there is the apparent risk of showing the King making errors of judgement. By the end of the play, however, he has apparently learned to act wisely, and in any case Skelton was not noted for his tact. Thus we find that the play does have a specific political context, but Skelton's objectives may not have been purely political. He seems to want to celebrate the King's new-found wisdom, and to hold out an ideal of princely behaviour based upon the proper exercise of royal power and the absence of political graft. Perhaps he meant his play to attract favour by supporting a royal policy of reform and renewal, with the implication that the old corrupt ways of the courtly vices might now be over and done with. For these he provides philosophical contexts in Aristotle and the Christian teaching on the cardinal virtues.[7] Most probably his concept of himself as a poet was that he should teach and advise, using some of the functions he perhaps had once exercised as the King's tutor long before. Even if such idealism seems eccentric, he found in his adaptation of the morality play and the *sottie* a remarkable dramatic device for expressing it. Indeed the critical problem remains that the theatrical skill revealed in the play has its own impetus which does not always match the political bearing.

There are no records of a performance of the play, though the stage directions, like the one quoted above, often suggest lively theatrical effects. Nor is it known whether the King saw the play. A clue for performance comes in the reference to the Taylors' Hall (l. 1404) which may suggest the Merchant Tailors' Hall, a sumptuous building off Threadneedle Street in London. An audience of merchants gathered there might have had a particular interest in the satire on extravagance. The play was not printed until *c*. 1530, after Skelton's death, by Peter Treveris, an associate of the Rastells, and not long before William Rastell began to print John Heywood's plays, with which there are some affinities (see below, pp. 117, 123).

John Heywood (1497–*c*. 1578)

The publication of *Magnyfycence* may well have given Heywood a lead. Though he did not follow the fall and rise structure, he saw in Skelton's application of the morality play to political circumstances that allegory could be used to particularise points of view which bore sharply upon the developing struggle within Church and state. Heywood was at court during the time we have been discussing: he received quarterly payments as a singer in 1519 and 1520 at the age of about 22, and a royal annuity presumably for his musicianship from 1521. A loyal Catholic, he was related by marriage to the Rastells and to Sir Thomas More. Through More there extends a link to Erasmus, who was one of the greatest intellectual influences upon Heywood: some of the distinctive features of the plays he began to write in the late 1520s point directly to the discrimination and inventiveness of the author of *The Praise of Folly*. As to Heywood's disposition, he was tactful and witty. His personal charm no doubt facilitated his survival as a courtier, in spite of the apocalyptic changes brought by four monarchs, until finally he went into exile in 1564.

The first known publication of his plays is clustered around the years 1533 and 1534, presumably because this might have had some effect on the political situation which from Heywood's point of view as a Catholic was rapidly worsening as the divorce crisis came to a head with Anne Boleyn's pregnancy in 1533. It was also the time when More, having given up the chancellorship, was waging a bitter, even vituperative campaign in his publications in support of the old religion, no doubt still hoping to avert the changes which were now coming to pass. Containing some mockery of abuses in the Church similar to passages in Chaucer or Erasmus, Heywood's plays are markedly different from More's polemics in their good-humoured tone, concentrating upon the dramatic resolution of conflicting but carefully balanced viewpoints. It is this which has led to their being dubbed 'debate' plays, though the term does less than justice to their dramatic dynamics if all it implies is a cool and reasoned presentation of opposites. For one thing, there is usually an implicit direction, reflecting Heywood's religious orientation, and for another the actions are endowed with surprises and contrasts, as well as distinctive development towards a conclusion which in itself is a statement of principle. In writing in this manner Heywood was influenced by the *Colloquies* of Erasmus, and beyond these the dialogues of the late Greek poet Lucian, but a comparison with them should start with Heywood's custom of establishing a plot which develops and shapes the argument of the contest. This is intensified by his sense of character as he usually endows his speakers with distinctive and skilfully contrasted personalities.

The chronology of his six extant plays is problematic, both in terms of exactly when they were written and in what order. *Witty and Witless* survives in a manuscript not written by Heywood. It is the simplest in staging terms since it consists of two consecutive dialogues on the subject of whether the witty man or the witless has more pleasure and less pain in life. The first leads to John admitting that James is right in arguing that the witless is the more fortunate, but it is succeeded by the dialogue between James and Jerome in which the latter shows James the errors of his arguments. Jerome ends in an orthodox Catholic position by advocating that the witty man may use his reason to bring about heavenly reward.

The elegant balance of this structure may not apparently be very dynamic, yet the interplay of minds is acutely phased to show how the upper hand is gained in each case. The exchange is livened by several verbal tricks including the use of 'leashes', by which an individual word is twisted about to yield shades of meaning, and also to offer skilful ingenuity. This is how John tries to establish the superiority of the witty:

Wytt hathe provytyon alwey for releefe
To provyde some remedy agaynst myscheef.   *harm*
Wytty take bysynes as wytty wyll make yt
And as wytty beate wyttles, wyttles must take yt.

(ll. 129–32)

There are moments when the discourse is rich in illustrative detail, as in the extended description of the fate of the mill horse. It seems likely too that this was a performance and that there would be plenty of mimetic action and position-play on the stage. Attention is drawn to the small stature of James, which suggests that here as elsewhere Heywood was interested in contrasts of size on stage: he is thought to have been a tall man himself, and to have appeared in his plays. *Witty and Witless* also has an extended view of folly, for which Heywood uses the French word 'sot', and which he may owe in part to *The Praise of Folly*. It is remarkable that one stage direction actually envisages the possibility that the King might be present at the performance.

Johan Johan, a translation of *La Farce du Pasté* (anonymous), shares with *Witty and Witless* a cast of only three, but its action and characterisation are determined by the source. It is apparently the closest of all his plays to a realistic situation in which John, the husband, is cuckolded by the local Priest, or at least he watches his wife share the pie she has baked with her lover, with outrageous sexual overtones. The characters are in fact established types, yet Heywood's version brings out the characters very boldly, and emphatically endows the action of the play with ultra-realistic significance, as the pie, and the wax which has to be chafed by John to mend a hole in his wife's bucket are repeatedly referred to verbally and in actions.

Apart from these aspects of the staging there is an effective division of the stage space, both in terms of the house where Johan starts the play, vowing to beat his wife – though he is too pusillanimous to do it – and the Priest's house whither he sent by his wife to invite the Priest to dine. There is a third divided location within the house. In this Johan is forced to watch and wait by the fire while the other two, some distance away at the table, consume the pie without giving any to Johan. Although these actions are determined by the source, it seems that Heywood's use of spaces and the interaction between them resemble closely his exploitation of stage space in the other plays, where a sense of balance and symmetry is usually developed. The essence seems to be that Heywood was able to imagine stage space(s) while he wrote the words and to create opportunities for actors.

In this translation Heywood does put his own language and ideas into the substance of the text. He carefully moves the scene to England by including English details especially English saints, and by introducing English proverbs and sayings. In dealing with Skelton we noted that he used some aspects of the *sotties*: with Heywood there is a much more deliberate and persistent use of the French material, but at the same time his Englishness is made doubly apparent.

What made Heywood choose to translate this farce? We can fit it into his work in the ways suggested in terms of the staging. The original gave him a chance to exercise that sense of oblique comedy which characterises his other fully original plays: the audience is put into the position of observer and judge. As Johan boasts of his intention to beat Tib, and fails, and as he threatens to intervene in the lovemaking or pie eating, and fails, the audience is invited both to sympathise with him and to laugh at him. The subject matter also makes the most of mocking the unpriestly character and behaviour of Sir John: a theme which undoubtedly fits in with Heywood's humanistic, Erasmian and even Chaucerian approach to failures by individual churchmen, and one which he exploited richly with the Pardoners who appear in *The Pardoner and the Friar* and in *The Four PP*. The author of the *Pasté* made use of the convention of the rondeau in which lines of verse are repeated according to a set pattern (ABaBabAB: capitals represent repeated lines). Heywood imported the patterning of key lines and their use interestingly matches the other verbal devices which he uses so effectively. For him, the words, with their power of cross-reference and of patterning, are an essential ingredient of the stage. Quite apart from the value we may place on the farcical qualities of this play when it is performed today, it is rich in its revelation of Heywood's dramatic priorities.

The Pardoner and the Friar and *The Four PP* share satire upon aspects of the Roman Catholic Church, especially Pardoners: for the characterisation of these Heywood drew directly upon Chaucer's *General Prologue to the Canterbury Tales*. But the tone of the two plays differs markedly. In the former the Pardoner is matched to an equally venal Friar with whom he is in direct competition for the attention of the audience. The action of the play consists of a gradually mounting rivalry which is characterised by a shouting match in which they address the audience simultaneously while at the same time seeking to outbid one another. This may sound a disastrous recipe for performance, but it has proved to be highly amusing if the two actors manage to pace the rising conflict. There are certainly variations in the way the sequence of five sets of speeches are arranged which suggest that Heywood considered the performance needs. The last phase of the play brings them to blows:

> *Then they fight.*

Friar   Lose thy handes away from myn earys!
Pardoner Than take thou thy handes away from my heres!
           Nay, abyde thou horeson, I am not downe yet –
           I trust fyrst to lye the at my fete!

Friar   Ye, horeson, wylt thou scrat and byte?
Pardoner   Ye, mary wyll I, as longe as thou doste smyte!

(ll. 539–44)

It is typical of Heywood's sense of performance that he actually writes dialogue for the fighting.

The satire in this play is directed against the Friar as well as the Pardoner, and in both cases it reflects the religious position we have already noted: the Pardoner, like Chaucer's, is attacked for his bogus relics and is seen as a blemish within the Church Heywood supported. On the other hand, the Friar is given words which specifically refer to Protestant doctrine such as the Word and the gospel (ll. 15–6, 62, 529–30), and the belief in the 'elect' (l. 42). Though we cannot be certain about the date, it seems likely that the play was generated in the late 1520s when the question of pardons and the growth of the Lutheran heresy (Luther was a friar) were matters of increasing conflict. The cacophany which drowns faith in venal controversy is exhibited, ridiculed and condemned in this play.

As we have seen, the blend of characters is an important part of Heywood's dramatic achievement. In *The Four PP* the Potycary (apothecary), the Pardoner and the Peddler seem to share various degrees of trickery, and the Palmer seems to balance this with his earnest faith. Once again there is a good deal of reference to matters of belief, but Heywood is skilful in matching the different approaches of his characters. The play is remarkable for many verbal devices which would no doubt be fun to do. This includes various rhyming games:

Potycary   Than tell me thys, be ye perfyt in drynkynge?
Peddler   Perfyt in drynkynge as may be wysht by thynkyng.
Potycary   Then after your drynkyng how fall ye to wynkyng?
Peddler   Syr, after drynkynge, whyle the shot is tynkynge
             Some hedes be swymmyng but myne wyll be synkynge,
             And upon drynkynge myne eyse wyll be pynkynge,
             For wynkynge to drynkynge is alway lynkynge.

(ll. 301–7)

There are some places where the argument is embroidered by movement games and devices, as when the stage direction says '*Here the Potycary hoppeth*' (l. 467). These features are clearly an important part of the entertainment of the play, as are the set-piece narratives of the Potycary who cured a young woman of the 'fallen syknes' by a 'tampon' (pessary), and the Pardoner who tells in a speech of 225 lines how he travelled to hell and used his credit there to retrieve a dead woman.

The plot itself consists of the management of two long conversations. The first juxtaposes the boasts of the participants in which they each strive to outdo the others. For example, while the Pardoner presses the value of his pardons for the dying, the Potycary replies that no one gets to heaven without help from his medicines. But as the boasts fail to resolve the problem of superiority, the Peddler proposes a competition to tell the biggest lie. This takes up the second main part of the play and it is followed by judgement by the Peddler. But these apparently trivial frameworks hide an underlying exploration of the values in these lives seen against a religious viewpoint which values responsibility to others and good Catholic practices. Such is Heywood's sense of irony that it is the earnest Palmer who wins the lying competition, and the Peddler, trader in trifles, who is made to bring out these serious values.

The balance of the characters is perhaps even more exact in *A Play of Love*. They are named for the four possible states of lovers: Lover Loved, Lover not Loved, Loved not Loving, and Not Loving Nor Loved. It has to be admitted that these can be very confusing on the page, but in performance they could be easily separated in visual terms based upon the following characteristics: Lover Loved is indefatigably, crushingly cheerful; Lover Not Loved is a misery; Loved Not Loving is the only woman; and Not Loving Nor Loved is a 'Vice' whose physical versatility and inherent mischievousness make him irrepressible. The characters could also be distinguished onstage by the colour of their costumes as an aid to the prevailing mood of each. Heywood builds his play as though he were a computer, combining and re-combining the characters in a variety of categories. Thus there are two who love, and two who do not love; two who are loved, and two who are not loved; two who consider themselves happy, and two who think themselves hard done by, and so on. It may be helpful to look upon this as a deliberate dramatic technique since it allows Heywood to present continuously changing perspectives. The contrasts in states and emotions are shown in dialogue in which the characters explain their own position and, as in *Witty and Witless*, the question of happiness is a key factor.

Not Loving Nor Loved provides a driving force for the plot. He takes exception to Lover Loved whom he characterises as a Woodcock (proverbially foolish), and his mockery is pointed by a series of performance devices verbal and physical. These lines combine both:

> Ye have ben before me before now,
> And nowe I am here before you,
> And nowe I am here behynde ye,
> And nowe ye be here behynde me,
> And nowe we be here evyn both to gether,
> And nowe be we welcome evyn both hyther;
> Syns nowe ye fynde me here with curtsy I may
> Byd you welcome hyther as I may say.

(ll. 705–12)

He performs a monologue of over 300 lines, in which he purports to show that in a love affair he had successfully bested his lover by not being truly committed to loving her. His theme is *mockum mockabitur* ('the mocker shall be mocked', Job 13:9, and proverbial). The recitation is another opportunity for virtuoso performance, especially as Heywood has the speaker take over the voices of others in the narrative. The final irony is that the woman does get the better of him, for he reveals inadvertently that he was more committed emotionally than he claimed: when she jilts him, he cannot conceal that it hurts.

As the argument about the traditional pleasures and pains of love comes to a climax in which the four characters are divided into two pairs, each to judge the other, Not Loving Nor Loved brings matters to a head by means of a theatrical display with a huge hat (called a 'copyn tank') and fireworks. He aims this at his usual victim, Lover Loved, whose lover, he alleges, is now in a burning house. Panic dents the latter's cheerfulness and so the Vice makes his point.

But these comic devices are also vehicles for more serious matters. The provenance of the play may well be legal since there are plenty of words from the law courts, and the word games might well reflect legal rhetoric. Possibly there is a satire on Wolsey, who personally sat in judgement. In the end all are reconciled and the Vice's mockery is nullified by an assertion of love, apparently Christian love from Luke 6:31:

> Gladly to wishe Christes precept doth bynde ye:
> Thus contentacion shulde alway prefer
> One man to joy the pleasure of an other.

(ll. 1547–9)

All Heywood's plays so far discussed have casts restricted to up to four actors. For *The Play of the Wether* he seems to have been able to draw upon a larger number, almost certainly a mixture of boys and adults, perhaps including himself in the role of Merry Report, the Vice of this play. This allows him much greater scope: although the play shows many of the devices we have already noted, it moves more ambitiously into a wider range of issues and is conceived to bring some influence to bear on contemporary events.

Ostensibly the plot is a series of petitions invited by Jupiter to advise him about the most desirable weather, a subject of perennial interest to the English. The petitioners, drawn from different ranks of society, are received by Merry Report who summarises them for Jupiter's decision. As all want different weather, Jupiter settles for the acclaimed solution that things shall remain the same. There are some ascertainable sources for this idea, notably the Greek poet Lucian's dialogue *Ikaromenippus*, which was translated into Latin by Erasmus and may have come to Heywood's

attention because of More's interest in it. The presence of Jupiter may be
a significant clue, leading interpretation of the play into deeper waters.
Skelton had identified Henry VIII as Jupiter in his court poem *Speke,
Parrot* (ll. 398–9). Besides other figures from the Pantheon which might
be identifiable, the play also refers, near the beginning, to recent parlia-
mentary activity. These are early clues as the play unfolds; later, more
complex suspicions are no doubt aroused and there persists a growing
feeling that all this cannot simply be about weather.

Most probably the play, which was printed in 1533, is an extended
commentary on the royal divorce, written, as we must expect, from the
Catholic view which Heywood espoused, and designed to encourage the
King to adopt a traditional line, discounting the babel of voices which
from various partisan points of view were urging change. The timing of
its publication, which may not have been long after performance thought
to be at Shrovetide, February 1533, was at the point when Henry's marriage had become public, chiefly because Anne Boleyn was now pregnant.
Heywood's dramatic skills, which we have observed in the other plays,
enabled him to intervene in an oblique and amusing way likely to avoid
retribution. He was certainly more tactful than More who, having given
up the chancellorship, was now engaged in a vitriolic defence of the old
religion.

Merry Report's behaviour shows that part of the play's topical interest
is control of access to the King. The suitors are arranged in rank order
(women and children coming last!), and he allows only the most superior
to speak directly to the monarch, who remains unobservable for most
of the play behind a curtain. But the structure of the play works against
this sense of hierarchy. The earlier suitors arrive and make their pleas
individually, but about halfway through the Wind Miller and the Water
Miller are allowed to argue out their respective claims together. This
episode intensifies the sex jokes which were already beginning to flow in
the play, and with the arrival of the Gentlewoman there is little doubt
that Heywood is wanting to suggest the King's sexual activity. Merry
Report makes his own sexual play before offering her directly to Jupiter
as a 'wife'. He is indignantly repulsed:

> Sonne, that is not the thynge at this tyme ment.
>
> (l. 786)

Whereupon Merry Report continues on his own behalf, tempts her into
a duet and tries a kiss. At this point in comes the Laundress, an outspoken
character who quickly reduces the sexual game to vulgar bawdy and
engages in a row with Merry Report. The Gentlewoman retires defeated.
The sex jokes are now at such an intensity that one feels that the audience
might be wondering whether everything they can hear might have a

double entendre. Even the name of the Boy who comes last of the suitors raises bawdy curiosity: why should *little Dick* be interested in snow*balls*?

Looked at from the twentieth century it is quite difficult to envisage how explicit Heywood's satirical, or indeed allegorical attack might have been. Tiny details of costume for Jupiter or the Gentlewoman now unknown to us might have created great hilarity, and potentially great danger over this sensitive issue. We can be fairly confident, however, that Heywood was well received at court at this time: he received a royal gift in the form of a gilt cup on New Year's Day, 1533, and his status and reputation were close to that of an allowed fool, one whose geniality and wit would cause him to be valued. This might allow him to get away with much that other more contentious figures like More, or even Skelton, could not achieve. It is interesting that the Catholic William Rastell printed the play, and in the colophon he is careful to claim that it is *cum privilegio*, a reference to the right to print for the King. Nevertheless he was interviewed by Cromwell not long after over other publications, and from that point ceased printing. Heywood himself remained at court until the reign of Elizabeth. He was particularly close to the Princess Mary: a few of his poems were written for her, and he arranged music for her in 1537 and an interlude, with 'Children' in 1538. When she became Queen, he delivered an oration as part of the coronation procession at St Paul's. His achievement as it survives was largely original and idiosyncratic in the best sense: he evolved a form of drama which was hugely entertaining because of its virtuoso effects and his penetrating irony. The techniques he evolved, perhaps deriving in part from Skelton, but also differing markedly, enabled him to comment searchingly upon contemporary conflicts.

John Bale (1495–1564)

Bale was roughly contemporary with Heywood and the extant plays of both come from the 1530s, an indication that the writing, the performing, and to some extent the publishing of plays was politically valuable at this period of intense crisis. Bale was educated as a Carmelite friar, and converted to Protestantism in about 1533. By the end of the decade, according to his own account, he had written more than twenty plays, most of them, it would appear, as part of Cromwell's propaganda in favour of the new Church. In the four surviving printed texts (1546–47), his name appears among the *dramatis personae*, suggesting that he was directly involved in performances. He may indeed have played the Vice in *Three Laws*, because the part is doubled with the Prolocutor in the printed text.[8]

Bale's plays owe much to earlier dramatic conventions, and in this respect he may be considered less innovative than Heywood. But his urge to use drama as overt polemic seems to have led to a vigorous approach to staging, and at times his concept of the established forms of drama is inventive and adaptable. There is considerable variety between his plays. His lists of his own plays show that he wrote a number to match the plays in the mystery cycles, presumably to re-create them in a Protestant idiom. The titles of the lost plays indicate that he concentrated upon Christ's ministry, from the episode with the Doctors through to the Last Supper, Passion, Burial and Resurrection. We have shown that the cycles were indeed traditional in outlook, and as the Reformation developed they came to be associated with the old religion: yet even in these plays we find some movement, however reluctant, in the sixteenth century to adapt parts of them towards new requirements, particularly in the suppression of Marian episodes, as in the York manuscript. Bale went very much further in his three surviving biblical plays: *A Tragedy of Interlude Manifesting the Chief Promises of God*, which is an adaptation of the Prophets' play, and is closely associated with the two plays of the ministry which survive, *John Baptist's Preaching* and *The Temptation of Our Lord*.

The selection of ministry plays is to be associated with fundamental aspects of Bale's doctrine: his sense that the role of the priest was to teach, and that the development of response to the scriptures was essential to the Protestant way of life. This and other Protestant objectives make the dramatic structures of these plays differ from those found typical in the mystery cycles.

A Tragedy of Interlude Manifesting the Chief Promises of God is divided into seven Acts which are composed in close parallel. In each, a significant and holy figure such as Abraham or David is given the opportunity to confess his faults and the fault of his time. God appears in a paternalistic and judgemental role, and gives pardon in response to the true repentance of the humans. By using such a powerful but rather anonymous figure, Bale probably sought to overcome the Protestant objection to the idolatrous portrayal of God on stage. Each Act ends with the singing of an anthem from the Advent liturgy: the stage directions are quite specific. This one is typical, giving information about stage movement as well as the music and language required:

> *Tunc sonora voce, provolutis genibus, Antiphonam incipit O*
> *Sapientia, quam prosequetur chorus, cum organis, in eo interum*
> *exeuente. Vel sub eodem tono poterit sic Anglice cantari.*
> (l. 178 s.d.: 'Then on bended knee he [Adam] begins in a
> loud voice the anthem O Wisdom, which the Chorus takes
> up, with an organ accompaniment as he goes out. Or with
> the same accompaniment it could be sung in English thus . . .')

The choices made here suggest that Bale is treading very carefully. He does use the Catholic liturgy, but he allows for the possibility of singing in English, at a date considerably before vernacular services or Cranmer's composition of the English *Book of Common Prayer* (1549). As the dramatic texture of the play leans heavily towards ritual, it seems possible that Bale was engaged in creating a Protestant form of worship, and one based upon distinctive Protestant traits. But the emphasis on human wickedness makes this a rather grim play, which may explain why Bale called it a tragedy.

The publication of *God's Promises* along with *John Baptist's Preaching* and *The Temptation of Our Lord* suggests that in some respects Bale saw these plays as a trilogy. Their performance together (in the open air) at Kilkenny in August 1553 may support this. He called these last two plays comedies. The differences are in doctrine, since these show the triumph of the Baptist and Christ, and in dramatic style since these two plays both involve satire and ridicule, the targets being traditional ecclesiastics represented by the Pharisees and Sadducees in *John Baptist*, and Satan himself in *Temptation*.

Bale emphasises the role of the Baptist as preacher inventing from tiny details in Luke's gospel three representative human characters: Turba Vulgaris (the Common People), Miles Armatus (the Armed Soldier), and Publicanus (the Tax Gatherer). John reproves them for their practice of the Deadly Sins, an interesting survival of traditional doctrine, and produces combined repentance. Each sinner then recounts his offences and each is baptised in turn. When, following the lead in the gospel narrative, the Pharisee and the Sadducee reprove John, he shows his superiority in scripture, but also in imagery. While they condemn 'hys newe lernynge', John replies with the 'baptyme of repentaunce'. As he turns attention to the coming of Christ he says:

> He wyll yow baptyse   in the holy Ghost and fyre
> Makynge yow more pure   than your heart can desyre.
> Hys fanne is in hande,   whych is Gods judgement
> Unto hym commytted   by hys father omnypotent.

> (ll. 326–9)

Bale's portrayal of Satan brings a sharp polemical tone into *The Temptation* since he associates him with the Pope. His main thrust is to show the deception which is directed against Christ. A good deal of the action comprises soliloquies of self-revelation by Satan and Christ, and there is also much stage time devoted to a close engagement in argument. This no doubt reflects Bale's persistent emphasis upon disputation as a means of revealing true religion. The biblical temptations are enacted: the stones to be turned to bread, the pinnacle of the temple from which Christ is urged to jump, and the mountain from which all the kingdoms of the world can be seen. But Satan appears in a religious garb:

A godly pretence,   outwardly must I beare,
Semynge relygyouse,   devoute and sad in my geare.

(ll. 74–5)

He tries to beguile Christ into mistrusting God chiefly by distorting
scripture, a device which Christ quickly demolishes. Bale handles very
carefully the issue of fasting, which he regarded as a Catholic abuse:
Christ's fast is scriptural, but Bale explained it by saying that it was not
intended to be followed by humans.

Three Laws and *King Johan* derive from the morality play conventions
which offered choices of moral and polemical themes: Bale concentrated
upon his denigration of Catholic doctrine and practices which had been
familiar to him for more than twenty years before his conversion. During
the 1530s Bale began his re-interpretation of history along Protestant lines.
In *Three Laws* he structures the play around the Laws of Nature, Moses
and Christ, each a personification. In turn they are physically damaged by
a pair of sins introduced by Infidelity: Idolatry and Sodomy, Ambition
and Avarice, and Hypocrisy and False Doctrine respectively. Nature is
afflicted with leprosy, Moses becomes blind and lame, and the Law of
Christ is degraded and sent for burning, the punishments for heresy. In
this last episode, Act IV, Bale criticised what he considered to be the evils
of his own time. Things are put right by Vindicta Dei (God's Vengeance)
who turns into God the Father and introduces Christian Faith. Thus the
allegory is a mixture of exhortation and the portrayal of Bale's understanding
of Christian truth.

This symmetry is fundamental to the demonstrative effect of the play.
There are significant costumes and properties which are endowed with
allegorical or biblical significance: Sodomy is clothed as a monk and
Idolatry as a magician, and Vindicta Dei drives Infidelity from the stage
by (scriptural) water, sword and fire. A great deal of the play functions
allegorically as the sins explain themselves, often with the vigorous language and rhythms characteristic of Bale's most pungent style. For example, since many people sought help for their illnesses by appealing to
the shrines of saints, Bale has Idolatry offer some remedies:

For the cowgh take Judas eare	*a fungus*
With the parynge of a peare,	
And drynke them without feare	
If ye wyll have remedy.	
Thre syppes are for the hycock	*hiccoughs*
And six more for the chyckock;	*choking*
Thus maye my praty pyckock	*peacock*
Recover by and by.	

(ll. 523–30)

The play was probably very important to Bale. It is mentioned in the first of his play lists, *c.* 1536; he had it printed in 1547 or 1548 at Wesel in a Protestant part of Germany; he sought to produce it in Hampshire in 1551; and it was reprinted in London in 1562 after his return from exile. The printed text has such a large number of stage directions that one may suppose that it was close to a performance, especially as this gives directions for costuming the vices, and a workable doubling scheme showing that Bale the Prolocutor also played Infidelity, the Vice.

Because it has been seen as an early example of a history play and a tragedy, *King Johan* has become important to theatre historians. But it appears that the play remained in manuscript, and although it was certainly performed in 1538, it could hardly have been as well known as his other four plays which did get into print. Nevertheless the play has a rich dramatic texture, and many of its characteristics indicate that Bale was able to develop the morality play conventions in a number of ways.

The manuscript was generated in a complex way which we cannot investigate in detail here,[9] but it reveals that Bale wrote the play originally at some point before 1536, and that he developed it further by about 1538 to fit a particular set of political circumstances, domestic and foreign. He again revised the play after the death of Henry VIII (1547), but he did not insert the modifications into the manuscript until after Elizabeth I's accession (1558). The manuscript as a whole contains many indications of performance, and the play was given for Cranmer in January 1539, Cromwell meeting the expenses.[10] It is not clear whether the revisions Bale subsequently made point to a later performance or publication; we have no evidence that either came about.

The play exhibits a close interaction of plot and character. The morality structure facilitates a process of moral decline which is eventually restored (fall and rise), but this is profoundly modified by Bale's choice of King Johan as a hero. On the one hand, this is a historical choice based upon Bale's intimate knowledge of chronicles (many of which he had himself collected), but the selection is such that Bale consciously suppresses details of what might be regarded as a rather unsuccessful reign in order to foreground one salient quality, Johan's resistance to the Papacy. This leads to the opportunity of dealing with Johan's death which, according to some chronicle sources, was caused by his being poisoned by a monk. Moreover, since Bale wanted to portray Johan as a good king, a victim of papal conspiracy, there could be no question of showing him falling into temptation. This particular morality device is transferred to the three estates characters, Clergy, Nobility and Civil Order (the law), which are not historical. It is they who have to be penitent at the end of the play and who have to be restored by the principal force for (political) good in the play, Imperial Majesty. This character is a kind of re-incarnation of Johan's virtues, without personal characteristics. Unfortunately, we do not know whether he appeared in the earlier version, but it is apparent that he was intended to represent the idea of a Protestant monarch which Bale wished to promote, following a lead by Luther. In the play he is firm, assertive and just, and sweeps away the base conspiracy of the villains. We do not know whether his costume would hint at Henry VIII who was the monarch towards whom the play was originally directed. There is some contrast with King Johan who is a pathetic, somewhat tragic figure, anxious to relieve Widow England from her sufferings but betrayed by the hostile or inactive estates, who in turn are misled and seduced by the real villain, Sedition.

Though he is not called 'the Vice', as Infidelity is in *Three Laws*, Sedition shows the characteristics of this stock theatrical type much used by later dramatists.[11] The evil which he embodies is a threat to the nation and a betrayal of kingly virtues. Because Bale's context is religious as well as political, Sedition advocates 'ear confession' as a means of controlling opposition to the King. This is typical of the issues in the play. Bale makes the most of the rite by ridiculing it, having Nobility make his confession to Sedition, and being incited to rebellion:

> The Pope wyllyth yow   to do the best ye canne
> To his subduyng   for his cruell tyranny.
>
> (ll. 1171–2)

This is done in a comic scene which might make this unpalatable idea a bit more acceptable. A similar mocking device occurs over the liturgy. When Dissimulation is heard singing the Litany offstage, Sedition says:

> I trow her cummeth sum hoggherd
> Callynge for his pigges: such a noyse I never herd!
>
> (ll. 637–8)

Sedition then sings a parody of the *Pater Noster* which is really a comic curse.

The morality play conventions gave a good theatrical stimulus to Sedition's actions onstage. As the conspiracy thickens Sedition 'brings in' the other villains, Dissimulation, Private Wealth and Usurped Power. This phrase means that one vice leads directly to another; but it is shown by a physical action. When Usurped Power asks what he must do, Sedition replies:

> To bare me on thi backe   and bryng me in also
> That yt maye be sayde   that fyrst Dyssymulacyon
> Browght in Privat Welth   to every Cristen nacyon,
> And that Privat Welth   browght in Usurpid Powre,
> And he Sedycyon.
>
> (ll. 792–6)

This implied stage direction is clarified by the copyist: *Here they shall bare hym in*. The point has added significance because this carrying in parodies the ceremonial carrying of the Pope or bishops, as for enthronement. The allegory is, however, developed further in a striking and original way, because shortly after there appears this direction:

> *Here go owt . . . Usurpyd Powre shall drese for the Pope, Privat Welth for a Cardynall and Sedycyon for a monke.*
>
> (l. 983 s.d.)

In subsequent action these new roles are employed to enact a piece of chronicle history from the reign of King Johan in which the Pope (Usurped Power) insisted on imposing his own nominee, Stephen Langton, as Archbishop of Canterbury (Sedition), aided by his Cardinal Legate (Private Wealth). The allegory is that these evil influences were manifested in these specific historical characters; but at the end, when Imperial Majesty administers justice, it is Sedition he punishes, not Stephen Langton. This emphasises the universality of the evils concerned, and it also bears upon the political situation in 1538.

Indeed, the play presents us with an intriguing tension between what might be termed ideological issues deeply involved in the Reformation, the strategy, so to speak, and the particular political situation for which the play was revised and performed in 1538 and 1539, the tactics. While on the one hand Bale condemned here, and in his many polemical writings, what he saw as the shortcomings of the Catholic Church, he was also intent in bringing influence to bear on King Henry to persist with reform. The Reformation had been carefully promoted by Cromwell as Henry's chief minister, but in 1538 things stood at a delicate point. Henry had used the Reformation to bring in the divorce, but he did not want to go too far for religious as well as political reasons. Cromwell's Injunctions of 1538 ordered that the English Bible be placed in churches, but Henry's personal revision of the so-called *Bishops' Book*, which codified changes, revealed that he was very reluctant over some issues, including what Bale called 'ear confession'. At about this time the European situation turned against Henry with an alliance between the Emperor and the King of France, and Henry took urgent steps to fortify the realm.[12] Among other things, this explains Bale's pillorying of the Clergy as traitors in *King Johan*, and his concern to bring the Nobility into line in support of royal supremacy, an issue which could be made a matter of patriotism. In fact the war never happened, but Henry would not promote the Reformation further, and on the fall of Cromwell in 1540 Bale went into exile in fear for his life.

Sir David Lindsay (1486–1555)

Ane Satire of the Thrie Estiatis was apparently written and modified, like *King Johan*, to meet changing political circumstance. Lindsay was a life-long courtier, serving as an usher to the boy James IV and working through the regency of Mary of Guise, a period from *c.* 1508 to *c.* 1547. There is no doubt that there was a theatrical tradition in Scotland, but little evidence of it has survived to support the lonely but monumental achievement of Lindsay's play. As it stands it has strong links with the morality play conventions, English and Continental, particularly in its partial use of the fall-and-rise structure and the devious inventiveness of the vices; but it also has marked similarities with French *sotties* and farces, and the exploitation of Folly as a stage practice.

The earliest reference to the play is the account by Sir William Eure, the English ambassador to the court of James V who saw a version of it in Linlithgow Palace in 1540. Eure was reporting on the King's attitude to the Reformation, and in support he includes Notes which describe the action of the play, here called an interlude. These show the action concentrating upon the issue of Spirituality and the failure of the Bishops to sustain it, being diverted by their own interest in worldly profit and sex. The key voice seems to have been that of the Poor Man who made 'a long narration of the oppression of the poor'. The Bishop's attempt to suppress these complaints failed, and he was overruled by the Man of Arms and the Burgess, who were in turn finally supported by the other-wise passive King.

One version of the extant text, the Bannatyne Manuscript (1568), relates to a later performance in 1552 at Cupar, Fife, Lindsay's home base, but it is incomplete. A fuller text was printed by Robert Charteris in 1602, and was used in London in the following years as a support for James VI and I's Protestant credentials.[13] The performance at Cupar was probably set up to help the shift towards Protestantism discernible in Fife at a critical time after a bitter struggle between opposing factions. About two years later it was done again at the Greenside on the side of Calton Hill, Edinburgh, in the presence of Mary of Guise, the Catholic Queen Regent, who at that time was interested in offering a measure of tolera-tion to the Protestant interests. This was a high-profile production, which is said to have lasted nine hours. In size and scope (the whole text has about 4,900 lines) the play matches *The Castle of Perseverance*, and indeed several of the large-scale *moralités*, especially as the two expanded versions, were done in the open air with a very large audience. For the Cupar performance Lindsay wrote a kind of local Prologue which mentioned many local names and locations: naturally this was omitted at Edinburgh, and though it appears in the manuscript it does not occur in the printed edition.

The play is divided into two Parts. Besides the Prologue, which contains some fooling about how the Fool gets Bessy, the Old Man's young wife, there is a break after Part One, for a meal during which an 'interlude' is played showing the crafty devices of a Pardoner getting the better of the Poor Man. In Part One, Rex Humanitas falls victim to the temptations of Sensuality and other fleshly vices while the good of the kingdom is engrossed by the Court vices, Flattery, Falset and Deceit. As a result, Good Counsel is driven away and Verity and Chastity are stocked. King Correction arrives to put things right. These episodes are related generically to some similar ones in *Magnyfycence*, *King Johan* and *Respublica*. Very little of this appears in the Notes provided by Eure and the extensive additions can be explained by changes in political circumstances. By 1552 James V was dead, and his infant daughter, Mary, was Queen. There was therefore no personal risk in presenting a King corrupted by Sensuality, but there was a need, in Lindsay's view, to keep up the pressure on Church abuses. His attack, however, is neither as aggressive as Bale's nor as oblique as Heywood's. The main effect is a kind of grim realism, as in the episode in which the Poor Man recounts how all his property and livestock were gradually taken in mortuary fees by the local clergy. The vices are comic characters who shock not only by their outrageous materialism, but also by their ignorance.

In Part Two, the King is a much less active figure, closer to the original version described at Linlithgow. Instead John the Commonwealth, perhaps like the original Poor Man, complains about Temporality and Spirituality. Correction has Flattery despoiled of his Friar's habit. He in turn betrays his companions, and Falset and Deceit are hanged, with some comic business. The Parliament by legislation puts right the abuses of the three Estates, and thus everything seems to be ending in an exemplary way. But Lindsay then introduces an episode in which Folly distributes fools' hats, first explaining his own matrimonial troubles, and then preaching a Fool's sermon not unlike the *sermon joyeux* of the contemporary French drama.[14] This sequence shares a moral ambiguity with the *sotties*. As an ending it has been much questioned, but in fact it functions as a means of emphasising that the long-term evils cannot be bundled too readily into an optimistic ending, and indeed so it proved, because the political strife in Scotland over the Reformation continued for some time afterwards, embittered by factions. Moreover, it provides a cautious ending which reveals Lindsay's considerable political sagacity, as well as enveloping the audience in a pleasing, comic *coup de théâtre*.

Notes

1. For Medwall's 'Life Records', see Alan H. Nelson (ed.) *The Plays of Henry Medwall* (Cambridge, 1980), pp. 163–9.

2. See R.A. Godfrey, 'Nervous Laughter in Henry Medwall's *Fulgens and Lucres*', in *Tudor Theatre* 3 (Bern, 1996), pp. 81–97.

3. R. Axton (ed.) *Three Rastell Plays* (Cambridge, 1979), p. 9.

4. G. Walker, *John Skelton and the Politics of the 1520s* (Cambridge, 1988), pp. 60–8.

5. *The Minor Poems of John Lydgate*, ed. H.N. MacCracken, 2 vols, EETS o.s. 192 (Oxford, 1934), II, p. 688.

6. Edward Hall, *The Union of the Two Noble and Illustre Famelies of Lancastre & Yorke* (London, 1548), fols 67ᵛ–68ᵛ; noted by Lancashire, no. 97. The latest date for composition of the play is 1523 when it was mentioned in Skelton's *Garlande of Laurell*, l. 1192.

7. W.O. Harris, *Skelton's 'Magnyfycence' and the Cardinal Virtue Tradition* (Chapel Hill, 1965).

8. For a fuller account of Bale's life, see Peter Happé, *John Bale* (New York, 1996), pp. 1–25.

9. The manuscript's evolution was first disentangled by J.H. Pafford and W.W. Greg (eds) *King Johan by John Bale*, Malone Society (Oxford, 1931).

10. Pafford and Greg, p. xxi.

11. For a fuller account of the Vice, see Chapter 9 below.

12. The political context is examined in detail by Greg Walker, *Plays of Persuasion: Drama and Politics at the Court of Henry VIII* (Cambridge, 1991), pp. 194–200.

13. Marie Axton, '*Ane Satire of the Thrie Estaitis*: The First Edition and its Reception', in A. Gardner-Medwin and J.H.Williams (eds) *A Day Festival* (Aberdeen, 1990), pp. 21–34.

14. For links with the literature of fools, see R. Lyall (ed.) *Ane Satyre of the Thrie Estaitis* (Edinburgh, 1989), p. xxiii; and Peter Happé, 'Staging Folly in the Early Sixteenth Century', in C. Davidson (ed.) *Fools and Folly* (Kalamazoo, 1996), pp. 73–111.

Chapter 9
Interludes

I

The term 'interlude' can only be used arbitrarily, but it facilitates an extensive consideration of a variety of plays through most of the sixteenth century until the development of the new styles of dramatic entertainment which followed the setting up of the Theatre in 1576 and the coming of the new professional mode of the Elizabethan stage. Historically, the term is an old one going back at least as far as *c*. 1300, when it was used in the title of an early play: 'Hic incipit *interludium de clerico et puella*' (Here begins the interlude of the clerk, i.e. cleric and the girl).[1] It continued to have currency in the fourteenth and fifteenth centuries, usually to indicate almost any kind of entertainment that was dramatic, though it was not often applied to the mystery plays. In the sixteenth century the term became much more common, but it remained rather elastic when one considers that of the plays discussed in Chapters 7 and 8, *Nature*, *Fulgens and Lucres*, *Magnyfycence*, *Four Elements*, *Wether*, *Love*, *Four PP*, *God's Promises*, *John Baptist's Preaching*, *The Temptation of Our Lord* and the early version of *Thrie Estaitis* were all called by this name, either as a title or in the text. It would be possible to multiply teasing instances which defy rigid categorisation.

From about 1540, when the control of plays because of fears of disorder, sedition and heresy increasingly became government concerns, the term 'interlude' appears regularly in official documents. This occurred, for example, in Proclamations of 1543, 1545, 1549, 1551 and 1559. Often it appears in the conveniently compendious phrase, 'interludes and stageplays', to make sure that nothing dramatic could slip by, though whether there is definite distinction between the two is problematic.

In more recent times it has been suggested that interludes may have originally functioned as entertainment at feasts or banquets: a possible reference of this kind occurs in the fourteenth-century poem *Sir Gawain and the Green Knight* (ll. 472–3), and there are a good number of other instances where interludes were performed in conjunction with a meal, as with Medwall's *Fulgens and Lucres*. But again there are so many exceptions that it cannot be seen as definitive. Nor has the suggestion that the sense of *inter* (between, as between meals or courses) been found sufficiently comprehensive. However, in the context of twentieth-century critical and scholarly writing the term has acquired a kind of working significance which can conveniently be adopted here: this is the notion of rather short plays (admittedly indeterminate in length) which might have been performed in the great halls of palaces and mansions, or indeed of such buildings as abbeys or guildhalls, or university colleges. Though there were performances by boys or school groups in such circumstances, there were often entertainments provided by itinerant players who would be paid for their performance during a brief stay. This means that adaptability to different kinds of staging is characteristic of interludes. The convenience of the term as a title for this chapter is that it suggests that many of the plays considered here were of this type, sharing a kind of transience or impermanence which is belied by their survival in print. The term may also be taken as an indication of scope, for many interludes, though they may deal with profound and vital subjects, are rarely of great length or requiring great complexity of performance.

We can perceive more about the development and working of interludes from the companies of paid actors who performed them, and the places where they played. As early as 1494 there is a record of regular payments by the royal exchequer to four named 'pleyars of the kyngs enterluds'. By comparison with many other actors, these four royal employees probably had a fairly secure status, but it is also obvious that the size of companies must have varied arbitrarily. Much later, in the manuscript play *Sir Thomas More* (*c.* 1594), there is a retrospective passage in which More discusses the activities of the company which has come to his house to help entertain the Lord Mayor with an interlude, the fictional time being about 1530. On that occasion the company consisted of four men and a boy, and the fact that the latter was to play three women led More to comment, 'Bir Lady, hees loden!' [*'By Our Lady, he's loaded!'*].

We should not, however, assume that all companies were limited to four adults. The strongest evidence about this comes in the doubling plans which were sometimes affixed to the title-pages of printed copies of interludes as part of the attraction for prospective buyers. These show that the number of players was often six, as in John Pikeryng's *Horestes* (1567), where they play twenty-seven roles; but for Thomas Preston's *Cambises* (1561) eight players are required to cover thirty-eight roles. There was also no reason why a company should not take on short-term extra players beyond its normal number for special occasions. Nor can it be assumed that the women's roles were played exclusively by boys. Nevertheless, there seems little doubt that in general the companies in midcentury usually worked with four to six players. There might well have been economic considerations here relating to how the income might be divided, a reflection of market forces and the profits which might be anticipated in relation to an acceptable living wage. By the end of the century with the establishment of the playhouses in London, the number in the companies increased to about twelve, no doubt a reflection of a change in economic circumstances as much as of a change in taste.

The relatively small numbers of actors would naturally influence the ways in which plays were constructed: part of the art of the writer was to make the most of his actor resources. David Bevington has pointed out that the effect of the smaller limits is that the arrangement for scenes in moral interludes has often been to show a good group of characters alternating with a bad, and that the two groups may never be scheduled to meet because the same actors are involved in both.[2]

Another significant effect of the small troupes may have been the development of the 'Vice'. We have noted in the previous chapter that both Heywood and Bale named a 'Vice', but there is a significant difference between them because Heywood does not use moral abstractions, good or bad, as characters. Bale, however, does, inheriting the practice from the earlier morality tradition. Both dramatists make the Vice a lively and influential character who makes a strong impact upon the spectators, often by speaking directly to them and by involving them in little bits of business. He may well be on the stage alone and be given extensive soliloquies which comment upon the direction of the action, and explain details of the plot. Such episodes are also characterised by high entertainment values which may depend on all sorts of tricks and word-play. Some of these devices may of course be found in other characters, but we may observe that there is a marked tendency for them to be confined to one. This in itself presents a challenge requiring the Vice to be played by a skilful and versatile actor. From this it may well have followed that the Vice's role grew to be the part given to the leading actor in the company, and, as many of the doubling schemes show, the Vice's part was not doubled, or, if it was, the other parts were usually very short, such as the Prologue. It is also true that if the alternating structure was adopted the Vice could be switched from talking to one set of characters to the other, perhaps by means of a soliloquy, while the others players changed their costumes and their roles. This in turn enhances the soliloquy of the Vice as a salient part of his performance.

Moreover, the role gained considerable moral ambivalence. It may well be that this owes something to the portrayal of Devils in the mystery plays and the moralities. From there would come the overriding need to sustain moral ideas so that even the Devil has to reveal the truth and what is ideologically desirable. It is not clear, however, that the Vice always acted as a tempter: sometimes his role was rather more concerned with embodying the principal evil in the play. The Vice has to be seen to be wicked and scheming, but he also has to reveal the truth in spite of himself. Part of the destructiveness may thus be associated with carnival, a kind of allowed licence which expresses discontent in the very process of supporting a moral order. The Vice is often associated with characters low in the social hierarchy. Added to this is the craftiness of the Vice whereby he may speak partial truths, often citing scripture with the appearance of holiness, in order to mislead. In his moral role he frequently adopts aliases whereby he first is reluctant to reveal his own name, and then assumes a falsely virtuous one. These last devices, being patent to the audience, no doubt have a mnemonic value. Some of the introductory devices, however, are less clearly related to the moral burden: for example, many Vices recount a strange and incredible journey, with the place names often alliterated.[3]

The theatrical usefulness of the Vice was enhanced by his verbal and physical dexterity. Many times his entry is given a special physical trait, like tumbling or dancing, excessive laughter or weeping, and the one may suddenly turn into the other. His speeches are rich with proverbs and puns, as well as slips of the tongue, bawdy jokes and various jingles: many writers who use him are quick to introduce changes of verse rhythm for his speeches. Singing is an important part of his role: there are many song cues, but at times the texts do not make it absolutely plain whether he sings or recites his jingles.

As to historical development, Bale and Heywood apparently played a significant part in his development in the 1520s and 1530s, establishing the centrality of the role. From about 1550, however, and for the next thirty years or so, many a dramatist found him to be useful or even indispensable: or, to put it another way, audiences came to expect him. In the revisions to *King Johan*, Bale added, in his own hand at some point after 1547, some performance details to the part of Sedition. A rough count shows that the Vice appeared in about thirty-five extant interludes during the period 1550–80, and there is no other conventional character who received such attention. The somewhat more regular status of acting companies after 1576 may have meant that gradually he was no longer in such demand or of such use. However, Shakespeare makes specific reference to him in his characterisation of Richard III, Falstaff, Claudius and Iago, all of them egregious villains, and Ben Jonson characterises him in 1616 as out of date in *The Devil is an Ass*. A measure of his attraction appears in a number of references to him in May Games and other related dramatic forms in popular entertainment at village level, but as no texts for these Vices survive it is difficult to be sure that he functioned in quite the same way in such festive gatherings. In such contexts it is less likely that he was part of a moral discourse, and it may well be that his role in these entertainments was closer to fooling.

As suggested above, songs were a common element in the part of the Vice, for he was able to use them to establish his identity, to show off his cleverness, and, because of his structural role to make significant steps in the development of the play. But singing is by no means confined to Vice solos. There are many instances where a group of sinful characters express their wickedness in company with the Vice, as in the drinking song by Newfangle, Cutpurse and Pickpurse in *Like Will to Like* (ll. 804–10). But characters of many other types also sing. Clytemnestra and Egistus have a love duet in *Horestes,* and there is a lullaby in *Pacient Grissell.* 'The Songe at the shaving of the Colier' in *Damon and Pithias* has the nonsense refrain:

> With too nidden, and too nidden
> With too nidden, and todle todle doo nidden.

There are songs associated with particular avocations as for pirates in *Common Conditions,* and for tilers in *Tom Tyler and his Wife*, where a trio begins:

> Tom Tyler, Tom Tyler
> More mortar for Tom Tyler.

There are street cries for a broom seller in *Three Laws* and in *Three Ladies of London*, and for a rat-catcher in *A Marriage between Wit and Wisdom*. The dead Wit is resurrected by a song in *Wit and Science*. Catholic liturgy is often mocked by singing it to inappropriate words as in *King Johan*, but Bale also uses the Antiphons for Advent in *God's Promises* quite seriously. The commonest songs are solos, but there are plenty which demand two, three or four singers. Often musical instruments were specifically required: viols, regalls, an organ, a gittern, bells, a fife and a 'tamboryne' (pipe and drum) are all mentioned.

Many interludes were apparently portable, or at least embodied the idea of doing plays in different locations, no doubt because of the absence of permanent bases for the actors. Some must have been performed in the open air: Bale's plays at Kilkenny were done at the market cross in 1553. Interludes are recorded in the churchyard of St Katharine's church, Aldgate, in 1565.[4] But indoor performances were the more common by far, and there is some evidence that there was government pressure to play within great houses where a person of importance might take responsibility for what went on. For example, in 1545 the Earl of Hertford's players were ordered to play only in the houses of the mayor, sheriffs, aldermen or substantial citizens.[5] This being so, one must presume that the great hall was the most likely place.

The advantages of this configuration were the closeness of the audience to the action, and the flexibility of the large acting space. Stage structures could be and were built in it at times, but they were not essential. The wall with the two doors could be made significant, either by the ways the actors conducted themselves, or by introducing a large stage property such as a throne or a seat of justice.

II

In this section we turn to a variety of interludes coming from the period 1510 to 1579. It is convenient to group them as follows:

- political allegories: *Youth, Hickscorner, Respublica*;
- the Wit and Science group: *Wit and Science, The Marriage of Wit and Science, The Marriage between Wit and Wisdom*;
- early tragedies: *Cambises, Horestes, Apius and Virginia*;
- moral plays: *Lusty Juventus, Enough is as Good as a Feast, Like Will to Like*;
- biblical plays: *The Life and Repentance of Mary Magdalene, The Virtuous and Godly Susanna*.

Political allegories

We have seen in Chapter 8 that deliberate political allegory became a significant part of the drama in the sixteenth century. Interludes, first by accident, and later under some pressure from the government, were often produced under the patronage and with the support of powerful magnates, and it follows that there would be many opportunities for powerful men and their supporters to make political comment through the entertainment they provided. The audience might be the target to be persuaded, or the fellow travellers who, like the party faithful of modern political conferences, needed to have their ideas and beliefs reinforced.

Youth and *Hickscorner* are similar in many ways, and there is now some evidence that the latter is an adaptation of the former, with a different political orientation.[6] Both plays are remarkable for their moral allegories which offer teaching about the life of virtue, intimately intertwined with the political circumstances of their individual contexts. In both interludes these allegorical meanings are enhanced by a great deal of circumstantial detail from contemporary life, to such an extent that the immediacy and vitality of their contents is one of their chief attractions.

The moral allegory of *Youth* restricts the character of the hero and the temptations which face him to a short period of life. The plot shows him indulging in the pleasures of youth, including the sheer delight in his own body:

My hearte is royall and bushed thicke,
My body plyaunt as a hasel styck,
Mine armes be bothe bigge and strong,
My fingers be both faire and longe,
My chest bigge as a tunne,
My legges be full lighte for to runne,
To hoppe and daunce and make mery.

(ll. 47–53)

Scorning the advice of Charity, a figure closely associated with Christ himself, Youth summons Riot, his brother, to help him beat Charity and Humility. Typically of allegory, his summons is not motivated: its value lies in the implied link, without an explanation. It rapidly becomes apparent from Riot's boasting that he has been in prison, and would have hanged at Tyburn had the rope not broken. This may well have been a popular motif, for it is the same for Newguise's escape in *Mankind* (l. 616). The moral decline takes a further step when Riot introduces Youth to his friend Pride. He in turn brings in Lady Lechery, and with her encouragement they all intend to go off to the tavern to indulge in a mixture of sex, drinking and gambling, all of which are graphically and enthusiastically described. Because he tries to prevent them, Charity is put into the stocks by Riot and Pride. Unfettered by Humility, he rebukes Youth who at first mocks the teaching but suddenly yields when Charity mentions the Redemption. Again the lack of motivation is allegorically effective: Youth is penitent, and the defeated Riot departs with the comment which speaks more truly than he intends:

But nowe I se it is harde
For to truste the wretched worlde.

(ll. 750–1)

Though this play has many details of London life, like its counterpart, there is some evidence that it was written in the North of England, possibly in the household of the Earl of Northumberland. Thought to date from 1513 or 1514, part of its purpose may well have been to criticise the Earl's son for riotous living, but the parallel with the young King Henry is hard to resist. Possibly the play expresses dissatisfaction with the way in which the young King's self-indulgent lifestyle had pushed into the background the influence which this important nobleman expected to have over him. It is a theme which may well be related to that taken up by Skelton a few years later in *Magnyfycence*.

Hickscorner follows *Youth* in its moral outline. Once again the hero is misled, and the chief virtue, Pity, is placed in the stocks by villainous company. When he is released he brings about the repentance of the fallen hero. But the allegory is made more complex, perhaps because this really is a revision: the hero is not a human figure but the abstract Freewill and he has a close associate in Imagination. These are neither vices nor virtues, but states of mind or soul, and what happens to them has to be applied to the human predicament.

This play is about salvation: its moral teaching and the threat of disaster, rooted in ordinary life are subject to the threat of damnation of the soul. The political context is less explicit, though its date around 1514 is beyond doubt. Ian Lancashire has suggested that the relevant circumstances may be the failed attempt by Richard de la Pole, the Yorkist pretender to the throne, who set up but failed to carry through an invasion from Normandy in the summer of that year. It certainly seems possible that an author basing his work initially on the structure of *Youth* might be attracted to this political variation, this time more clearly in the interest of King Henry. Like the author of *Youth* this playwright is working on both moral and political levels.

For some years it has been thought that the author of *Respublica* was Nicholas Udall. This has yet to be confirmed, but there are circumstantial details which are suggestive. The play was written to be performed by boys probably at court: in his career as a schoolmaster Udall worked at both Eton and Westminster. The heading of the only surviving text gives some unusually specific details, especially as it has remained in manuscript:

> *A mery entrelude entitled Respublica made in the yeare of oure Lorde 1553 and the first yeare of the moost prosperous reigne of our moste gracious Soverainge Quene Marye the first.*

The emphasis upon the first year of the reign may well suggest that the author was conscious that what he had to show had a direct bearing on the changed politics of the Tudor dynasty, now that the crown had returned to a Catholic monarch. As we shall see, there are references to traditional moral allegory, but the main purpose is political. Respublica, the protagonist of the play, laments the state of the country and in this she is echoed by the complaints of People about poverty. The villains are seen to be exploiters who, having gained the confidence of Respublica by means of the aliases Reformation, Policy, Honesty and Authority have collected the wealth for themselves. In the end things are put right by Nemesis, described as 'the mooste highe goddesse of correccion' (l. 1783), and the prologue sets up a link with Queen Mary whom God has sent 'to reforme thabuses which hithertoo hath been' (l. 50). But if the play is in some sense celebration of the way Mary has, or might, put right the errors and abuses of the Protestant reign of her brother, Edward VI, it is remarkably mild and unvindictive in tone. The prevailing dramatic effect is one of ingenious and resourceful comedy which relies upon some very effective character types, and skilful word games and stage business.

The plot itself is straightforwardly typical of the political morality play in its presentation of how the vices take over the running of the country and how the deception of Respublica is carried out: *King Johan* and *Thrie Estaitis* have some similar features, as in the deception of King Johan, and the poverty caused to Lindsay's Pauper by those who exploit him. The scene in which the villains take up their aliases is a set-piece of comic conspiracy, as they keep forgetting to be consistent, a weakness which even affects Avarice who is the driving force and who is specifically called 'the vice of the plaie' in the manuscript. His alias, Policy, is frequently associated with Vices in other interludes (as with Politick Persuasion in *Patient and Meek Grissell*). The action which follows contains repeated protests by People, the anticipation that Truth, the daughter of Time, will come to reveal all, and a traditional dramatic motif of the medieval drama in which Truth and her sisters Mercy, Justice and Peace embrace, as in the Bible (Psalm 84:11, Vulgate) and bring an end to deception. The punishments are more symbolic than realistic: Avarice will be squeezed like a sponge to make him give up his ill-gotten wealth.

The possibility that this play has school auspices, even if it were performed at court, is enhanced by the division into five Acts, a feature which marries classical to morality-play methods, and one which emphasises the simplicity of the outline. The absence of any doubling scheme suggests that the play was more likely to have been performed by boys than by travelling companies on the road. The strong but simple characterisation is very effective. Adulation (Honesty) has a quickly persuasive tongue; Oppression (Reformation) is a cruel bully, quick to offer brute force; and Insolence (Authority, 'the chief galaunt') adopts a haughty manner which is most in evidence in his dealings with People. Though the latter has genuine and substantial grievances arising from his increasing poverty, he is a strongly comic type. He is given a rural speech and in his conversations he frequently falls into malapropisms and other misunderstandings. At his first entry he is looking for 'Rice puddingcake' (= Respublica), which excites the scornful Adulation to interrogate him:

Adul.	Who hathe wrought to youe suche extremytee?	
People.	Naie to tell how zo, passeth our captyvytee.	*capacity*
Res.	It passeth anie mans imaginacion.	
People.	Youe zai zouth, yt passeth anie mans madge mason,	
	Vor we þynke ye love us as well as ere ye dyd.	

(ll. 652–6)

'*Beano*' jokes, no doubt enjoyed by the young performers, but it is interesting that the author clothes his political intentions in such harmless nonsense.

The comic tone is even stronger in Avarice, who is onstage for much of the play. Though he embodies one of the Deadly Sins, his part is sustained by stage business associated with a miser. His costume is apparently hung with purses: he talks fondly to them:

> But in faithe goode swete fooles yt shall cost me a fall
> But I will shortelye fyll youe, and stoppe youre mouthes all.
>
> (ll. 467–8)

He becomes so absorbed in this that the other villains have difficulty in gaining his attention. At one point he gives names to thirteen of them ('leases . . . interest . . . perjury . . . bribes . . . benefices . . . rents', ll. 855–84); at another he has to turn his coat inside out to conceal them. These jokes could no doubt be worked up to be good stage fun, but we should not overlook their appropriateness to the allegory of Avarice, and to the contemporary financial abuses which interested the author.

One last speculation is engaging: in discussing Heywood we found that there was a possibility that he played Merry Report himself alongside the boys in his company: it would have been quite appropriate for Udall, the schoolmaster, to adopt the same technique here. If the play were done at court, there is also a good chance that Heywood would know about it, especially because he was apparently close to Queen Mary. And we have noted that the use of cheerful comedy in connection with a carefully modulated point of view is another of his characteristics. Udall was Protestant in sympathy, but here, in the first year of Mary's reign, with the future uncertain, the need for a Protestant to be persuasive would be just as great as that which lay behind Heywood's moderating tone when he wrote *Wether* at the time of the Divorce. The techniques in Heywood's plays and in *Respublica* form a sharp contrast with those noted in *Youth* and *Hickscorner*: in the latter the question of salvation and its moral imperatives are made to work quite differently from the more worldly-orientated moral issues in these later plays. This shift is accompanied by a much greater theatrical sophistication. The difference illustrates in a striking way the variety of scope possible in the interlude.

The Wit and Science plays

This group of three plays is a fortunate survival as they dramatise the same theme: the marriage between Wit, the natural endowment of mental ability, and Science, true knowledge or wisdom. Taken together they reveal different origins and dramatic registers that were possible for the interlude, and since they were written over a period of about thirty years they also give some evidence about development. *Wit and Science* was written by John Redford, presumably while he was the Master at St Paul's choir school between 1530 and 1547. Since Redford, as an educator, is concerned with humanist ideals and methods for his pupils, he is much closer to Heywood than to Bale. However, his method is undeniably allegorical, indicating that we should not see humanist drama as exclusively dealing with human characters. The plot itself is not about salvation so much as about the acquisition of earthly wisdom, albeit with the noblest of aspirations towards learning. Wit, the hero, must study and listen to good advice to deserve the love of the lady Science, daughter of Reason and Experience: she will bring the benefits of learning 'unto Godes honor and profit' (l. 1056).

As in a moral play, the plot shows the failure of the hero to live up to his initial aspirations: he has to suffer mentally and emotionally, by being rejected by Science, and physically by being killed in a rash and premature encounter with the monster Tediousness. He is miraculously revived and shows repentance, after being flogged by Shame, as though he were a sinner. These strong and effective motifs from the moral play are intermingled with elements from quite different dramatic provenances. The story is a romance which ends at the altar, and the action is partly drawn from the way the hero should show his worthiness by a chivalric encounter. His revival after his death – and it appears that the allegory works on the assumption that he really does die – is rather like the revival of St George who is killed by the dragon (or the Turkish Knight) in the folk play discussed in Chapter 10. At the second attempt, urged on by the right advice and assisted by Instruction and Diligence, he makes no mistake, triumphantly carrying in the monster's head upon a pole. At his worst moments Wit becomes involved in a comedy of folly, a sufficiently rare element on the English stage at this period. He is betrayed by Idleness, who puts on to him the fool's clothing of Ingnorance (sic), blackening his face to make him unrecognisable to Science. Though this episode does bear the moral identifier of a change of costume to illustrate a change of state, it is really an exploitation of the comedy of folly, especially in the lesson which Idleness tries to give to Ingnorance. This passage, which hilariously reveals the latter's inability to remember from one moment to the next, ends with her putting Wit's coat on to Ingnorance, whom it does not fit and who does not know how to keep it on.

The musical content of the play is lively and varied. When Wit dies he is revived by a quartet sung by Honest Recreation, Comfort, Quickness (Life) and Strength. As it progresses, different parts of his anatomy are revived – ear, eye, hand and foot in turn, presumably with accompanying business as the singers kneel around the corpse. Later he sings a duet upon his reconciliation with Science: 'Welcome mine own.' These items suggest that one of the objectives was to make the most of the musical talents of the choir boys. At another point, Science's devotion to Wit, who is in disgrace, is made clear by the quartet of Fame, Riches, Favour and Worship, who come in with viols. Possibly these are the same musicians doubling for the revival quartet.

In modern performances this play has proved very lively and entertaining, a feature of the inventive theatricality of the author over situations, such as Science's failure to recognise the blackened fool Wit as the lover she longs for, and the monstrous incomprehension of Ingnorance as he tries to learn his lesson 'on my thumbs'. Reason's gift of a mirror to Wit at the beginning proves a rich allegorical and theatrical device. It is through this that Wit finally realises his mistake. Apparently he has not looked after it very well: 'This glas, I se well, hath bene kept evill' (l. 803). And after polishing it up he sees that he does indeed appear a fool when he checks with the audience:

> How looke ther facis heere rownd abowte?
> All faire and cleere, they ev'rychone;
> And I, by the mas, a foole alone.

(ll. 809–11)

Inevitably, such a device makes the audience question the selves they see reflected.

The allegorical outlines of the other two Wit plays are similar and both contain incidental derivative details. The anonymous *Marriage of Wit and Science*, printed before 1570, is the closer (for convenience, *MWS* in this chapter). It has been suggested that the author was Sebastian Westcott, who was Redford's successor at St Paul's. A play called *Wit and Will* was performed at court in 1567–68.[7] It uses the romance and chivalric outline, including the two battles with Tediousness, the revival, and the seduction by Idleness in much the same way, but there are interesting shifts of emphasis.

The play is intended for performance by boys, and there is an unusual concentration of women characters which they would undertake. The occurrence of many highly serious female parts for boys on the Elizabethan stage means that dramatists came to rely upon a high degree of skill. But even Shakespeare, whose managing of Flute's incipient beard and a squeaking Cleopatra, relished some ambiguity, and indeed sheer fun over such transsexual impersonations. The concentration of female roles in *MWS* may thus have been delightful as comedy. In parallel, the dramatist uses the youth and small stature of Will, a new and mischievous page given by Nature to Wit. Will admits to being 11 or 12 years old and his contribution to events is usually destructive. In this respect he resembles a Vice, though, like its predecessor, *MWS* uses the morality play techniques for matters of secular education rather than salvation. Perhaps too much of a human character to be a Vice, he is one of the most marked innovations of this play and his activities illustrate the difficulty of being too categorical.

The inclusion of Will is also part of a shift in the allegory. In this play Nature is given the most influential thematic role. She introduces the play and gives Will to Wit as he sets out to win Science. The betrothal which begins *Wit and Science* is reached later in *MWS*, and part of Wit's task is to use but also to control his will which may lead him into disaster. As the play progresses Wit is deceived by Idleness, and she changes his clothes with those of Ignorance, but the extensive comic discourse of folly and ignorance is much reduced. The role of Shame is enlarged and there is a much more ritualistic element in his beating of Wit. Science actually watches the second battle with Tediousness, who is beheaded onstage. Nevertheless, the musical element is sustained at a comparable level, with new lyrics. In general the revisions have the air of a sympathetic re-working of the original, perhaps well-loved, material: it is a process which apparently makes the most of opportunities, especially the presence of the youngster who could be so engaging in the part of Will.

The curious manuscript of *The Marriage between Wit and Wisdom* (*MWW* hereafter) has both a known author, Francis Merbury, and a date, 1579. Merbury is known to have been at Christ's College, Cambridge, between 1571 and 1578, and he later became a well-known preacher, but the manuscript of *MWW* is not in his hand. Its most peculiar feature is that it appears to be a copy of a printed play, even to the point of incorporating the phrase 'never before imprinted'. Its titlepage, which has a doubling scheme for six actors, is laid out as though copied from a printed sheet, and it has been suggested that this layout is reminiscent of John Allde's for his known printings of *Like Will to Like*, *Cambises* and *Enough is as Good as a Feast*. As it happens, the play does include borrowings from other interludes, including *Cambises*. There is, however, no mention of the play in the Stationers' Register, and there is no record of performance.

The original plot of *Wit and Science* survives clearly enough. Wit, encouraged by his father and mother, Severity and Indulgence, is seeking to marry Wisdom, and the moral allegory supports this in a mode which remains essentially humanistic. He is misled by Idleness, who befools him. The monster, re-named Irksomness, at first lays Wit out with his club, but he is beheaded shortly afterwards by Wit using the sword called Perseverance provided by Wisdom in reviving him. This is all compressed into the earlier half of the play. Eventually Wit does succeed in marrying Wisdom, but only after he has been further deceived by Fancy who plays upon his sexual fantasies and has him cast into prison. This shift in structure enables the author to make much more of Idleness who is here male, and performed as a fully-fledged Vice, so that the amorous and instructional activities have to be carried out by his whore, Wantonness.

It is she who sings Wit to sleep and blackens his face, sustaining the idea of folly in her song:

> Lye still and heare nest the;
> Good Witt, lye and rest the,
>   And in my lap take thou thy sleepe.
> Since Idlenis brought the
> And now I have caughte the,
>   I charge the let care away creepe.
> So now that he sleepes full soundly,
> Now purpose I roundly
> Trick this prety doddy,   *blockhead*
> And make him a noddy,   *fool*
> And make him a noddy!
>
> (ll. 423–33)

Idleness no doubt fits in with the educational allegory in as much as he is a threat to learning and may prevent Wit from marrying Wisdom. But his influence upon the action is more apparent than real. The date of the play is significant for his role as Vice, and the recognition characteristics come thick and fast from his first entrance. He is quick to establish a relationship with the audience, but it is one which draws attention to the dramatic environment and to his own skills:

> Ah, sirrah! My masters, how fare you at this blessed
>   day?
> What? I wen all this company are come to see a play!   *think*
> What lokest the, good fellow? Didest the nere a se
>   man before?
> Here is a gasing! I am the best man in the company,   *gazing*
>   when there is no more!
> As for my properties I am sure you knowe them
>   of old:
> I can eate tell I sweat and worke tell I am cold.
>
> (ll. 178–87)

His allegorical significance is established by a game over his name: he first admits it and then gives his alias Honest Recreation, which seems to be directly inspired by the character in *Wit and Science*. But having established this, Merbury concentrates on making the most of his performance characteristics. He appears successively as a Doctor (perhaps a folk-play analogue), a rat-catcher, a crier (in which role he performs the joke of reducing his proclamation to nonsense),[8] a beggar with a stolen porridge-pot about his neck, and a priest ('the purveyor here in earth for the devil'). The text is rich in stage directions, many of them concerning the farcical activities of the Vice, as in:

> *Now shall Search rune away with his mony and he shall cast*
> *away his stilt and run after him.*

(ll. 1048–50)

Many of the directions are strictly functional and informative to would-be actors:

> *Here he washeth his face and taketh of the bable.*

(ll. 475–6)

The existence of this manuscript of *MWW* and of the putative published text associated with it suggests that Merbury was sharp enough to see the possibilities of adapting a successful amateur boys' play to a more public arena, and it is a significant move towards the London-based professional theatre which was to develop after 1576.

Early tragedies

The influence of classical conceptions and methods in tragedy, discussed in Chapter 7, persisted through the sixteenth century, sometimes fuelled from abroad and from contemporary tragedy written in Latin. The popularity and flexibility of the interlude in the early years of Elizabeth I's reign, and the associated experimentation with the physical circumstances of staging, provided further scope for the exploration of tragic material. For the most part this development depended upon classical plots, though these were not always in dramatic form originally. Many arrived in the Elizabethan period by way of a number of non-dramatic medieval poets who put their mark upon them and showed their interest in tragedy: chiefly Boccaccio, Chaucer and Lydgate. In the work of these poets is expressed not only the fearful falls of great men and women, occasioned by divine wrath over wickedness, or the terrible intervention of Fortune, but also two important philosophical motifs in contempt for worldly things (*de contemptu mundi*), and a lament for lost glories (*ubi sunt . . .*).

The publication of the English versions of Seneca's tragedies began with Jasper Heywood's *Troas* in 1559, and the three interludes to be considered here were all written within a few years of this. Thomas Preston's *Cambises* was printed by John Allde between 1561 and 1570, and John Pykeryng's *Horestes* by William Griffith in 1567. *Apius and Virginia*, written by 'R.B.' (*c.* 1564), was entered in the Stationers' Register in 1567, though the extant edition, by William How, did not appear until 1575.

While each of these plays addresses a different story in individual ways, their close origin in time is complemented by many similarities of outlook and technique. All three plays follow in the path of earlier moral interludes, and they all seek to reflect a moral universe which is underpinned by religious and political security. The presence of abstract characters indicates this didactic purpose, as does the commentary on the actions and the moral issues involved. But the access to tragedy leads to an interest in moral ambiguity or paradox, to ways of presenting moral dilemmas, to the expressing of extremes of emotion, and to the extensive presentation of violence and suffering on the stage.

The moral paradox in *Cambises*, which derives ultimately from Herodotus, and appears in Richard Taverner's *Garden of Wisdom* (1539), concerns the contrast between one exemplary act of justice carried out by Cambises, followed by a series of tyrannical acts which expose him to the destruction of the Gods. The good deed is pertinent to the role of kings since it shows the condign punishment Cambises visits upon his corrupt deputy, Sisamnes. When for his own advancement the latter abuses the authority deputed to him, he is summarily executed and flayed on stage. Cambises' subsequent tyrannical actions, which perpetrate several further murders, including those of his cousin-wife and his brother, are universally condemned. Though he starts off acting justly he becomes more and more an embodiment of injustice. Thus this tragedy is largely a matter of just retribution.

In *Apius and Virginia*, for which the main source is Chaucer's *Physician's Tale*, the original being in Livy, the tragic effect is divided between the eponymous characters. Though at one point Judge Apius suffers a dilemma which includes warnings from Conscience and Justice, he pursues his lust for Virginia. When Claudius, his associate, alleges in court that Virginia, his child-slave, was abducted by Virginius (in reality her true father), Apius gives instruction that Virginia must hand her over. On hearing of this Virginia, fearing shame and dishonour, begs Virginius to kill her. When Virginius presents his daughter's head to Apius he is overcome by guilt, condemned by Justice and Reward, and finally he kills himself. The tragedy of Apius is thus somewhat similar to Cambises', since he is a person in authority who is overthrown by his own wickedness. Virginia, on the other hand, is a pathetic but courageous victim who cannot escape from the dilemma which encompasses her. In order to increase the tragic effect and to develop her character as admirable, the author alters his source so that the initiative for her decapitation is her own.

In *Horestes*, the dilemma of the hero is central to the plot, and, as in the *Oresteia* of Aeschylus, the ultimate source, his actions in killing Clytemnestra, his mother, and Egistus, her lover, are ultimately vindicated. This is interwoven with another tragic element in the downfall of these lovers who, by the murder of Agamemnon, the father of Horestes, and the pursuit of adultery bring just destruction upon themselves. The story of Horestes is one of the earliest examples of the revenge tragedy which was to become so popular a few years later under the impact of Kyd's *Spanish Tragedy*. The outturn, however, is a strengthening of Horestes as king, and this emphasis upon the power of the monarch, if rightfully maintained, is embodied inversely in the failures of authority shown by Apius and Cambises. This is undoubtedly a theme which had great contemporary importance on the accession of Elizabeth I. It is likely that *Horestes* had a specific application to the murder of Henry Stuart by Mary Queen of Scots and her subsequent marriage to the Earl of Bothwell.[9]

In all three plays there is a taste for revealing the extremes of emotion, as in the erotic fantasies of Apius:

> Ah Gods, would I unfolde her armes complecting of my necke?
> Or would I hurt her nimble hand, or yeelde her such a checke?
> Would I gainsay hir tender skinne to baath where I do washe?
> Or els refuse hir softe sweete lippes to touch my naked fleshe?
>
> (ll. 363–6)

The grief of the wife of Praxaspes, whose son is shot through the heart by Cambises in drink, is sustained over a long speech:

> With blubbered eyes, into my arms from earth I wil thee take,
> And wrap thee in mine apron white! But, oh my heavy heart,
> The spiteful pangs that it sustains would make it in two to part,
> The death of this my son to see!
>
> (ll.583–6)

Clytemnestra makes a fruitless plea for mercy from Horestes:

> Pardon I crave, Horestes myne, save now my corpes from death;
> Let no man saye that thou wast cause I yeldyd up my breath.
>
> (ll. 731–2)

Indeed, a substantial part the action of all three plays is given over to similar expression of feelings, but it is supported by violence in physical action in all three. The stage directions make clear that terrible events were to be enacted explicitly. For Virginia the pathetic aspect is emphasised: *Here tye a handcarcher aboute hir eyes and then strike of her heade* (l. 835, s.d.). In *Cambises*, Sisamnes is skinned on stage: *Flay him with a false skin* (l. 464, s.d.). The death of Egistus in *Horestes* is to be witnessed by his lover and fellow victim: *Fling him of the lader, and then let on bringe on his mother Clytemnestra, but let her loke wher Egistus hangeth* (l. 790, s.d.).

Ambiguous elements related to the main action of these early tragedies are to be found in the subplots which they all contain. These are usually associated quite closely with the Vice's mischief with low characters who are comic. Their presence makes for an intriguing impact on the main business. Sometimes they underline the moral issues, as in the case of Mansipulus and Mansipula (male and female servants in *Apius and Virginia*), who are tempted by the Vice, Haphazard, to take a chance on not being spotted if they take time off. Such a proposal seems to echo his advice to Apius, who is also to take a chance on achieving his desires. On the other hand, a good deal of the business in which these low characters are involved seems to be a kind of low comedy of crime. They indulge in all sorts of misbehaviour, sexual or violent: there is a bout of fighting in each play, and in *Horestes* and *Cambises* a woman gets the better of men in a brawl. These characters also sing as part of their vulgar and licentious behaviour: the refrain of one song by Mansipulus, Mansipula and Subservus is:

> With thwicke thwack, with thump thump,
>> With bobbing and bum,
> Our syde saddle shoulders shal sheilde that doth come.
>> Hope so, and hap so, in hazard of thretninge,
>> The worst that can hap, lo, in end is but beating.
>> (for whole song see ll. 285–318)

The contribution of the Vice in each play is related to the moral issues, both in terms of the way these are expressed allegorically, and also in a more general sense of tragedy. In addition to the function of Haphazard as mentioned above, Ambidexter, who deceives by playing with both hands, reflects the contrast between the one good deed by Cambises and his tyrannical ones. The full title of Pikeryng's play gives his Vice prominence: *A Newe Enterlude of Vice conteyning the History of Horestes . . .* When Horestes at the beginning is doubtful about the unnaturalness of killing his mother it is the Vice, posing as Courage, who brings him a message from the Gods to urge him to proceed. Taken together with his later admission that his real name is Revenge, this suggests that Pikeryng wanted to present revenge as ambiguous, a position which reflects traditional theological teaching on this subject,[10] and one which has enormous potential in the uncertain and shifting values of the tragic world.

The Vices do not carry the general reflections upon tragic experience which are commonplace for the Chorus in classical tragedy. Such reflections are usually given to other characters. But the Vices do draw attention to moral failings, whether the evils which they themselves embody, or other greater ones like lust and tyranny. They also have a facility for anticipating the action which increases both the moral conflict and a sense of inevitability. Such interventions, often in the form of a soliloquy which gives them a special authority, also have an important shaping role in the exposition of the narrative. Thus Ambidexter, before the final disaster overcomes Cambises, says:

> Hear ye? I will lay twenty thousand pound
> That the king himself doth die by some wound.
> He hath shed so much blood that his will be shed;
> If it come thus to pass, in faith, then he is sped.
>
> (ll. 1148–51)

The Vice has a bearing on the emotionalism of these plays noted above. One of the Vice characteristics apparent in many plays in which he appears is his ability to turn quickly from laughing to weeping or vice versa. This facility is used for remarkable effect. Revenge comments heartlessly on the condemned Clytemnestra:

> A pestelaunce on the, crabyd queane! I thinke thou do delyght
> Hym to molest. Com of, in hast, and troubel me no more.
> Com on, com on, ites all in vaine, and get you on afore.
>
> (ll. 832–4)

Ambidexter is prone to weeping, as he does for Smerdis, the brother whom Cambises has murdered; but it is superficial:

> With sorrowful lamentations I am in such heat!
> Ah, my heart, how for him it doth sorrow!
> Nay I have done, in faith, now, and God give ye good morrow!
> Ha! ha! Weep? Nay laugh with both hands to play!
>
> (ll. 741–4)

Though such contrasts may have prompted Sir Philip Sidney to characterise these plays as 'mongrel tragi-comedy',[11] the mixture is actually a potent one which these writers are consistent in using. Their success probably depends more than anything upon the sheer inventiveness of the writing for the Vice's part.

As the printed texts of all three tragedies are supplied with doubling schemes, those responsible for them must have hoped that they might be performed by small professional groups. But there are hints that for *Horestes* and *Apius and Virginia* the auspices may have been private and that the original performances were by boys. There is a record of a production of an *Orestes* at court in the winter of 1567–68, but this cannot be definitely linked to Pikeryng's play.[12] The chief points are the large size of the cast, the elaboration of the music – *Horestes* has so much that it is almost a musical play – and the possible application of the moral and political to circumstances at court and to royal authority. The staging requirements are not complex: *Horestes* uses some kind of high place for the ladder employed at the execution of Egistus; *Cambises* needs a banquet scene, and *Apius and Virginia* requires a judicial court. Where a sense of location is necessary, as in the separate places in *Apius and Virginia*, this could be achieved quite adequately by the dialogue itself without the necessity of special structures. All three plays, even if produced with the help of the resources at court originally, would be in their printed form sufficiently flexible for occasional presentation by independent and itinerant companies. The tragic effects, and the associated moral and emotional dimensions, are here given a very practical treatment.

Moral plays

Here we shall consider three interludes which are largely concerned with moral doctrine. They are representative of many others, but in each case it is possible to suggest something about a political context and to note some information about authorship, a process which in itself also helps to place these interludes in a social context.

All three playwrights were clerics. Richard Wever, whose *Lusty Juventus* was printed *c.* 1550, may have been the Oxford scholar who was a prebend at Bubbenhall in the diocese of Lichfield, and who was examined for heresy during the Marian regime in 1556 according to Foxe.[13] William Wager had a lively and influential career in London, holding livings there from 1567 to 1591, and perhaps more significantly lectureships at St Mary Woolnoth and other parishes in the 1570s. Two plays bear his name: *The Longer Thou Livest the More Fool Thou Art* was printed by William How, probably in 1569; and *Enough is as Good as a Feast*, printed by John Allde, followed shortly after. Ulpian Fulwell, whose *Like Will to Like, Saith the Devil to the Collier* survives in three separate editions, spanning 1568 to 1587, was a country parson at Naunton in Gloucestershire. His patron was Burghley, and after the play was first published Fulwell seems to have wanted further patronage: though married, with a number of children, he went to St Mary's Hall in Oxford in 1579 and was Master of Arts by 1584.

Lusty Juventus, printed in the reign of Edward VI, but perhaps originating in the last years of Henry VIII, is closest to Bale's plays, and part of the formulation of Protestant doctrine and the attack upon Catholicism.[14] It may also have been influenced by *Youth*, in that its subject matter is in part the follies of the young. This aspect is no doubt related to the Prodigal Son, a motif which became popular in the second half of the century. The orientation of the play is unexpected because the Vice,

Hypocrisy, is impressed by the interest the young are showing in the new religion. This is a neat connection between the traditional need to correct the extravagance of the young with the idea that reactionary forces sustaining the old religion are to be found among the old. From his Catholic point of view he must distract Juventus (*Latin*, Youth) from his new ways and teach him to respect the religion of his elders. He is aided in his purpose by the Devil, who laments that he is losing his power over the world, another anti-Catholic stab typical of Bale. This characterisation sets up a Protestant theme much exploited by dramatists subsequently: the use of a comic Devil who could be used as a means of ridiculing Catholicism.[15] Hypocrisy tries to cheer up the crestfallen Devil by his account of the many different ways he has sought to sustain the old faith. He speaks better than he knows, and his catalogue is of course an indictment of itself. The list which begins:

> As holy Cardinales, holy Popes,
> Holy vestimentes, holy copes . . .

goes on for another 35 lines (ll. 408–44). It must also have been fun to do, a performance opportunity suitable for a Vice.

The text is rich with Protestant doctrine. In the opening exposition both Good Counsel and Knowledge refer to St Paul, and they give Juventus the New Testament. Juventus, perhaps too confident that he will never leave Good Counsel and Knowledge, is distracted by Hypocrisy from his intention to hear preaching and falls into company with Abhominable Living, who tempts him to kiss her. Restoration is achieved by Good Counsel, who condemns fleshly indulgence and introduces God's Merciful Promises, a character perhaps suggested by Bale's *God's Promises* (printed in 1547), but in any case one who represents a fundamental part of the new covenant valued by Protestants. The dramatic impulse wavers at this point as Wever gives full scope to a sermon-like ending: the Vice and the Devil disappear after the temptation, though they are mentioned.

The other two plays were apparently written after the Elizabethan settlement which changed the nature of public religious controversy by accepting state Protestantism. This affects their Protestant orientation in different ways. Wager's attention is partly upon economic problems and how to square them with doctrine; Fulwell accepts Protestant teaching, almost as though taking it for granted, and his interest lies in an elaborate theatrical exploitation of some comic types and situations.

Wager draws on the older morality play in making his protagonist very much the centre of the action, but, perhaps influenced by a somewhat pessimistic and Calvinistic approach he avoids a redemption, and offers hope by having his main fatally sinful character, Worldly Man, shadowed by Heavenly Man. This is not so much an equal division of protagonists as in the French *moralités*, like *L'Homme Just et L'Homme Mondain*, but rather the arrangement of the action places much greater dramatic emphasis upon Worldly Man than on his counterpart. This is seen in the sequence of his death. Once he begins to feel ill he is overshadowed by God's Plague, who recalls Death in *Perseverance* and the Messenger in *Everyman*, and the medieval Dance of Death:

> I am the plague of God properly called
> Which cometh on the wicked suddenly;
> I go through all towns strongly walled
> Striking to death, and that without mercy.
>
> (ll. 1243–6)

At this point, in response to Worldly Man's request, the Vice, Covetous, brings in Ignorance, the chaplain, whose comic ineptitude and pro-Catholic ideas give no comfort to the failing man: Ignorance has 'spouted with the Genevans, twenty on a row' (l. 1259). Worldly Man is 'haunted with the mare' (*nightmare*) and raves:

> O what great pains and torments I thought myself in
> Lying in fire which to burn did never lin.   *cease*
>
> (ll. 1299–1300)

The Physician, another comic type called Flebishiten, can do nothing for him, and as Worldly Man realises that death is inevitable he begins to make his will, encouraged by Covetous. But he is overcome by his sufferings and dies without completing it. Significantly, he makes no mention of God at the last. Altogether this is a powerful scene which makes the most of serious and comic ingredients to press home the horror of this sinful death. For doctrinal reasons it exploits the emotion of fear, closely associated with ridicule.

Though Fulwell gives his play a framework of Protestant doctrine, as evidenced by mockery of Latin prayers, the presence of God's Promises and the praise of virtuous rulers, the main allegory turns on the proverb in the title. This is broadly interpreted as meaning that evil consorts with evil. Since the Devil and the Collier (both black) appear in the full form of the proverb, they dance together in the introduction. There is no central human figure: the action is episodic, showing how different groups of characters, such as Tom Tosspot and Rafe Roister, misbehave together, and then picking up later on the misfortunes which have ensued, with the aid of Hankin Hangman. Nichol Newfangle, the Vice, who is appropriate to such ephemeral similarities, is one of the most vigorous and inventive in the canon, a feature which argues that in spite of his provincial background Fulwell had a strong sense of theatrical effects. He sings, dances, plays with the audience, and heartlessly makes fools of all the shady characters in the cast. One marked feature is that the text and the stage directions are rich in suggestions about physical movement about the acting space – fighting, riding, dancing, kneeling, falling over, carousing, as well as singing and playing instruments (the Vice plays a 'gittorn [*early guitar*] or some other instrument').

There is a hint that the play may have been performed by the Paul's Boys in the reference to something 'in the shrouds', a part of St Paul's churchyard where their theatre is thought to have been. The intellectual content of the play is certainly not very demanding and the lively action would be appealing. But the repeated publication and the doubling scheme on the title page suggest that the author or his publisher thought there might be a professional market for these comic antics. Considered with the other two moral interludes in their differing ways, Fulwell's play is a pointed illustration of the changing theatrical times which offered opportunities for the inventive. But it also underlines that political and religious purposes remained a continuing consideration whether the author chose to exploit his material actively in this direction, or remained content to accept an orthodox expression. No doubt the growing concern by the government for control of the stage through censorship was a factor. Fulwell, with his apparent need for patronage, as evidenced in his non-dramatic work, *The Flower of Fame* (1575) praising the Tudor dynasty and the Protestant faith, needed to be wary.

Biblical plays

The new religious climate at the beginning of the reign of Elizabeth I saw an interest in biblical plays under various auspices. Though the mystery cycles were still being performed, the new religion had different requirements, particularly over the relation of the individual to God. The different emphasis on scripture shows itself in many plays. There were several based upon the parable of the Prodigal Son, including *Nice Wanton* and *The Disobedient Child*. A fragment of *The Cruel Debtor* (1565), possibly by William Wager, shows it to be a version of the parable of the unjust steward (Matthew 18:23–35). Further biblical plays have survived from this period, including *The Resurrection of Our Lord* (1545), *Jacob and Esau* (1554), and *King Darius* (1565). References exist to lost plays: *Samson*, at the Red Lion in 1560/61, Thomas Ashton's *Passion of Christ* (1560/61) at Shrewsbury School where he was headmaster, a court masque on *Wise and Foolish Virgins* (1561), and a play on *Two Sins of King David* entered in the Stationers' Register in 1562. A translation by Arthur Golding of *Abraham's Sacrifice* by the French Protestant Thomas Bèze was printed in 1575.

The two biblical plays to be considered here are about women who were seen as exemplary in medieval and Renaissance times, and their stories became so popular that each became a cultural icon, though for interestingly different reasons. Both are ultimately derived from biblical sources, though it is notable that these were extensively developed by the dramatists.

Lewis Wager, the author of *The Life and Repentance of Mary Magdalene*, was educated as a Franciscan at Oxford, and made subdeacon in 1521. The date of his conversion to Protestantism is unknown, but he became rector of St James, Garlickhithe, in 1560. He died in 1562, leaving a widow. These similarities with the life of Bale are paralleled in his work, which shows the influence of Bale's plays. His play, printed in 1566 and again in 1567, takes the outstandingly popular story of Mary Magdalene and adapts it to Protestant ideas and to the style of production associated with interludes in the 1560s.

Though she is named in the Bible when Christ speaks to her in the garden after the Resurrection, traditional Catholic teaching, as exemplified in *The Golden Legend*, had conflated her with the woman who washed and anointed Christ's feet, the woman from whom Christ exorcised seven devils, and the sister of Lazarus. The medieval Digby play, *Mary Magdalene*, embodies these elements, as well as accretions about her castle at Magdalo, her journey to convert the King of Marseilles, and her apotheosis at the end of her life when she was taken up into heaven from the desert by divine means. Most of these items, which were not only non-scriptural but also encouraged the worship of the miraculous in sainthood, were rejected by Protestants. The essence of the cult which grew up around her had been penitential and devotional, and the climax of earthly activities was the moment of supreme penitence in the washing of Christ's feet. At this point, the ointment, her hair and her tears acquired devotional significance which was partly erotic.

Though Wager's education had familiarised him with the extended versions of the story, he concentrates upon a few incidents and takes a strictly Calvinist line: typically, he omits the meeting with Christ in the garden. For him the wickedness of the original Magdalene becomes a figure for unredeemed humanity which needs Christ's direct intervention for salvation. This involves the central Lutheran doctrine of Justification by Faith. In her unredeemed state, Magdalene is shown concerned with makeup, clothes and hairstyle, and under the Vice's encouragement she avoids marriage to make the most of her other advantages: the traditional erotic elements are thus transformed into exploiting herself – 'Hold up the market, and let them pay for the ware' (l. 786).

It cannot be shown that Wager knew the earlier Digby version, but his methods of staging are strikingly different. The earlier Magdalene is tempted by the Devil, who encourages her pride and persuades her to follow his

ways from choice. Her conversion comes as an act of will. For Wager the
disaster is occasioned by the Vice called Infidelity (the name of the Vice
in Bale's *Three Laws*). He signifies her turning away from faith and he
encourages her worldly ways, accompanied by other vices who are reminiscent of the Seven Deadly Sins: Pride of Life, Cupidity and Carnal
Concupiscence. Instead of the medieval staging of the Digby play, which
the stage directions make clear are a series of houses around an area large
enough for a sea voyage in between, Wager adopts the linear structure
characteristic of the interlude, with less specific reference to locations. The
key sequence shows that Law, another reflection perhaps of Bale from
Three Laws, gives Magdalene the Knowledge of Sin, whereupon Christ
intervenes, leading to the appearance of Faith and Repentance. The meal
at the House of Simon is then used to show Magdalene's now exemplary
state:

> To all the world an example I may be
> In whom the mercy of Christ is declared.   *revealed*
>
> (ll. 1769–70)

The stage direction shows how closely Wager sought to rely upon scripture:

> *Let Marie creepe under the table, abydyng there a certayne space*
> *behynd, and doe as it is specified in the Gospel.*
>
> (l. 1818, s.d.)

When Magdalene has washed Christ's feet the allegory is completed by
Justification, who shows that love is insufficient until Christ bestows
grace: it is only then that the character Love enters: 'I am named Love,
from true faith procedyng' (l. 2093). Thus Wager changes the function of
love on theological grounds.

The story of Susanna appeared in the Vulgate, but because it was found
not to have a Hebrew original it was placed in the Apocrypha by the
Protestants. Nevertheless they sustained its enormous popularity as a subject for drama which, it has been shown, extended to at least seventy
dramatisations in Europe as a whole up to the seventeenth century.[16]
Again there is an erotic element in that she takes a bath and excites the
lust of two untrustworthy judges who try to force her submission: but this
may be used in different ways on ideological grounds. The surveys of
Susanna plays show that she was of interest to Protestant and Catholic
alike, the latter tending to stress her saintly qualities even though she lived
before saints were invented.

Very little is known about Thomas Garter, the author of *The Comedy
of the Virtuous and Godly Susanna*, though the legal discourse in the play
gives some support to the idea that he had a legal training. The Protestant

aspects of his thinking are palpable, and his management of dramatic effects and staging are of interest. The extent of the parts of the young Daniel and Susanna herself may mean that the play was originally done by boys, though the play is unusual in that there are apparently no songs.

In this play the theme of the responsibilities of leaders or judges is interwoven with ideals of behaviour concerning female honour and marriage. Both were of great interest to the Protestant ethic. The former is related to the emphasis Luther put upon the role of the nobility and the special responsibilities of leaders towards God and their subjects. It is intimately bound up with the political effect of royal supremacy, and it is not surprising that it might be of interest to lawyers. The plot shows two versions of the matter in Joachim, Susanna's husband, who is loving and supportive for most of the time, but who is severely threatened when she is alleged to have been disloyal. The unjust judges who conspire against Susanna, here called Sensualitas and Voluptas, are the reverse of Joachim. Trusted because of their office, they seek to force her by the legal device of acting as one another's witness against her alleged adultery. Following the account in the Bible, they are broken by the young Daniel who reveals an inconsistency in their testament. The irony of justice is maintained as they are stoned to death instead of Susanna.

Her conduct is exemplary throughout, even though all the characters seem convinced by the allegations of the judges. Joachim relies on her obedience, which is demonstrated early on. The attack upon her is extensive. It is initiated by a comic Sathan who sets his son, Ill Report the Vice, to undermine her. The choice of name is apt because the Vice does seek to destroy her reputation, but on the way he also notes the destruction of that of the judges and takes part in their death. In his trickery of them he takes on the role of quack doctor who comes to assuage the pangs of love. The judges themselves are sinister, but they are cleverly managed by the author in the way they rather reluctantly reveal their lust to one another.

The text is notably rich in stage directions, which suggest that the author went some way towards envisaging how things might be done on stage effectively. The following occurs near the beginning of the play, before the conspiracy against Susanna is really under way:

> Note that from the entraunce of Susanna, the Judges eyes shall never be of [f] her till her departure, whispering betweene themselves as though they talked of her.
>
> (ll. 359–61, s.d.)

The style and language of this makes it unlikely that it was written by the actors themselves: it looks as though the author is helping the reader to imagine what is going on. Two lines later another follows, again with a sense that it is meant to be read as part of a narrative:

With this Joachim, Susanna and her two Maydes go to the Table
to the two Elders.

(ll. 364–5)

This play is one of the few interludes considered here to have been performed in modern times.[17] The production admirably revealed how the verse can convey the serious preoccupations of state and private honour, and the action showed the vulnerability and constancy of Susanna. The comic effects of the Vice were highly successful, and so was the ridiculousness of the Devil and the judges in their different ways. The performance put it beyond doubt that the presence of such comic elements, conventional and repetitive though they may seem on the page, is a positive element in the ideas and emotions aroused by the play, and a rich theatrical embellishment. For all their apparent limitations as to size and scope, the interludes can be seen as flexible and coherent.

Notes

1. A fuller discussion with relating examples is given by Nicholas Davis, 'The Meaning of the Word "Interlude"', *METh* 6 (1984), 5–15, 61–91. The standard work on interludes is T.W. Craik, *The Tudor Interlude* (Leicester, 1958).

2. See, for example, his discussion of *Lusty Juventus* (*c.* 1550) in *From 'Mankind' to Marlowe* (Cambridge, Mass., 1962), pp. 144–5.

3. This peculiar or astounding journey turns up in the folk play discussed in Chapter 10 below.

4. Lancashire, no. 1121.

5. Lancashire, no. 1046.

6. The following account reflects many of the conclusions of Ian Lancashire's radical re-reading of these plays in his 1980 edition.

7. See Arthur Brown (ed.) *The Marriage of Wit and Science*, Malone Society (Oxford, 1960), pp. v–vi. The play presents a peculiar textual difficulty in that a passage of some 160 lines out of a total of 1,548 was printed out of order. Brown first identified the error correctly in his edition, but in accordance with the practice of the Malone Society he kept to the incorrect order of his exemplar. In the absence of any other reliable edition, references here follow his numbering.

8. This device is played by Cain and Garcio in *Towneley* 2.421–39.

9. See J.E. Phillips, 'A Revaluation of *Horestes*', *Huntington Library Quarterly* xviii (1955), 227–44; and K. Robertson and J-A. George (eds) *Horestes* (Galway, 1996), pp. 1–4.

10. For the view of Aquinas, see R.S. Knapp, '*Horestes*: the uses of Revenge', *English Literary History* xl (1973), 205–20 (210).

11. *Defence of Poesie* (1582), ed. A. Feuillerat (Cambridge, 1923), p. 39.

12. Marie Axton (ed.) *Three Tudor Classical Interludes* (Cambridge, 1982), pp. 29–30.

13. J.M. Nosworthy (ed.) *Lusty Juventus*, Malone Society (Oxford, 1966), p. xxii.

14. For similarities with *The King's Book*, 1543, see H.S. Thomas (ed.) *An Enterlude called Lusty Juventus* (New York, 1982), pp. xviii–xxviii: references are to this edition.

15. Apart from *Like*, and *Susanna* discussed below, this motif appears in *The Disobedient Child*, *The Conflict of Conscience* and *All for Money*.

16. J. de Rothschild (ed.) *Le Mystère du Viell Testament* (Paris, 1885), pp. lxvi–cvii. Paul Casey notes 71 performances of Susanna plays in German-speaking countries between 1532 and 1636, *The Susanna Theme in German Literature* (Bonn, 1976), pp. 241–6.

17. It was performed by Joculatores Lancastrienses at various locations, including Perpignan, in 1986, directed by Meg Twycross.

Chapter 10
Other Dramatic Forms

Though there is always a significant amount of our experience of drama which arises outside the strict limits of what can be found in the written text, the dramatic forms to be considered here have the special feature that very few of them have survived in written form. The chief evidence comes from records, whose value has to be appraised carefully as they were often not made to give specific details about the nature of plays, but only to refer to them obliquely and for some purpose not directly concerned with what went on in performance. For example, the object of such records might be to show what performances cost, or to deal with dramatic events in terms of legal problems arising, or even of social disturbance. Of the three kinds of dramatic performance to be considered here, the local or parish drama has least in the way of texts, though records are copious. The traditional or folk play closely related to it has some textual survivals but these do not go back beyond the eighteenth century. And the civic shows and public entries and processions are well enough served because of the importance to the state of their chief protagonists, monarchs, their families and guests, but the nature of this particular dramatic experience requires special consideration because it is not quite like that which we normally associate with plays and their audiences.

Parish drama

This title has emerged from the work of the Records of Early English Drama project (REED) to express the change in our understanding of drama at local level which has developed since the systematic collection and publication of early records of drama began in the 1970s.[1] Although there was some local drama which was analogous to the major religious cycles in cities like York, the quantity is much less than might have been anticipated, and where new information has been found it is largely about secular kinds of dramatic activity rather than about drama based upon biblical subjects. Though the systematic investigation and evaluation of records is by no means complete, it is clear that dramatic activities were widespread and plentiful, and also that local traditions and customs played a large part in determining the forms dramatic entertainment was to take. Shot through this mass of information are questions about the nature of the performers themselves. A good deal of money was paid to them at various times by official bodies like local councils and by individuals, but their organisation varied remarkably. On the one hand, there were travelling companies under noble patronage which were autonomous, but on the other hand these were supplemented, if not outpaced, by many *ad hoc* groups which were clearly amateur at base but which nevertheless collected money from spectators for good causes such as the Church itself. Some of these went on short local tours, and it is apparent that the custom of exchanging dramatic entertainment between parishes was widespread.

The nature of these performances makes us consider what we actually mean by drama, because boundaries of genre are not always conveniently precise. One feature is undoubtedly putting on special clothes which may hide the identity of the performer, and give a new one. These may show membership of a group or distinguish it from others. Costumes or masks may follow conventional types like devils and fools, and they may indicate a participation in conventional or even ritualistic activities. Then again they may facilitate practices which support the existing social structures or undermine them. To assume another identity may enable a collection of funds for good causes, or permit activities which transgress normal social behaviour in sexual, religious or social terms. Moreover, a new identity achieved by costume, language or gesture will almost always be entertaining to those who know or who may suspect the person who is concealed. In some forms there is the pleasure of revelation. Along with this comes the role of the audience, who must on the one hand be entertained, but who may also be instructed, induced to worship, or led to a release of behaviour which they would not dream of in their normal lives. The audience may also be stimulated to practise its own skills in singing and dancing or in competitive activities such as wrestling or archery. As a result, the conclusion of such quasi-dramatic activities may not be constrained within the limits of a plot but remained open-ended in order that competition or display may take place. It is clear too that large parts of these activities were not always solely or primarily dependent upon words.

Turning to the specific forms of drama, we may first consider that which is substantially religious. Much of it took place in the churches, both before and after the Reformation, and it worked because the clergy were sympathetic to it and indeed were able to participate as performers or as part of the invention of what was to happen. It may well be that specifically religious texts which have survived, such as the *Abraham and*

Isaac play from Brome in Suffolk, were written by the clergy and performed by the parishioners. In many places drama was associated with
Corpus Christi, though not in the form of a cycle or an extended series
of plays. It is often quite difficult to determine whether what happened
at Corpus Christi was a procession or a single play or a series. The case of
the Resurrection play at New Romney in Kent is notable because being
such a small place the village might not have been expected to have a play
cycle, yet this is in fact what was performed in 1555, with four plays and
a total of fifteen episodes from the Baptism of Jesus to the Ascension.[2]

The custom of electing a Boy Bishop at Christmas, usually in connection with the feast commemorating the slaughter of the Innocents, is
documented from 1221 at York. It is found at St Paul's in London from
1225, and there are elaborate regulations dating from 1263 regarding
procession, sermon and feast. The custom is traceable at many other
places, including Hereford, Gloucester, Thetford, Louth and Exeter, as
well as at Selby, where a visiting Boy Bishop from York was paid over
the period 1398 to 1533. Special attention was given to the installation
at some schools such as Winchester and Eton in the fifteenth century.
This particular custom was rejected at the Reformation, but the sustaining
of plays on Corpus Christi persisted rather later in the sixteenth century
and beyond at a local level. There is a report of a Corpus Christi play at
Kendal from the beginning of the reign of James I.[3]

In many places, religious guilds were also an integral part of local
religious drama. These were often serviced by clergy acting as chaplains.
One of the most conspicuous is the St George guild at Norwich which
supported the Corpus Christi celebrations in the sixteenth century, but
there is evidence of others promoting the celebration of other saints. At
York in 1554 there was a St George procession or riding with a mass, a
sermon and a play.[4] The events enacted are unknown, though a dragon
was paid for. At New Romney in Kent the St George play is known for
1458 and 1468, and it appears to have been exchanged with Lydd in
1490. Saint plays in general, though still in evidence in the 1520s when
there are records of eleven performances, suffered much at the Reformation when the play books were destroyed as idolatrous and the guilds
were usually suppressed. In spite of the patriotic associations of St George,
the plays associated with him mostly disappeared at this time, though we
shall find echoes of him in the folk play discussed below.

The practice of observing the Entombment and Resurrection of Christ,
usually known as the Easter Sepulchre, was another casualty at the Reformation, though it was apparently widespread, and sometimes supported by
specially dedicated Resurrection Guilds. It was centred on a tomb, or
shrine with a canopy, on the north side of the church which could stand
for Christ's tomb. Payments were made for constructing or adapting the
sepulchre where necessary. There is substantial evidence about the physical

properties that were used for the ceremony, which had liturgical elements, and there was a strong representational aspect which could be considered dramatic. Thus people provided in their wills for their own tombs in churches, and specifically required that they be used to represent the Holy Sepulchre in Jerusalem. As the ceremony developed, a cross, sometimes with a Christ-figure affixed, was placed in or on the tomb on Good Friday, as though to recall the buried body of Christ. It remained there until Easter Sunday when, in some places, it was silently removed to the altar so that the Sepulchre could then appear empty when visited by the three Marys.

There is very little evidence, however, that beyond the ceremonial representation of these actions there was any substantial dramatic activity or encounter by actors. It is intriguing that the Sepulchre was adorned with iconographical images in stone, or specially painted pictures which might be carried in procession and represented elements from the biblical narrative. It is also apparent that there were models of angels, devils and human characters, rather like puppets, which must have provided a kind of still-life image. Some of the details of this are to be found in wills. The records at Bristol in 1470 suggest a mimetic element since there were payments for wigs, wings and weapons and that thirteen devils, four knights and four angels were present, but, in the absence of corroborating evidence elsewhere, it is not possible to be certain that these apparent stage costumes and properties were actually designed for human actors. However, payments were made at Gloucester between 1546 and 1559 to those who (mimetically) watched over the Sepulchre and the candle that burned there between Good Friday and Easter Day. It seems though that for Protestants the misguided representation in the ceremony was a matter for complaint, as John Hooper, Bishop of Gloucester, indicated in 1547:

> What resemblance hath the taking of the cross out of
> the sepulchre and going a procession with it, with the
> resurrection of Christ? None at all: the dead post is as dead,
> when they sing *iam non moritur* ['now he is not dead'], as it
> was when they buried it.[5]

Because the Church, as a building and as a social organisation, was central to parish life it is not surprising that many activities apparently of a non-religious kind were drawn to its influence or made to serve its needs. The custom of holding church ales, or Whitsun ales, drinking parties with miscellaneous entertainment, was widespread. Sometimes these are called King ales in reference to the May King discussed below. The outcome was a contribution to Church funds even if the clergy had to monitor and reprove unseemly behaviour. Later in the sixteenth century as the Protestant reaction intensified there are many reproofs recorded for making merry in the churchyards, especially when such activities attracted the faithful from their attendance at services. As to church ales, these were no doubt an important economic support for church expenses.

The custom of rush-bearing was popular, especially in the North of England, where it survived in a revised form to modern times. It was a summer festival whose practical purpose was to bring new rushes for the floor of the church. These were often decked with flowers, but it also true that the event attracted dancing and even mimetic or parodic activity. There are records from Cheshire of carts being used, booths constructed and payments for food.

The substance of many popular festivals, however, is somewhat more remote from a Christian purpose. It is likely that the occurrence of the giant Gogmagog, at Newcastle, and the procession of Yule and his wife in York, prohibited in 1571, were survivals from earlier rites. There were four giants in the Chester Midsummer Show in the sixteenth century, along with characters from the mystery plays such as devils, and Balaam and his ass. Underlying the Church's year with its regular festivals was the natural cycle of cultivation, which perhaps gave rise to customs at Plough Monday, the first after 6 January. A Plough song is recorded at Snettisham, Norfolk, in 1500. The activities of Hock Monday and Tuesday (in the second week after Easter) were said to derive from a historical feat of women in the wars with the Danes before the Conquest. The essential action involved mock battles in which the women captured the men for ransom, and vice versa. Apparently the former was the more profitable to the parish funds. The event was reproduced before Queen Elizabeth I in July 1575 at Kenilworth and described in a letter by Robert Laneham.[6]

The importance of these customs in the history of drama lies as much in their contribution to social cohesion as in their quasi-dramatic features. The former are significant because they suggest that most people would see such entertainments as having a neighbourly purpose, as well as possibly a financial contribution to the parish. In some activities 'liveries' were used as a sign that contributions had been made. But the dramatic element must have given experience of public participation and the development of performing skills and also the development of a relationship with an audience. It is apparent, as the political and religious controversies developed through the Reformation, that many of these activities were used for partisan or ideological purposes. While the Protestants suppressed some of them in the 1530s, many were revived under Queen Mary. Under Elizabeth some were again suppressed, but Archbishop Grindal's West Riding Injunction of 1571 suggests that the ideological battle against Lords of Misrule, Summer Lords or Ladies, disguised persons in Christmas or May games, morris dancers, and others at rush-bearings was still in progress.[7] We now need to turn to two rather more elaborate activities which embrace many of the characteristics noted somewhat sporadically so far. These are the Robin Hood plays and the folk play.

Robin Hood became a myth in the Middle Ages and he lasted long enough to be remembered in the professional Elizabethan theatre, as well as surviving into children's stories for centuries thereafter. It is characteristic of myth that heroic deeds should be acted and recognised, and that though there may be some meaning attached to the character and the narrative it is not purely allegorical or moral. The myth of Robin Hood was manifested in ballads and plays, which were contemporary and probably developed alongside one another. As we shall see, there are very few plays which actually survive to illustrate how he might have been enacted. Nevertheless at the core of this mythic material we have a young man who may be both good and bad, who is an outlaw, and who is not always as successful as a hero should be. His paradoxical nature is shared with Maid Marian, a man/woman figure, Friar Tuck, who is lecherous and drunken in spite of his vows, and Little John, the skilful warrior who is always subordinate. These paradoxes give greater strength to the myth because they defy simple moral interpretations and add independent vitality to narrative.

In the records which deal with entertainments in parishes, Robin Hood is one of the commonest characters. Not only does he have the three associates just mentioned: there is often a May King and Queen, who preside over the core activities, which involve fighting and feasting, and there may also be sundry fools, devils and vices. Since the outcome of the fighting may not have been predetermined, it follows that the plot is not always dominant: indeed, at times it seems that the words of the play or ballad might just be a means of setting up physical conflict. There is no doubt that the prowess of those taking part was important and competitive, especially in the skills of archery and wrestling, both of which were valued nationally.

Let us now review the historical and geographical extent of the Robin Hood plays, bearing mind that the records are incomplete. As always, a record of an event or some transaction is a positive indication, but the absence of a record does not necessarily mean that nothing happened. The close connection between the Robin Hood play and the May game is particularly intriguing because there are plenty of records of the latter which do not actually mention Robin Hood. There is, for example, an early prohibition in 1240 at Worcester. In the fifteenth century there was a play containing Robin Hood before the Mayor of Exeter in 1427. A letter of Sir John Paston written to his brother in Norfolk in April 1473 mentions W. Wood, a servant: 'I have kept him this three year to play St George, and Robin Hood and the Sheriff of Nottingham.' Perhaps associated with this, there is among the Paston papers, in Norfolk, on the reverse of household accounts from May 1475 à text of 21 couplets from a Robin Hood play, having two episodes. It is untitled and undivided for speakers but clearly a dialogue containing performed events typical of the combat associated with Robin Hood, who is named in the fragment.

Under a linden tree, an unnamed Knight and Robin shoot (archery), cast
the stone, cast the axle-tree, and wrestle. When Robin takes a fall, he
blows his horn and they fight to the death:

> Lat us fyght at ottrance.
> He that fleth, God gyfe hym myschaunce.

This is followed by:

> Now I have the maystry here,
> Off I smyte this sory swyre.   *neck*

As the episode ends Robin puts on the Knight's clothes and carries off
his adversary's head in his own hood. In the second episode Robin and
some of the band are imprisoned by the Sheriff. Little John and Friar
Tuck are surprised by the Sheriff while engaged in archery, arrested and
condemned to 'be hangyde and y-drawe'. The text ends without reaching
a proper ending: perhaps we may suppose that by some device or feat of
arms Robin would make good his escape.

   In the sixteenth century Robin Hood plays an increasingly identifiable
part in local festivals. The geographical area of his activities has been
described as from Cornwall to Aberdeen, though the records show a
concentration south of Nottingham, especially in the Thames and Severn
valleys and in Devon. By contrast, there is not much to back up the
Paston items noted above from the rest of East Anglia. Evidence from
Henley-on-Thames between 1499 and 1520 shows a continuing association between Robin Hood and the King Game. Whatever activities these
quasi-dramatic events presented, the collection of money was an important part. Payments for play books for Robin Hood at Lydd in Kent
support the idea of a written text. In Devon, where Robin Hood appears
in at least ten places, there are provisions for (Kendal) green costumes and
a silver arrow. But the ever-present possibility of the fighting getting out
of hand persists. In 1498 a Star Chamber case over breach of the peace
shows that William Milner from Wolverhampton (formerly Staffordshire)
calling himself the Abbot of Marham (or Mar-all), a local variant of the
Summer King, brought eighty armed men to the Willenhall Fair. The
threat to the peace came with Roger Marchall of Wednesbury, who called
himself Robin Hood and was followed by a hundred men. However
violent the ensuing encounter, Marchall's defence shows how the Robin
Hood activities might credibly be used to claim a beneficial outcome:

> It hath been of old times used and accustomed on the
> said fair day that . . . the inhabitants of the said town of
> [Wolver]hampton, Wednesbury and Walsall have come to

the said fair with their captains called the Abbot of Marham
or Robin Hood to the intent to gather money with their
disports to the profit of the churches.[8]

Other characters in the Robin Hood story also caused problems, as at
Chagford in 1509–10:

There shall be no riot kept in any parish by the young men
of the same parish, called Robin Hood.[9]

William Dyke, when examined about his preaching, criticised the Whitsun
ales, speaking of

Maid Marion coming into the Church in the time of prayer
and preaching to move laughter with kissing in the church
besides other sundry abuses.[10]

As noted above, it was common for plays to be taken through a series of
parishes, and Robin Hood is no exception. In spite of the robust nature
of his entertainment, in 1513–14 Robin Hood paid to Kingston what
he had gathered in Croydon, and Henley-on-Thames received money
collected by Robin Hood at Reading.[11]

Against this background of vigorous activity which was profitable but
which also shows much evidence of being socially disruptive, we must
also consider that there is a certain amount of more literary evidence in
the form of written-up entertainments or printed texts containing Robin
Hood through to the 1590s. It appears, in short, that there was a very
large amount of Robin Hood activity in local circumstances that was both
persistent, but also ephemeral because it was not written down, and it
must have contained a great deal of fighting and other competitive activities whether well-intentioned or not.

The court of Henry VIII took notice of some possibilities in the
tradition. The King himself visited the Queen in the guise of Robin
Hood in 1510, and he was entertained in 1515 by Robin in archery
contests.[12] Later, in about 1562, the publication *The Play of Robin Hood,
very proper to be played in May Games* shows that the material was becoming part of a written or print culture, and also suggests that performance
might be a matter of interest to the growing links between print and
performance. This is sustained by the inclusion of Robin Hood episodes
in three plays written for the London stage: *George a Green, the Pinner of
Wakefield* (1590), George Peele's *Edward I* (c. 1591), and Antony Munday's
Downfall of Robert Earl of Huntingdon (1598).[13]

In the first of these, George, the hero, accompanied by his beloved,
meets Robin Hood and his men, and successively defeats Will Scarlet and
Much, the miller's son, and is holding his own with Robin himself, when

the latter stops the contest. He introduces Maid Marian, and George entertains them to a banquet. Peele shows how Lluellen, in flight from King Edward, assumes a disguise as Master of Misrule, Robin Hood, and his companions assume corresponding disguises. The story is complicated by the presence of Mortimer, who takes on the disguise of a Potter, which leads to his discomfiture as a suitor for Maid Marian. The episode ends with a beating. In Munday's play, the Earl of Huntingdon, outlawed by Prince John, becomes Robin Hood and proclaims his independence. He vows to live an outlaw until the return of Richard I from the Crusade, and he introduces an egalitarian theme, including defence of the poor, and of women, and resistance to usurers and clerics. This later version of some of the traditional motif shows that Robin's outlawry and threat are purged to something more socially acceptable, and given a flavour of chivalry which would outweigh the ignominy or indeed the risk of being considered an outcast and vagabond. These plays are close in time, suggesting that at this point in the 1590s the idea of Robin Hood was both fashionable and useful ideologically.

In comparison with this fairly secure evidence for the widespread interest in the Robin Hood plays and entertainments, that for the traditional folk play which centres on St George is rare and late. What survived until the twentieth century and can still be seen in revivals cannot be surely traced back into medieval times, though some elements probably did exist then. In the surviving version of the play, as used in Book 2, Chapter 5 of Thomas Hardy's *Return of the Native* (1878), the mummers arrive in disguise for an indoor performance, associated with Christmas festivities. The play, beginning with simple boasts, shows a crude fight, by no means as 'serious' or skilful as in the Robin Hood plays, in which St George is slain by the Turkish Knight. His subsequent revival by a comic Doctor using grotesque tools such as a saw and a brace and bit, and a magic juice called elecampane, is followed by another bout in which he is successful, and the whole thing ends with a merry dance and a collection. At times there was a long but rather inactive cast with comic or outrageous names such as Big Head, Pickle Herring, Blue Breeches, Beelzebub and Father Christmas, as well as suitable costumes, usually designed to obliterate the identity of the persons acting.

The study of this form of drama has sought to relate it to the dying of the old year and the coming of the new. Some fertility or perhaps sexual reverberations are found in the presence of Maid Marian among the characters, and some versions encompass or substitute a wooing dance. These wooing plays, with a Bessy usually played by a man, were concentrated in the East Midlands, whereas the St George play, often known as the combat play, ran up the spine of England from the Isle of Wight to the North-west. But such a distribution can only be reasonably certain for the nineteenth and twentieth centuries. The literary quality of the texts, none of which goes back before the eighteenth century, is decidedly poor – one might even think this deliberate. They show no sign of the learned and clerkly authors we have found in the bulk of medieval and Tudor drama. There remains 'a serious chronological gap' between these earliest written versions and what we may deduce from the records in the REED volumes about the parish drama, especially as the folk drama as such appears primarily an indoor entertainment, while the Robin Hood and other parish plays were usually outdoors.[14] Nevertheless it would be unwise to assume that the parish plays and the folk plays were entirely separate and unconnected.

If, therefore, some earlier form existed which may have been related to winter festivals, or some death and rebirth ritual, it seems likely that the versions which can be discerned from the eighteenth century onwards may have been influenced by the parish drama of various kinds. This could include the morris dances and perhaps the older sword dances confined to north-east England with the spectacular lock of swords around the neck of the fool. The more literary forms which are dealt with in Chapter 9 on the interludes would also provide a reflection of this. Indeed, some of their effects do seem detectable since some speeches from *Youth* are to be found in the *Revesby Sword Play* as written down in about 1779.[15] The behaviour of some of the folk-play characters with their 'Make room!' entry routines and their topsy-turvy language also suggests the Vice and perhaps other boastful stock types.

To take the argument a little further, it is true that although the St George form of the folk play is hard to find in the medieval and Tudor canon, there are other details in the surviving dramatic texts which are remarkably similar to folk-play ingredients. These include the comic Doctor in the Croxton *Play of the Sacrament*, and in Thomas Garter's *Susanna*, where he is one of the Vice's Protean roles. Dances by disguised figures are intruded into the action of *Wisdom* and *Fulgens and Lucres*, and in the latter play there is a wooing of the Maid by the two Players A and B, as well as the coarse combat called 'fart prick in cule'. The death of Wit at the hands of the giant Tediousness and his subsequent revival and success-ful return to the fray in *Wit and Science* suggest the main element in the plot of the folk play. In *Mankind*, the masked devil is inserted like a mumming, and the audience have to contribute to a collection before he will come on. This play contains a comic combat and cure sequence, and a scatalogical Christmas song. In the biblical cycles there are some ele-ments which recall popular entertainment associated with folk plays. These include the wrestling contest of the Shepherds in Chester, the abusive Pikeharness, servant of the Towneley Cain, and the abuse of the soldiers by the mothers in the Slaughter of the Innocents.[16]

All this suggests that there may have been a number of verbal and dancing episodes which were of traditional and perhaps ritual origin, and that they found their way into the lively mixture of dramatic styles in the interludes and the earlier drama. The routines may have continued throughout the Tudor period, and finally found their way into a more formalised folk play later, so that by the eighteenth century it was established as a recognisable form and one that could be written down. Because it was so adaptable (for some, under the Hanoverians St George became King George), it continued to spread and develop up to the First World War. The impact of this upheaval brought to an end a rural, village-based culture which had been largely unchanged for more than a thousand years.

Public entries and state entertainments

In what was perhaps one of the simplest ways of recognising and saluting the importance of royal visitors, individual plays from the mystery cycles were sometimes specially performed, as at Chester in 1498. The play of the *Assumption of the Virgin* was produced for Henry VII at the Abbey gate in the unusual month of August. For Richard III the city of York put on a special performance of the Creed play on 2 September 1483.[17] But the history of such welcomes goes back well before these – at least as far as to the entry of the Emperor Otho to London in 1207. They later reached a conspicuous complexity and extravagance, and combined many aspects of Church and state, and issues national and local. When Henry VIII visited York in 1541, the Lord Mayor, in his address, was decidedly uneasy about the difficulties of previous years over the pro-Catholic rebellion known as the Pilgrimage of Grace. He speaks of the King's mercy and pity extended to subjects who were 'late offenders in these northern parts'.[18] The ingredients of such procedures could be drawn from many different sources, and it is apparent that some of the material discussed in the previous section could readily be thought appropriate. King Arthur, St George, Robin Hood and various giants, fools and vices, were all made to play their part. The element of participation is also found in that the royal celebrations often included tournaments and disguisings, the former involving complex rituals with some role-playing, and the latter often leading to dancing by some or all of the spectators, who became participants.

The City of London had a specially important contribution to make as the capital city, and also as a centre of wealth and urban culture which could not be rivalled elsewhere in Britain. The Mayor and Corporation can be seen jealously guarding their privilege to control and manage what went on in their streets, as is apparent in the tension which arose with the court over the reception of Katherine of Aragon in 1501 discussed below.

By contrast, the tournaments were more a matter for the nobility: for these, the commoners were only spectators.

There were so many entries into London over the years that a traditional route was evolved. The entry began across London Bridge, where there were suitable pageant sites at the Southwark gate, and halfway across before the drawbridge gate. Proceeding north up Gracechurch Street, a stop could be made at the Conduit. At the end of Gracechurch Street a left turn, westwards, led to the Tun in Cornhill, the Great Conduit, the Standard, the Cross in Cheapside, and the Little Conduit which stood near to the entrance to St Paul's churchyard, the final site. The various permanent structures at these sites had some space around them to accommodate events and could be adapted to give a valuable vertical dimension; several of them had battlements. The entry was essentially a procession, with the visitor as the chief member. He or she encountered various quasi-dramatic welcomes at each station. It is worth noting that the usual route of the mystery plays at York was also used for royal entries, as for Henry VII in 1486. Probably the route was first developed for entries though Mickelgate from the south, and the pageants, when they evolved, followed the precedent.

There are a great many records of such entries in our period, but it is not always possible to be sure exactly what kind of drama was enacted. This is attributable to the records' differing perspectives: some detail expenses; some give technical information about constructions, some give quotations of the speeches; and some, in specially elaborate manuscripts which are really 'books', attempt to give a narrative account of the events of the procession.

The following selected occasions illustrate some of the dramatic characteristics of these events. For the coronation of Richard II in 1377 a castle was constructed in Cheapside with wine flowing from it on two sides. It was surmounted by a mechanical golden angel who bent to offer a crown. In 1432, for Henry VI's return after his coronation in Paris, John Lydgate had constructed a historical and scriptural allegory which took in the trades of the City, and used the motif of the Jesse tree to show his origins. The text for Margaret of Anjou's arrival in 1445 stressed the theme of peace and saluted her as a daughter of Jerusalem, in respect to her father's claim to the Christian kingdom established during the Crusades. This was built into an allegory of an ascent to Jerusalem by Margaret herself. Each of the pageants had a specifically scriptural theme, with appropriate words of a scriptural quotation on display. The visual aspects reflected the theological message. On London Bridge a ship representing Noah's Ark, at the topographical point where working ships were to be found in real life, was accompanied by verses drawing attention to the Dove bringing the 'branch of peace'. The quotation was 'I will not rage further upon the earth' (Genesis 8:21).

On similar lines, though with markedly different components, the welcome for Katherine of Aragon (1502) portrayed the sequence of the
procession as a dream vision, with Katherine herself as a kind of protagonist. She gained Virtues in the Tabernacle of the Saints and the castle
of Policy and ascended by the spheres of the Moon and the Sun, until,
blessed by the Lord, she might take her place on the Throne of Honour.
Among the benign influences was Prince Arthur, her husband-to-be,
who was associated with the constellation of Arcturus. This fascinating
mixture of elements from different cultural *schemae* is thought to have
been influenced by Burgundian models.[19] At the sixth pageant, by the
Little Conduit, there were many pillars with pictures of lions, dragons and
greyhounds. There were stairs on each side, at the head of which stood
the Three Theological and the Four Cardinal Virtues, surrounded by many
virgins in ermine. Above them were three seats: in the middle sat Honour,
while the other two were empty, each with a sceptre and coronet of gold
as a token that they were reserved for Arthur and Katherine. At the top
were canopies and pinnacles with emblems. In his speech Honour made
the allegory apply to all people as well as specifically to the principals:

> Also your self see weell that in the wey
> And in iche stappe toward us ascendyng
> There dwellith a vertue, so that no man may
> Asspire to us for any maner of thinge
> But sith they be ever more dwellyng
> In the wey. All folkes of necessitie
> Must come by thise vertues or thei com at me.   *before*

> Wherfor, noble Princes, if that ye persever
> With your excellent spouse, than shall ye
> Reigne here with us in prosperite for ever.
>
>   (ll. 792–801)

The welcome for Katherine is certainly a high point in the quality
of these processions, but they continued for the rest of the sixteenth
century. In 1511, to celebrate the birth of a son, a tournament was held
at Richmond in honour of Queen Katherine. This had the usual ritual of
competition between the champion and the challengers, but there is also
a note of fantasy and allegory as the challengers were called Coeur Loyal,
Valiant Desire, Bon Voloir and Joyeuse Penseur.[20] The welcome for the
Emperor Charles V to London in 1522 was similarly spectacular, and
drew upon a huge range of analogous figures who shared qualities with
the honoured guest: Jason, Charlemagne, John of Gaunt (an ancestor),
King Arthur, King Alphonsus and the Four Cardinal Virtues. It was
furnished with Latin verses by William Lily.

At Anne Boleyn's coronation entry in 1533 the traditional Judgement of Paris was transformed into a debate between the three goddesses who, on this occasion, presented the prize of the golden apple to Anne herself. It is intriguing to find John Heywood, the dramatist discussed earlier, under a canopy at St Paul's reciting verses as part of the welcome at the coronation of Queen Mary in 1554. As we know something of his special loyalty to her before her accession, there is a personal note here: it is not clear whether they were his own verses. There are sometimes extensions of pageantry on to the royal boats. In June 1539, to entertain the French ambassadors an anti-Catholic river battle was staged at Westminster. After various nautical manoeuvres the Pope and his cardinals were thrown into the Thames. The witness carefully explained that those in the defeated crew were specially chosen because they could swim and the triumphant King's barge hovered to pick them up afterwards.[21]

The high status accorded by Queen Elizabeth to her own image is much reflected in the ceremonial entries. At her coronation she was welcomed along the usual route. She is said to have added to the entertainment by responding with some comments at most of the shows – something Katherine of Aragon could not have done in 1501 because she knew no English. Elizabeth went on many progresses during her reign, during which she was welcomed in ways closely associated with those in London. Among her later journeys there was the entertainment at Kenilworth in 1575, and her visits to Cambridge in 1564 and Oxford in 1566, where she was entertained by a very concentrated series of academic dramas. Indeed, when, in spite of her intellectual and cultural distinction, she fled from Cambridge exhausted, she was pursued to her next destination by the loyal but disappointed participants of one play she had not stayed for.

These sample details from a multitude may enable us to see the strength and quality of the contribution of this dramatic mode. Though some conventional elements are absent, there are many things which are characteristic of dramatic experience. Among these come impersonation and performance before an audience. The latter is interesting because the audience is complex in terms of class, and also in its differing relationships to what went on. The principal is the honoured visitor, but everyone present is also part of the experience, and in this aspect the performance has parallels with the performances of the mystery cycles in the cities of the North. In 1501 Henry VII and Queen Margaret watched the entry of their future daughter-in-law from a haberdasher's house.[22] But the spectacle itself, very costly as it was, gives continuing vitality to allegory especially as it draws upon both the spoken word, including musical settings, and upon elaborate visual effects. The vertical dimension of the playing spaces seems impressive in itself, and seems likely to suggest hierarchy and interrelationship between components. It is not surprising that the records frequently refer to trees and mountains as the form in which allegory was presented. There are also the resonances of conflict, victory and harmony which may be later played out more fully in tournament.

The nature of a procession is that it confers some significance upon those who take part and also upon those who watch, significances which may be related to order and sequence. As these large-scale formal entries were often engineered to have a climactic ending, they could express the structural function which is inherent in much drama. It is not just a question of a plot or narrative: the dramatic process in these processions implies change and development for those taking part, and the implementation of this is the result of the imaginative contribution of the designers: the largely unknown authors. To this we might add that although each entry had to bear directly upon the immediate circumstances of its inception, the methods were developed from one place to another, and in the bourgeois culture of the City there was no doubt a conservative element which carried forward from one event to another – as indeed the route itself suggests. But this was informed by the extraordinary wealth and variety of the cultural material which could be drawn in – from learned and from popular culture, so that the giants were mixed with the Christian Virtues, the classical gods and figures from contemporary events. This mixture was characteristic of the English dramatic tradition through the period and beyond, and it may well be that the evolution of civic pageantry which involved a heavy commitment of resources, both financial and intellectual, and of performance skills, made an indispensable contribution.

Taken in addition to the dramatic forms in the earlier part of this chapter, these performances show the importance of stage techniques in the sixteenth century. There is the important link between what is said and what is seen in both costume and setting. There is the increasing sense that stage figures (or characters) may speak with their own voice, or they may express indirectly the intention of the author, this being a salient characteristic of drama universally. There is always an emphasis upon allegory, which gives enormous resonance to both speakers and setting because one characteristic can stand for one or more others. The growing sophistication in the use of stage allegory became increasingly important as the sixteenth century progressed, and the observation of the forms discussed here suggests that it was a growing Renaissance and Reformation form rather than a dying medieval one. Because the royal entries and ceremonial were part of court culture, they could become more and more a vehicle of royal policy as well as being highly entertaining for participants and spectators alike. This was no doubt stimulated by the artistic skills involved – mimetic certainly, but also musical, choreographic and those using the plastic arts. Because of these skills and the theological, political and philosophical commitment of those involved, the drama became a powerful medium of ideology and a rich aesthetic form.

Notes

1. See the collection of essays edited by Alexandra F. Johnston and Wim Hüsken (eds) *English Parish Drama* (Amsterdam and Atlanta, 1996). For details of REED volumes, see Abbreviations. Some counties are in *Malone Society Collections*: VII for Kent (1965); VIII for Lincolnshire (1969); XI for Norfolk and Suffolk (1980/81).

2. James M. Gibson, '"Interludium Passionis Domini", Parish Drama in Medieval New Romney', in *English Parish Drama*, pp. 138–44.

3. *MS* I, 352–8, 364–5; II, 373.

4. REED *York* I, 310.

5. Modernised from a quotation in Pamela Sheingorn, *The Easter Sepulchre in England* (Kalamazoo, 1987), p. 60. I acknowledge a more general debt to this authoritative study.

6. *MS* II, 264–6.

7. Barbara D. Palmer, '"Anye disguised persons": Parish Entertainment in West Yorkshire', in *English Parish Drama*, p. 84.

8. Modernised from REED *Shropshire* II, p. 658.

9. REED *Devon*, p. 119.

10. Peter H. Greenfield, 'Parish Drama in Four Counties Bordering the Thames Watershed', in *English Parish Drama*, p. 113.

11. Alexandra F. Johnston, '"What Revels are in Hand?" Dramatic Activities Sponsored by the Parishes of the Thames Valley', in *English Parish Drama*, pp. 100–1.

12. *MS* I, 180.

13. Relevant extracts are printed in D. Wiles, *The Early Plays of Robin Hood* (Cambridge, 1981), Appendices 4 and 5. There is a list of dates on pp. 64–6.

14. T. Pettitt, 'Tudor Interludes and the Winter Revels', *METh* 6 (1984), 16–27.

15. E.K. Chambers, *The English Folk Play* (Oxford, 1933), pp. 104–20.

16. See R. Axton, *European Drama of the Early Middle Ages* (London, 1974), pp. 175–94.

17. REED *York* I, 130–1. Richard saw the whole of the Coventry Corpus Christi plays on 2 June 1485, as did Henry VII in 1487 and 1493, REED *Coventry* 66–8, 77.

18. REED *York* I, 274.

19. Gordon Kipling, *The Triumph of Honour* (Leiden, 1977), pp. 79–93. For the full text see Kipling's edition, *The Receyt of the Ladie Katerine*, EETS 296 (Oxford, 1990).

20. C.E. McGee and John C. Meagher, 'Preliminary Checklist of Tudor and Stuart Entertainments: 1485–1558', *RORD*, xxv (1982), 31–114 (p. 63). This catalogue contains bibliographical details of a large collection of events.

21. S. Anglo, *Spectacle, Pageantry, and Early Tudor Policy* (Oxford, 1969), pp. 269–70.

22. Wickham I, 61.

Part III

Professional Theatre

Chapter 11
Theatres and Companies: The Context of the Professional Stage – James Burbage and John Lyly

When James Burbage began the construction of the Theatre in 1576, he inaugurated a new era in the history of English drama. From his establishment of a specially built theatre there developed a way of life on the stage which comprised a much greater concentration of resources, human and financial, than had existed before. From now on, whatever the difficulties, it was possible for an increasing number of actors, writers and entrepreneurs to hope to make a livelihood from the theatre, and this meant ultimately an enhancement in the quantity and quality of what could be presented and what audiences could expect. It also meant that the stage might become more influential, or, as some might consider, more dangerous in ideological terms.

But there is another underlying factor against which such developments should be considered. However enormous the changes inaugurated by Burbage, there was also a continuity in many traditions of entertainment, and of the skills of performers and playwrights alike. The art of theatre may have been rejuvenated as a result of Burbage's new building, but the rich and complex achievement described in the earlier parts of this book did not suddenly disappear. It is not possible to evaluate properly the changes which now came about without being conscious that many inherited aspects of the nature of plays and their performance helped in the development of the new drama. Indeed, as has already been suggested, it is one of the features of this particular study that it can give a sense of the continuities between medieval and Renaissance drama.

The years following the building of the Theatre yield far more information about theatrical activities, and more London plays are recorded than ever before. It is perhaps worth recalling that, just as this expansion was about to begin, the old art of the mystery cycles was being brought to an end, largely by government intervention. The last performance at Chester was in 1575, the last in York was 1569, with further unsuccessful attempts up to 1580.

In this chapter we shall look at the buildings, the companies, the audiences and some conditions of performance which make up the context of the theatre in the years immediately preceding the arrival of Shakespeare in London in the early 1590s. This includes some of the physical changes which arose, and also a look at the ways in which the profession of acting developed as a result of having permanent theatres which could be the centres for many new undertakings. It is significant that this third section of our study is as long as the two previous ones even though it is centred on only fourteen well-packed years. In essence it is an account of ways in which thinking about drama were renewed.

Theatres

Burbage's Theatre was not the only kind of place for performance open in London in 1576. There were amateur companies having various degrees of continuity performing at the Inns of Court, and in private houses of the nobility. There were productions at court which could draw upon extensive financial support. These might be by the Children of St Paul's or of the Chapel Royal under the control of the Master of the Revels, who began operating on a permanent basis from 1545. These two companies each had their own regular place of performance within the precinct of St Paul's cathedral and at Blackfriars respectively. It was also customary for the court to reward adult companies for putting on special performances of plays which had been written for other contexts. At different times the great halls at Hampton Court, Greenwich and Whitehall were used for such occasions. It is apparent that performances at court took place annually at certain seasons. Most of these ways of presenting plays had been going on for years.

The adult companies at work before 1576 may have been professional, in the sense that some of the successful members earned most of their living from acting, but it is apparent that the organisation was intermittent and that the groups were too unstable to last very long. The instability was a feature of the necessity to be itinerant. Such groups would have been responsible for less prestigious performances at inns, some of which were within the City of London. By 1576 players had performed at the Boar's Head in Aldgate, the Saracen's Head in Islington, the Bel Savage on Ludgate Hill, the Red Lion in Stepney and the Bell Inn in Gracechurch Street. Of these the Red Lion is most noteworthy, since John Brayne, a grocer, paid in 1567 for a 'wooden scaffold or stage for interludes or plays'. The legal document in which this is mentioned gives the dimensions as 40 feet by 30 feet, and 5 feet high. Brayne was the brother-in-law of James Burbage, and later he helped with the financing of the Theatre.[1]

Such performances may well have been quite frequent, though it seems likely that the boothed stages they employed were movable. One feature of these inns was that the open-air courtyards where performances took place could accommodate spectators looking down from galleries and upper windows. These performing spaces were shared with other forms of entertainment such as displays of fencing or prize-fighting. The multiple use of buildings could also have operated in reverse: it is possible that on the south bank of the Thames the pits used for bull- and bear-baiting were used for plays, hired out to the company for the occasion.

Burbage built his Theatre about a mile to the north of the City of London in Holywell Lane, off Shoreditch, no doubt because he wanted to be free of the jurisdiction of the City authorities which often bore heavily on players. It was an open-air building, polygonal in shape, made largely of wood (Burbage was trained as a carpenter), with three layers of galleries of seats surrounding the paved central area where many stood to watch the play. Part of one of these layers was designated a lords' room for wealthy patrons. To one side of the central space was the fixed stage, which was itself partly roofed by the 'heavens' supported on pillars, and at the back of this was the tiring house for the players. The stage was raised above the level of the courtyard and its back wall had doors into the tiring house which were thus the primary means of entry on to the stage. The 'heavens' could accommodate lifting gear, and there was probably a trap in the stage floor.

From these details it is apparent that the Theatre was an imaginative combination of features previously found in inn-yards, pits for animal baiting, the screens of great halls, and the commonplace demountable booth stage. The arena structure whereby an audience in a circular configuration looked down into a performing area, as in an amphitheatre, is virtually too ancient and too widespread to be attributed to any particular precedent. Burbage's originality lies in this very combination of pre-existing elements: it proved so effective that the Theatre became a model for other playhouses which were built in London in succeeding years. They all followed the Theatre in being located outside the City limits: most of them were on Bankside, which was accessible via London Bridge or by boat across the Thames. Initially, and falling within the scope of this volume, they were:

1577   The Curtain in Moorfields, south of the Theatre, and used in close collaboration with it;
1587   The Rose on Bankside, built by the entrepreneur Philip Henslowe and enlarged and refurbished by him in 1594.

Later, as both the business and the art took greater hold, there came a second phase of construction. These theatres were similarly outside the City and showed some variations derived from the experience of a generation of playing, but still substantially they followed Burbage's combination:

1595   The Swan on Bankside;
1599   The Globe on Bankside, built by Cuthbert and Richard Burbage from the timbers of the Theatre – burnt down in 1613, and rebuilt;
1600   The Fortune at Cripplegate, built by Henslowe and Edward Alleyn, the actor;
1614   The Hope on Bankside, built by Henslowe on the model of the Swan, with a movable stage to accommodate bear-baiting.

From a financial point of view, the Theatre had the enormous advantage that access could be controlled and indeed graded according to entrance charges. This method was much preferable to the traditional but uncertain collection from the crowd, and it no doubt played a part in stabilising the companies. The performance advantages, on the other hand, centred on a number of features which undoubtedly left their mark upon how plays were to be written. There was virtually no scenery, though furniture and properties could be brought on stage. This helped rapid transitions between scenes. The location of scenes could be very flexible, ranging from the virtually unspecified to the highly atmospheric, conjured up chiefly by language. In this respect the plays at the Theatre followed the practice of many earlier performances. The details given above about doors, the heavens, and the trap indicate that entrances and exits remained a major resource making possible such things as surprise, or indeed its opposite, as comment could be made on characters approaching or leaving the action. It was also possible to play on two levels, giving an important vertical dimension – one found also in the use of pageant carts for mystery cycles – and this facility contributed much to the convention which we shall consider in the two following chapters of framing the action with fictionalised onlookers. The open stage encouraged processions, marches and battles, including sieges: theatrical devices going back as far as *The Castle of Perseverance*. One of the characteristics of the Theatre which has emerged at the New Globe in recent months is that the actors seem very close to the audience. This is made very plain if one stands on the stage and looks up at ranks of spectators banked in the facing and surrounding galleries. From such a position it is plain why soliloquies were so favoured.

Because of the entrance charges and the fact that the Theatre and its progeny took in a socially diverse audience – whoever wished to pay – they have come to be known as the public theatres. By contrast, the private theatres were more selective in that they charged more. They were also roofed, and had smaller audiences, who were all seated. Since they were inside it was also possible to use scenery and to make the most of unexpected revelations and changes. That they were under the control of the Master of the Revels may also have meant that there was money for scenic effects, especially when productions were translated to court.

Essentially, these private theatres were used by boys who were amateurs, but since both the Children of the Chapel Royal and the Paul's Boys came together for the purposes of education as well as to sing at services, the role of the schoolmasters who led them was very important. As these men tended to serve for many years, their professional status gave continuity in management and expertise. At St Paul's the work of John Redford, author of *Wit and Science* and associate of John Heywood, was continued by his successor Sebastian Westcott, who was Master from 1547 until 1582. Working with the Chapel Children, Richard Farrant took over the Blackfriars in 1576, where were presented some of the plays of his associate, John Lyly, whose work we shall consider later in this chapter.

Although the Paul's Boys were well known and certainly attracted an audience within the City, the exact location and nature of their playhouse is somewhat obscure. In an accusation against Westcott in 1575 it is alleged that he 'kepethe playes' as though he had been doing so for some time. The playhouse was somewhere in the precinct of old St Paul's, probably in the cloister, partially in the undercroft ('the shrouds') of the chapterhouse: almost certainly it was completely roofed. In such a place, access could be fully controlled as in the public theatres.[2]

The Children of the Chapel, together with their associate company, the Children of the Windsor Chapel, performed in the Blackfriars: an upper storey in the old Dominican priory within the west wall of the City. Richard Farrant took this over in 1576 for the purpose of public performances by the Children. He used it until his death in 1580, and his successor continued until trouble arose over the lease in 1584. It was at this period that some of Lyly's plays were done at the Blackfriars. The Children of the Chapel were sometimes joined by the Paul's Boys and together they took performances of Lyly's *Campaspe* and *Sappho and Phao* to court. As the difficulties over the lease at the Blackfriars continued, performances were stopped. For this brief period, 1576–84, this so-called First Blackfriars offered entertainment to audiences drawn from within the City in parallel with the Paul's playhouse. Many years later, in 1609, the King's Men, Shakespeare's company, under Richard Burbage gained access to a different part of Blackfriars and used it as a seasonal alternative for their Globe: this is known as the Second Blackfriars, but its history is beyond our scope here. The impact of these private theatres must have been an important complement to that of new public playhouses, even though the First Blackfriars, and presumably Paul's, were both quite small, accommodating up to 200 spectators. By contrast, the Rose is thought to have had room for up to 2,000, and the Globe for 3,000.

The plays done at the First Blackfriars suggest that there was a raised platform for the stage and that there were two doors at the back into the tiring house. There was probably an inner stage, as used for *Sappho and Phao*, and a trap is required so that a tree can be raised in Peele's *The Arraignment of Paris*.[3] The performances could take place after dark and in the winter, and the theatre had the added advantage of being within the City. The private theatre arrangements no doubt contributed a great deal to the development of drama at court, and especially to the evolution of the court masque which was to be so successful after the accession of James I.[4]

To return to Burbage, however, his creation at the Theatre was the central act in a remarkable period of expansion: but the physical characteristics of these buildings were not the only innovations. Because they concentrated players together it became possible and necessary to develop new ways of operating the financial business of acting; and there were also influential extraneous factors.

Companies

On 6 December 1574 an Act of Common Council was promulgated by the City of London severely restraining the activities of players. It is an elaborate document, which in its first part dwells upon perceived abuses encouraged by the performing of plays in inns and public places.[5] The hostility to acting exhibited there may have been based upon some genuine difficulties, such as the undesirability of allowing gatherings during times of plague, or even the possibility that acting plays might encourage people not to go to work or not to go to church; but there are also indications of further prejudice against acting on moral grounds, a theme which, as we have seen elsewhere, can be traced far back in Christian thinking. It was now re-surfacing in the developing Protestant, or even Puritan, ethos. There is no doubt that the city housed many people who were chronically circumspect if not hostile towards performing plays. The prejudice was expressed, for example, by Stephen Gosson in *The School of Abuse* (1579) and *Plays Confuted in Five Actions* (1582), and Philip Stubbes in *The Anatomy of Abuses* (1583). Stubbes says, 'Plays were first invented by the Devil, practised by heathen gentiles, and dedicate to their false idols, gods and goddesses.'[6]

Against this, it is manifest that there was a huge amount of dramatic activity of many types all over the country, as the REED volumes indicate. One of the chief means by which this was delivered was by the well-established activities of itinerant companies of actors working under the patronage of the nobility. Such patronage was a function of power and thus it served the political ambitions of individual nobles as well as offering protection for the players against criticism and interference. This meant that to preserve troupe solidarity was desirable and necessary, and that patrons would continue to support it if possible. The arrival of the Theatre implied the idea of a physical base for such groups, and from then onwards the London-based acting companies carried out a major role in the presentation of plays.

In the years immediately preceding the opening of the Theatre, there was action by the government on a national scale which militated against the activities of itinerant players. This manifested itself in the Statute against Unlawful Retainers (3 January 1572), and the Act for the Punishment of Vagabonds (29 June 1572) directed against Rogues and Sturdy Beggars, in which the prescribed punishments for not having a proper licence to be on the roads were gruesome, and ultimately capital. However, on 10 May 1574 the Patent issued to Leicester's Men enabling them to perform plays allowed by the Master of the Revels in London and elsewhere may have helped to create an opportunity for Burbage.[7] Presumably it was the political influence of Leicester which enabled him to go against the palpable trend towards suppression.

For some companies, like the Queen's Men, established in 1583, or the Admiral's Men, first known to be active as Lord Howard's at court at Christmas 1576, continuity over a long period was possible, but there were plenty of others which came and went as patronage or business competence wavered. The records show that the most successful companies performed at court regularly, had opportunities to perform in the new public theatres, and were occasionally licensed by the authorities to perform within limits of the City itself in spite of the 1574 Act. They had many long and complicated itineraries throughout the country taking in the houses of the nobility and gentry as well as being rewarded for performances at inns and other public places. As time went by, there were plenty of changes in the configuration of the companies, and they seem sometimes to have co-operated and sometimes to have been rivals. For example, the Admiral's Men played at the Theatre at times, but after a quarrel with James Burbage, Alleyn and others moved into the Rose in 1591, where they worked in close association with Henslowe.[8] So successful were these companies that by 1599 Thomas Platter reported:

> Thus daily at two in the afternoon London has two,
> sometimes three plays running in different places,
> competing with each other, and those which play best
> obtain most spectators.[9]

The consumption of plays was enormous and the repertory was built up very rapidly in the 1580s. Some popular plays were repeated, but by the 1590s Henslowe was financing thirty-five new plays a year.[10]

The financial organisation of the companies depended upon a hierarchy in which the 'sharers' formed the core and derived the largest financial benefit. They hired journeymen for individual performances on a specific wage and made arrangements for apprentices. The journeymen moved from company to company and some of them had other employment, while the sharers' investments kept them in the home company. The profits had to be shared with the entrepreneur who leased the theatre to the company. This meant that he might take a large part in management, and it does appear that over the years Henslowe became more and more involved in specifics. The evolution of such a financial system was an indispensable part of the development of the professional stage. Significantly, it is a direct development of the medieval guild structure. It systematised the need to please audiences and in doing so it helped to set up a remarkable feature of the Elizabethan stage: the sustaining of certain well-tried plays, such as the anonymous *Mucedorus* and Kyd's *Spanish Tragedy*, which came to be favourites over a long period.

The main income of the companies was taken at the door of the theatres, which were vulnerable to closure by the City authorities, usually on grounds of the danger from plague. There is a formidable list of such interventions: plays were restrained seven times between 1572 and 1583, and almost continuously from August 1592 to the end of 1593.[11] On such occasions there were two ways of filling the income gap: by taking the company on tour, and by marketing play texts. The long plague closure of 1592–93 was followed by a flurry of publication in 1594 of plays many of which had been performed several years earlier, and might otherwise have now been lost to us. For an extra attraction it was a frequent recommendation on title pages to refer to performance by an eminent company. It is apparent, however, that the plays as printed texts were given much less recognition than the plays when performed, and sometimes the printed versions were truncated and ill-prepared. As to the travelling, the details given by E.K. Chambers (*ES* 3.1–261) show that the companies went up and down the country in complicated journeys. Unfortunately we do not usually know how many players went on each journey, and it is unwise to assume that the number was consistent. This naturally would mean that texts were often cut or enlarged in order to adapt them for local performance, a process which makes for intriguing problems about the consistency of texts.

Before 1576, many plays had been printed with doubling schemes, the number of players required varying from four to nine. After 1576, the companies grew in size, presumably as a result of the settled base and the more sophisticated organisation and finance. Doubling schemes appeared less frequently as a recommendation for purchase. But the practice did continue in the new companies even with their greater resources. The Queen's Men comprised twelve members in 1583, and T.J. King has shown that the average number of players in the performance of Shakespeare's plays was just under ten adults with three or four boys (apprentices, not sharers) for the women's parts.[12] The number of sharers and the number of players in a specific play need not necessarily be the same, but it is clear that the new arrangements offered much greater freedom to playwrights.

Audiences

Even though the theatres were placed outside the City of London, Burbage's intention must have been to attract city-dwellers, who formed his main constituency. As far as the public theatres were concerned, the Bankside gradually became a centre for a variety of amusements including the plays, and the price of entry remained low enough to enable even apprentices to afford it. The lowest charge for standing entry in the pit was one penny, and the galleries could be entered for twopence or threepence. There was more expensive provision for eminent or affluent spectators in the lords' room. Though there was much contemporary criticism of the behaviour of audiences, much of it comes from groups hostile to the stage, and therefore it cannot be assumed that the audiences consisted entirely of low-class rowdies. There are certainly legal cases about disorder, mostly after 1600. The presence of women cannot be doubted. In spite of the efforts of those interested in denigrating all females at plays, it is clear that respectable citizens' wives attended throughout the period.

The private theatres do seem to have admitted all comers, though there must have been a tendency to exclude the socially undesirable. Several times Lyly shows uneasiness about audience reaction. He asks that the players 'may enjoy by your wonted courtesies a general silence' (*Campaspe*, Prologue at the Blackfriars, l. 35). In *Sappho and Phao* he asks for 'soft smiling, not loud laughing' (Prologue at the Blackfriars, l. 9). Higher entrance fees might have been a deterrent. The experience of being present in a small audience, and in an indoor auditorium must have been remarkably different from that at the Theatre, and it is most likely that performance in these theatres would have required a different style of acting. Because of their educational and humanist inheritance the subject matter was also different. One special feature was that in these theatres the cheapest places were furthest away from the stage, in direct contrast to the practice in the public playhouses.

If audiences at both kinds of theatre came from different social classes, the expectations of the playwrights and the actors must have been that the spectators would be prepared to take in a fairly sophisticated diet. We shall note in some individual plays that there was knockabout fooling and often a good deal of fighting including prolonged swordplay. But in contrast there is much language which is fascinating in its complexity and which reflects rhetorical skills of a high order. Playwrights consciously assailed ears as well as eyes.[13] Most of the audience must have been educated enough to enjoy what they heard. Many of them would be literate, London having a higher rate of literacy than elsewhere.[14] It is clear, however, that the aural culture of sermons and public speaking presumed that even those who could not read would still be able to respond to the complex material they were accustomed to listening to. The palpable pressure from Marlowe and other dramatists about the nature of the language they were using indicates that expectations were high. As most of the audience were city-dwellers, the success of the stage derived in part from the concentration of wealth and expertise in a thriving city. Gosson contemptuously stigmatised the playgoers as 'the common people which resort to theatres being but an assembly of tailors, tinkers, cordwainers, sailors, old men, young men, women, boys, girls and such like'. Take away his prejudice and this seems a very varied audience.

Alongside the developing interest in drama there was naturally a variety of other forms of entertainment. Many of these activities had a long ancestry, and they were drawn into the city by the same concentration of people, wealth and opportunity we have been considering for the plays. The Bankside housed bull- and bear-baiting. There were frequent displays of warlike arts, including fencing and archery. Magic, usually known as conjuring, and other demonstrations of skills attracted attention. There was music in taverns and on the streets. Dancing was popular, and perhaps one of the most interesting forms of entertainment was the jig. Its origins lay in popular folk festivals before the middle of the sixteenth century. It was a combination of song, in ballad form, with an accompanying dance. It was much developed by Richard Tarlton, who included a variety of popular entertainments in his performances as a clown. Many early plays contain dances which are forms of jig, such as the dancing Devil and Vice in *Like Will to Like*. In the 1590s, after Tarlton's death, jigs were entered increasingly in the Stationers' Register. Sometimes they were performed as an after-piece of plays. The following is a refrain from the dialogue between a lady and her lover in *A New Northern Jig called Dainty come thou to me*, registered in 1591:

> Cast no care to thy heart
> From thee I will not flee
> Let them all say what they will
> Dainty come thou to me.[15]

The activities of clowns and fools had been encouraged in the houses of the nobility for generations. The Tudor monarchs had court fools, including the famous Will Summers (d. 1560).[16] No doubt these different forms of entertainment were all available to playwrights. Indeed, all the ones mentioned found their way into plays in some form or other.

Most of what has been said here concentrates upon the City of London. The vigorous drama away from the capital must have been fed and stimulated by the performances of the London companies on tour. Unfortunately, we do not usually know exactly what the itinerant players brought to provincial towns, but there are indications that the popular *Mucedorus*, for example, was performed outside London. According to Nashe, Tarlton went on tour with the Queen's Men.[17] Such performances were done under the auspices of the local civic authorities, or in the houses of the affluent. It barely needs saying, however, that there is hardly a watershed comparable with that in London to be found in the provinces. Away from the capital the presentation of plays had for centuries depended upon either local amateurs or travelling companies, and we have no reason to suppose that these practices changed very much, except that the companies from London now could bring richer and more varied fare. The May games and the church ales continued, and Robin Hood was still popular. Some of these para-dramatic activities, indeed, fed back into the popular plays of the London stage, and we find traces of them in the repertory to be considered in the next two chapters. Before turning to these, however, we shall consider the plays of John Lyly, who made a significant individual contribution before 1590.

John Lyly

In many ways Lyly's plays are a continuation of the work of playwrights like John Heywood and John Redford, for all his surviving dramatic work is closely directed towards court performance. Like these predecessors a generation earlier, he worked with the boys' companies, and it is probable that the performances were given by boys with some adults in key roles – a practice which Heywood is thought to have adopted. Only with *Mother Bombie* (printed 1594) is evidence lacking of presentation at court: *Campaspe* and *Sappho and Phao* were given there in 1584, *Love's Metamorphosis* in 1586, *Gallathea* and *Endymion* in 1588, *Midas* in 1590, and *The Woman in the Moon* in 1593.[18] As we have seen, Lyly had the special advantage of being able to prepare some of his plays by showing them beforehand to audiences at the Blackfriars. His response to the circumstance of court performance followed the others in the sense of propriety which governs all his writing. He was prepared to open up topical or delicate issues, but his handling of them suggests that he was aware of the need to be circumspect. In this he showed a courtier's judgement comparable to Heywood's, though Lyly was not as successful at surviving in court circles as Heywood had been.

The subjects of his plays revolve around characters and episodes drawn from classical myth, and in this he shows his preoccupation with humanist education such as was desirable for young men. Indeed, he is master of managing events, topics, plots and language which were appropriate to this end. But his interest in myth reveals one of its great strengths: its potential for use as allegory. In this Lyly manifests his medieval inheritance, and shows that allegorical modes could still be used successfully to expose philosophical issues, and as a means of presenting and analysing characters or situations. There are places where his use of allegory also has political dimensions, though it is not apparent that all his plays, or that everything in any one of them, should necessarily be read in this way.

The classical influence can be found in several aspects. All his plays are comedies: though the endings are not necessarily smooth resolutions of all difficulties, they are chiefly concerned with love, and often involve Cynthia, Cupid and Venus. At times, as in *Mother Bombie*, the intrigue shows distinctly classical motifs. Here, there are two wealthy fathers, one with a foolish son and the other a foolish daughter, who wish their children to marry. There are also two other not so wealthy fathers of an intelligent son and daughter who wish to marry their offspring to the wealthy but foolish heiress and heir. The sorting out of this elegantly balanced plot is the result of the activities of the four pages who work for each of the four fathers. Mother Bombie herself is a very wise English woman who tells fortunes, but her predictions are given the authority of a classical oracle.

In other plays, however, the classical setting shows itself in the interaction of gods and goddesses in human affairs, and the familiar device of the impact of dissension between them upon human affairs is the substance of the plots. This is found in the even more elegant balances of the plot of *Love's Metamorphosis*, which turns on the conflict between Cupid and Ceres. This plot is thought to be largely original, but its nature suggests the complexities and attractions of classical myths. The setting is a pastoral one in which Erisichthon (*Gk*: angry and earthy), a farmer, furious with Ceres, cuts down a tree sheltering her nymph Fidelia whom he kills. He is punished by Famine, who gives him an insatiable appetite. Nisa, Celia and Niobe, three other nymphs devoted to Ceres, anger Cupid in disdaining their rural lovers, Ramis, Montanus and Silvestris. This rejection is a material part of the play, giving scope for witty and ingenious speeches explaining the grounds for rejection. But the inventive ingenuity is situational as well as linguistic. Nisa is cruel, Celia coy and Niobe inconstant. Cupid transforms them into symbols of these Petrarchan dispositions as a stone, a rose (which fades), and a bird of paradise (which, according to contemporary belief, lives only by air and dies if it touches the ground). In doing this Cupid is moved by the faithful love exhibited by Protea, daughter of Erisichthon, for her beloved Petulius. When Ceres begs Cupid to relent, a bargain is struck whereby Erisichthon is pardoned in return for the acceptance of their lovers by Ceres' three nymphs. But at the last moment the nymphs themselves resist the deal, and they are only persuaded to relent when each of their lovers in turn accepts the respective natural flaws as part of what he has to enjoy and love. Thus the psychology of love is cleverly entangled with the quasi-mythic framework. For example, Celia and Montanus finally agree to love in spite of difficulties:

Celia	I consent so as Montanus when in the midst of his sweet delight shall find some bitter overthwarts [*frustrations*] impute it to his folly in that he suffered me to be a rose that hath prickles with her pleasantness as he is like to have with my love shrewdness.
Montanus	Let me bleed every minute with the prickles of the rose so I may enjoy but one hour the savour.

(5.4.140–5)

These complexities of love, so carefully balanced and so neatly interactive, are well within the capabilities of young male actors. The emotional range is limited, and yet the powerful expression which relies heavily but dazzlingly upon carefully modulated sentence structure is well suited to youngsters carefully schooled in speaking as well as in singing. At the same time, it is obvious that here and elsewhere Lyly is able to exploit the physical presence and attributes of these young men. The overall effect, therefore, is that the ideas about love and its discomforts are intellectually well explained, while the appearance of the young actors in costume exhibit elegance and attractiveness. It must have been a very effective dramatic mixture. No doubt the sexual aspects of these characterisations were played up, and, though it is always difficult to be certain about matters of taste, it would seem that this was a much enjoyed combination since the plays were done so frequently at court.

At the same time, there is a political dimension which does much to explain both their success and Lyly's motivation. In several plays there are powerful authoritarian figures, either monarchs, gods or goddesses, who dominate the action. There have been attempts to identify Cynthia in *Endymion* and Sappho in *Sappho and Phao* with Queen Elizabeth and other figures, in consequence with courtiers interacting with her, but these have not proved convincing. The only real exception is Midas, whose ambition to conquer the islands north of his kingdom, whose lust for gold and whose folly can be identified with Philip II of Spain. *Midas* was performed at court not long after the Armada of 1588.

Nevertheless, the plays are often concerned with the relationships between the superior and powerful and those of lesser stature as with Cynthia, the goddess who is loved by Endymion, and Sappho who is presented as a princess loved by Phao, a humble ferryman. In such cases the social distance between the two lovers is material: Endymion is rescued from his sleep by a kiss from Cynthia, but she does not love him in return, and Sappho, though she did return the love of Phao, cannot respond to it fully and she lets him go:

> for destiny calleth thee as well from Sicily as from love.
> Other things hang over thy head which I must neither tell
> no thou inquire.
>
> (*Sappho and Phao*, 5.3.27–9)

Alexander the Great does love Campaspe, one of his Theban captives, and the action of the play shows how the great conqueror pauses briefly in his military campaigns to show how she has impressed him. But when she, in her turn, falls in love with Apelles, whom Alexander has commissioned to paint her portrait, Alexander withdraws and continues with his conquests, finally seeing love as beneath him:

> Well enjoy one another. I give her thee frankly, Apelles.
> Thou shalt see that Alexander maketh but a toy of love and
> leadeth affection in fetters, using fancy as a fool to make
> him sport or as a minstrel to make him merry. . . . Alexander
> is cloyed with looking on that which thou wonderest at.
>
> (*Campaspe*, 5.4.145–57)

That Lyly took plays dealing with such situations to court is an indication that he is concerned with more than trifles. The politics there were still intimately involved with Elizabeth's political and psychological exploitation of her femininity, even though the possibility of marriage receded during the 1580s on the grounds of her age. There was still flirtation in her affairs, and there was also the question of how those seeking to influence her – mostly men – could manage a situation dominated by a woman. To entertain such a person with elegant fictions about love and to show the pains and perhaps the rewards of amorous relationships between those of unequal rank was more than titillating. It must have been an attempt to use such material to win influence for Lyly himself, or perhaps for his patron the Earl of Oxford who supported the court performances.

The plays exploited the imagery surrounding the Queen, especially by their humanist tone, with the discussion of such philosophical issues as chastity versus true love. They show characters, human as well as divine, struggling with virtue and honour in their love affairs. These are accompanied by a discourse of power, but the interesting dramatic aspect of this is that the Queen herself was expected to be present at performances and to see an image of herself both as monarch and woman in the business of the plays. She is to be complimented by the action, though her direct involvement in it, as in Peele's *Arraignment of Paris*, is avoided.

Lyly goes near to idealism. He presents a partly magic and partly supernatural world which is simplified. There are a few touches of earthy realism, but in general he portrays a rarefied society concerned with honour and perfection. Much of the action of the plays is verbal exploitation of ideas in highly decorative ways, often using repetitive devices which turn ideas inside out and upside down. Yet the flaws in this world, the love affairs uncompleted, the rage and frustration, the disappointed affections, suggest that the superficial gloss is a deliberate artifice – attractive in itself no doubt – aimed at hinting or reflecting an underlying disturbance.

One of these is the failure of court life to meet the real aspirations of Lyly himself. It has been rightly noted that his exploitation of it was ultimately unsuccessful and that some of the plays show a disenchantment in spite of the apparent elegance. The elaboration of the plays betrays a high intelligence, one which might be expected to see through the worship of the chaste Queen, to perceive the power struggle underneath in the court intrigues. He was not the only court poet to have played with idealism and to have presented grim authority. He may even have been partly concerned to support such a structured hierarchy even though he was conscious of flaws within it.

Disturbance shows itself at another level, however: in the presentation of women in the plays. Here the rather stereotyped masculine view is offered that women are fickle, changeable, corrupt even, and the contrast between female failings and the unsullied devotion which men offer is much emphasised. On the one hand, this may lead to the loving embrace of human weakness noted above in *Love's Metamorphosis*, but it may also be an index of apprehension about the power of women and be the result of a need to portray unfavourable feminine characteristics. To this we should add that the image of woman in authority recurs again and again in the plays. Sometimes she is endowed with insight, but more often figures like Sappho and Endymion's Cynthia are a threat to masculinity. One intriguing detail, for example, is that ferrymen such as Phao were noted in London for the way in which their powerful and attractive physiques were sexually attractive to the noble ladies they served. Lyly's plays undoubtedly reflect a conflation of sexual and political attraction and power.

If this is so, it can be seen that the dramatic forms he employs are effective as ways of embodying these preoccupations, even if Lyly is working partially at an unconscious level. We have already noted the particular effect of using boys as performers. The impersonation of women of various ages by young males is sexually challenging. This is most striking in *Gallathea*, in which the two daughters of shepherds disguise themselves as males, and each in her disguise falls in love with the apparent masculinity of the other.

The reason for the disguise of Gallathea and Phyllida as young men is a version of the beast-from-the-sea myth. Although the setting is the English River Humber, it is an offence to Neptune by the locals which has led to the imposition of the obligation to sacrifice annually the most beautiful virgin to Agar, Neptune's sea-monster. The disguises are an attempt to deceive Neptune, but early in the play the theme that destiny overrules everything and cannot be deceived is firmly stated. These disguises have counterparts in the disguise taken by Cupid in order to catch Diana's nymphs, and the disguise of Neptune that seeks to uncover the trickery which is being played against him.

The conflict between Venus and Diana, which is really another debate between love and chastity, is made sharper by the activities of the disguised Cupid. He brings tormenting pleasures:

> A heat full of coldness, a sweet full of bitterness, a pain full
> of pleasantness, which maketh thoughts have eyes and
> hearts ears, bred by desire, nursed by delight, weaned by
> jealousy, killed by dissembling, buried by ingratitude, and
> this is love.
>
> (1.2.16–19)

Such passages illustrate how skilfully Lyly adapted the decorative prose style he had used in his *Euphues* novels (1578–80) to dramatic speech. Though Cupid is disgraced by the power of Diana, in the end she herself is matched by Venus who represents true love, differentiated from lust. This philosophical framework is presented wittily and ironically in the play, so that the idea of love is at least ambivalent. The same may be said for the love between the two girl-men: they approach each other warily and distrust their own feelings. Here Lyly makes the audience fully aware of the circumstances so that their hesitancy is appealingly comic, but he is careful to keep the tone light, and here he avoids the bawdy suggestiveness which is found elsewhere in the play among the male characters.[19] Part of the dramatic effectiveness lies in the way each mirrors the other, giving a typical balance to their dialogue:

Phyllida   Suppose I were a virgin (I blush in supposing myself one), and that under the habit of a boy were the person of a maid: if I should utter my affection with sighs, manifest my sweet love by my salt tears, and prove my loyalty unspotted

	and my griefs intolerable, would not then that fair face pity
	this true heart?
Gallathea	Admit that I were as you, would you have me suppose that
	you are, and that I should with entreaties, prayers, oaths,
	bribes, and whatever can be invented in love, desire your
	favour, would you not yield?
Phyllida	Tush, you come in with 'admit'.
Gallathea	And you with 'suppose'.
Phyllida	(aside) What doubtful speeches be these! I fear me he is as
	I am, a maiden.
Gallathea	(aside) What dread riseth in my mind! I fear the boy to be
	as I am, a maiden.
Phyllida	(aside) Tush, it cannot be; his voice shows the contrary.
Gallathea	(aside) Yet I do not think it, for he would then have
	blushed.

(3.2.17–34)

The audience is hardly likely to be deeply involved emotionally in such an exchange, but the closeness of the dialogue and its stylistic ingenuity encourage the appreciation of wit. The experience of a play by Lyly is thus more a matter of intellectual engagement set up by his interest in structural parallels and contrasts. No doubt the classical humanist subject matter and the ideological approach implied in this also helps. The fact that he used the Boys' Companies also meant that he could use larger casts than had been the case with the interludes acted by adult companies, and this facility broadened the range of his structures.

These considerations suggest that Lyly was a dramatist of skill and experience. Modern criticism has tended to stress his small stature and limited achievement, but in fact his approach to the subject matter of love and authority shows that he is not merely a decorative dramatist. His treatment of both is extensive and it brings out conflicting elements. Although there are similarities between the plays and we have found themes and techniques which link them, there is a notable variety in the way he sets about his dramatisations, and his approach to each play has a strong element of originality in both design and execution. He may have been conscious of the limitation of writing plays for boys, but in fact he seems to have made this into an opportunity for exploring the differing possibilities of comedy. He was sufficiently aware of the traditions of classical comedy to realise the importance of decorum and this may have been of considerable help to him in preparing his work for court performance.

The printing of Lyly's plays in his lifetime suggests that he was held in high esteem. The texts give us enough evidence about their staging to indicate that he had an imaginative grasp of how his plays were to be performed. As far as we know, the First Blackfriars was used for public performances which were in effect rehearsals for subsequent court production, and the assumption must be that the acting spaces were comparable in size and configuration. We must also assume that the performances at the Blackfriars and at court were very much alike, even if the latter was in the great hall at Greenwich on one occasion, and Whitehall on another. For the later plays, however, the Blackfriars was not available for rehearsal, and Lyly may have moved into the Paul's acting area which, as we have seen, is less easy to identify and describe. At court, the Queen's presence is often implied, as in the Court Epilogue of *Campaspe*, which refers to 'your Highness' (l. 7).

Whatever the difficulty in specifying details now, his general concept of the stage is a combination of the Terentian street and the medieval unlocalised central playing space. The former used a series of doors, each leading into an unseen interior which was identified as the house or base of one of the characters.[20] Lyly chose two or perhaps three such locations as in those identified as Sappho's or Cynthia's palaces. However, the Revels documents show that payments were made quite frequently for the construction of houses, presumably three-dimensional, in preparing court entertainments. This tradition of erecting such free-standing structures was well established: it could have been appropriate for both *Apius and Virginia* (*c.* 1559) and *Horestes* (1567). In this way the Terentian street would be modified because it becomes undetermined and unidentified.

This space is much used by Lyly in the action, as for the boasting of Sir Tophas in *Endymion* (2.2), which could be demonstrated anywhere. It is also the place for enacting movement between one house and another, during the course of which journeys, dialogues could take place, as when Cynthia wishes to visit the bank where the sleeping Endymion lies (4.3.57). During such movement there is also the possibility of the passing of time. Lyly owes much to medieval precedents in this feature, particularly as it was applied to indoor staging in great halls. The principle behind it is not realistic but symbolic or allegorical: it does not really matter how far Cynthia has to walk. The effect, however, may be to change the perspective and in this way to enhance the balance between parts of the play, which was so important in Lyly's dramatic style. In *Love's Metamorphosis, Gallathea*, and *Endymion* Lyly makes various uses of a tree so as to suggest that it was the same property which could be invested in different but appropriate meanings from play to play. The contrast in *Campaspe* between Alexander's palace and the studio of Apelles on either side of the stage has an imaginative significance. As to the houses themselves, some of them had interiors, as is implied in the stage direction – *Sappho in her bed* (3.3.1) – from which she speaks. Endymion needed to disappear within the bank on which he fell asleep, for he had to age before being 'discovered' in order to be awakened.

The plays are rich in musical elements, and no doubt the boys would be adept in singing. The Master of the Chapel had the right to recruit boys from anywhere in the kingdom, a bit like a press-ganging. In Act 5 of *Campaspe* there is provision for one character to do some tumbling and for another to dance. This variety of activities suggests that Lyly realised the importance of entertainment in commanding attention at court. It is a striking enhancement of the intellectual pleasure of debate and the emotional ones which would arise from seeing boys evoke the conduct and experiences of women.

Notes

1. The legal plea is given in full by J.S. Leongard, 'An Elizabethan Lawsuit: John Brayne, his Carpenter, and the Building of the Red Lion Theatre', *Shakespeare Quarterly* 34 (1983), 298–310.

2. R. Gair, *The Children of Paul's: The Story of a Theatre Company, 1553–1608* (Cambridge, 1982), pp. 44–9.

3. I. Smith, *Shakespeare's Blackfriars Playhouse* (London, 1964), pp. 137–43.

4. D. Lindley, *Court Masques* (Oxford, 1995).

5. The Act is printed in full in *ES* 4.273–6.

6. Substantial passages from these works are in *ES* 4.203–5, 213–9, and 221–3; see also p. 223. For the link between theatre-going and the perceived and dangerous loss of social identity, see J.E. Howard, *The Stage and Social Struggle in Early Modern England* (London, 1994), pp. 26–40.

7. Details of this legislation are in *ES* 4.268–72.

8. *ES* 2.138. In fact Alleyn was married to Henslowe's step-daughter.

9. *Travels in England*, pp. 166–75, quoted in A. Gurr, *Playgoing in Shakespeare's London* (Cambridge, 1987), p. 213. For afternoon performances, see *ES* 2.543.

10. Gurr, p. 118.

11. *ES* 4.346–9.

12. *ES* 2.106; and for later years T.J. King, *Casting Shakespeare's Plays: London Actors and their Roles, 1590–1642* (Cambridge, 1992), pp. 254–5.

13. On hearing as opposed to seeing, see Gurr, pp. 85–97.

14. Gurr, p. 54.

15. C.R. Baskervill, *The Elizabethan Jig* (Chicago, 1929), pp. 107, 377–8; for further information, see pp. 12 (origins), 81 (types) and 85 (plays).

16. E. Welsford, *The Fool: His Social and Literary History* (London, 1935), pp. 159–70.

17. A. Gurr, *The Shakespearean Stage 1574–1642* (Cambridge, 1980), p. 86.

18. References are to *Campaspe* and *Sappho and Phao*, edited by G.K. Hunter and D. Bevington (Manchester, 1991); *Endymion*, edited by D. Bevington (Manchester, 1996), and for the remainder, *The Complete Works of John Lyly*, edited by R.W. Bond, 3 vols (Oxford, 1902).

19. The playing of women's parts by boys attracted unfavourable comment from Puritans: 'When I see . . . young boys, inclining of themselves unto wickedness, trained up in filthy speeches, unnatural and unseemly gestures, to be brought up by these schoolmasters in bawdry and idleness, I cannot choose but with tears and grief of heart lament', Antony Munday, *A Second and Third Blast of Retreat from Plays and Theatres* (1580), *ES* 4.212.

20. See the edition of a slightly earlier English version of Terence's *Andria*: *Terence in English: That Girl from Andros*, ed. M. Twycross (Lancaster, 1987), pp. 1–5.

Chapter 12
Kyd and Marlowe

The new circumstances described in the previous chapter provided opportunities for dramatists like Kyd and Marlowe who could now write for a specific market. Even though the personal rewards for dramatists may have been unconvincingly small, theatres and companies now needed plays in quantity, and the result was an outpouring of work designed to hold attention, amuse and even instruct. The plays of these two writers were among the most successful of their age, and they were performed for decades after their first presentation. They are still part of mainstream theatre today.

Though several playwrights of this time have been given the name 'University Wits', the term is of limited value. It does indicate that some of them, having had a formal education to university level, were in touch with the literature of other cultures, particularly Greece and Rome, but in fact the requirements and opportunities of the new theatres were probably just as important in inspiring and moulding their work. If we did not know they had had university education, it might be very difficult to distinguish their plays from those of writers who had not. For all his devotion to Seneca there is no evidence that Kyd went to university. Moreover, the new theatres were businesses which had to please audiences and from them produce incomes. This meant that the concept of 'popular drama' took a new turn. But in the work of Marlowe, Greene and Peele there was a continuity with some aspects of medieval dramatic forms, including the morality plays, the folk drama and the entertainment of the streets.

A glance at the stage chronology of the 1580s and 1590s reveals that this was a period of intense productivity for the stage, no doubt in response to an increasingly keen demand. The texts were produced specifically for performance and to that extent they were largely ephemeral. Printing was a supplementary activity which lagged behind the performances, and it is often difficult to tell how long the gap was between performance and printing because the dates of performances in the 1580s are obscure. Usually the publication of a play was a quite different business enterprise from its performance. Apart from Henslowe, who was keeping daily accounts in the 1590s, we have limited indications of day-to-day procedures, but his records do not begin until 1592. This means that we may not be able to use external evidence about how and when playwrights may have influenced one another. Even so, there was undoubtedly much cross-reference which can be substantiated by direct quotation and also by many broad similarities in the works produced in this period. As a rough guide it is possible to say that Peele began to write in the early 1580s, that he was joined by Kyd, Marlowe and Greene from about 1585 and that all four continued for about a decade, and that in this time a significant number of anonymous plays were also written. The position is slightly distorted by the long closure of the theatres in 1592–93 because of plague, for this seems to have triggered the publication of a number of texts in order to produce income, and many of these originated some years earlier. Thus for convenience we shall deal first with Kyd and Marlowe who were probably the two most influential playwrights and whose work sets modes for many others, particularly in tragedy. They have also become culturally important in recent years.

Thomas Kyd (1558–94)

Thomas Kyd's reputation rests upon one play: *The Spanish Tragedy* was written between 1585 and 1587, and the first known printed copy has been dated 1592. It was both popular and influential, and is known to have been performed at a number of different theatres before 1642. Henslowe's records indicate that he received profits for twenty-nine performances between 1592 and 1597, making it second only to Marlowe's *The Jew of Malta*, which reached thirty-six.[1] It was reprinted in 1594 and 1599, and Ben Jonson was paid for additions in 1602. Kyd's other known work consists of *Cornelia* (1594), a translation from the French tragedy by Robert Garnier, and *Soliman and Perseda* (printed *c.* 1592). This is attributed to him, mainly on the grounds that its plot is a vital part of the climax in *The Spanish Tragedy*: it does have some stylistic similarities, and there is a framing device consisting of Love, Fortune and Death who are in dispute.[2] The evidence is that *The Spanish Tragedy* preceded *Tamburlaine* by a short while. There is little doubt that there was some interaction between the two men. At one point in the 1590s they shared a room and they were together under suspicion by the authorities.

Kyd's plot is framed by Revenge and the Ghost of Don Andrea of Spain who has been recently and dishonourably killed in battle by Balthazar, Prince of Portugal: Andrea now seeks revenge. Balthazar, himself captured in the war with Spain, falls in love with Bel-Imperia, Andrea's former lover, but she now prefers Horatio, one of the captors of Balthazar. Lorenzo, her brother, conspires with Balthazar, and when it is obvious that her love for Horatio has been consummated, they kill him. The discovery of his corpse drives Hieronimo, his father, mad. The latter seeks revenge upon the murderers, but the King of Spain is indifferent to his pleas, and in a critical move Hieronimo takes the task upon himself, aided by Bel-Imperia. Together they cast themselves and their enemies into roles for a performance at the Spanish court of *Soliman and Perseda*. During the action the villains, acting their parts, are stabbed in reality and Bel-Imperia kills herself. Hieronimo is arrested, but he bites out his tongue rather than explain, and using a knife given to him to sharpen his pen he stabs himself. This story, with its horrific incidents and fatal momentum, is in itself a major resource for tragedy, but its management reveals that Kyd had a rare gift for dramatic techniques, as well as a highly suggestive philosophical and ideological grasp upon the significances he wanted to reveal.

The staging is a rich texture of effective and often innovative devices. The action is watched by Revenge and Andrea who intervene from time to time in a choric manner, but it is made clear to the audience that we too are to watch them and not necessarily to see things as they do. This sense of the watcher watched permeates many other situations in the play, and it is one of the chief devices by means of which its stage perspectives are developed. Thus there several episodes comprising onstage performances with onstage audiences. Hieronimo, before the death of his son, prepares a dumb-show involving three Kings (1.4); there is a dumb-show in which nuptial torches are extinguished in blood (3.4); and there is the climactic performance of *Soliman and Perseda* (4.4). In this last, the distancing of the audience is enhanced because Hieronimo bizarrely arranges that the actors in his production should speak in different languages. As the watching King and Viceroy make comments which remind the real audience of the identity of the actors, the deliberate sense of unreality is intensified. While this is a highly effective stage device, full of the unexpected and the intriguing, it also has a thematic significance which shows that Kyd knew how to manipulate the staging. The unreality and uncertainty are linked with the pervading sense that human fortune and experience are determined not by human choices, but are subject to terrible and inexorable forces which take away human identity. Kyd's interest in the metatheatrical aspects of his drama is enjoyable as a staging experience for the audience, but it also has a strong suggestion of the impermanence of what is portrayed and adds much to the play's significance. In structural terms there is a further way of sustaining comment upon the main action by means of contrast. The secondary plot, in Portugal, where the Viceroy believes he has lost his son Balthazar, and suffers excessive grief, is managed to reflect grimly upon the sense of loss experienced by Hieronimo. The audience know that Balthazar is not dead but a captive. In his misery his father points to the uncertainties of Fortune:

Fortune is blind and sees not my deserts,
So is she deaf and hears not my laments:
And could she hear, yet is she wilful mad,
And therefore will not pity my distress.

(1.3.23–6)

Kyd is able to turn things like properties and costumes into stage icons. For example, the scarf given by Bel-Imperia to Andrea is taken from his corpse by Horatio; when he returns it to her, Bel-Imperia gives it back to him as a sign of her changed love; Hieronimo takes it from Horatio's corpse, thus linking the two revenge stories. And later when he is administering justice he draws it from his pocket as he considers the plea of an Old Man who has also lost his son through murder (1.4.42; 2.5.51; 3.13.85, s.d.). Another example of such symbolism comes with Hieronimo's death. As already noted, when he is apprehended for the slaughter in the play within the play, he is threatened with torture to make him reveal why he has acted so violently. Biting out his tongue, which then becomes a stage property, makes an emblem of his refusal; and this is immediately followed up when the knife he is given to sharpen the pen in order to write the truth becomes the weapon by which he frustrates his interrogators and silences himself forever. The gap in the explanation of his actions is part of the moral ambiguities of the play which Kyd deliberately underlines. The special role of individual stage properties is indicated by specific instructions about how they fit into the action. This may be an accident of playhouse management by which a meticulous stage keeper kept his preparations up to the mark: but it looks suspiciously as though the dramatist himself may have been acutely aware of this potent means of suggestion.

The staging is further enhanced by Kyd's extensive use of onstage narratives and of soliloquies. The former owe much to his interest in classical sources both in epic poetry as well as in the conventions of ancient tragedy. The epic narratives, as with Andrea's accounts of his own death and his fate in the underworld (1.1.15–85), the General's report of the arrest of Balthazar (1.2.22–94), and Horatio's description of Andrea's death to Bel-Imperia (1.4.6–43) are valuable because of the contribution of the speaker to the narrative as well as for the way the style enhances detail and gives it emotional impact. The response of those who listen on stage is also material: after Horatio's narrative, Bel-Imperia shows her new-found love for him. There is also the malevolent distortion in Villuppo's account of the 'death' of Balthazar (1.3.59–95). Kyd's use of this dramatic convention derived perhaps from Seneca: he may well have been aware of the publication of Newton's collected translation of the *Tenne Tragedies* which appeared in 1581. One of the functions of these narratives in accordance with neoclassical principles seems to have been to avoid the presentation of violence on the stage: but Kyd is so deeply interested in the effect upon the imagination that he both describes it and has it horrifically enacted as in the stabbing by Lorenzo of the hanging body of Horatio. This emphatic treatment of violence was a landmark for the following years when tragedy and violence became synonymous, even though Kyd was by no means the first to do it, as the spectacular death of Egistus in Pikeryng's *Horestes* (1567) shows.

As with the watcher watched noted above, the soliloquies make the audience witness something which they cannot take as realistic, or accept at face value. In many of them the audience has been given information which leads them to interpret what is said differently from the speaker's intention, as is the case with Pedringano's expectation that Lorenzo will protect him (3.3.1–16). There are seventeen soliloquies in the play, of which nine are spoken by Hieronimo. Since he is not on stage very much before the death of Horatio, this is a remarkable concentration, and most of these speeches are very long, some of them being accompanied by significant properties. They involve a suspension of the normal sense of stage time and, becoming a key feature of our experience of the play, operate in a privileged way to deepen the portrayal of Hieronimo's emotional stress. The decision to concentrate so many of them in Act 3 means that the nature of the play changes emphatically at this point. Kyd no doubt found precedents for them in both medieval drama and Seneca. There is at times direct reference to the latter, but more extensively Kyd works on the rhetoric of the soliloquies, giving them a poetic of their own. For example, Hieronimo addresses a series of different imaginary listeners:

> O eyes, no eyes, but fountains fraught with tears;
> O life, no life, but lively forms of death;
> O world, no world, but mass of public wrongs,
> Confused and filled with murder and misdeeds!

Then he speaks directly to heaven for several lines, and the first half of his speech ends with an appropriate climax which is both a summation and an indication of incoherence:

> Eyes, life, world, heaven, hell, night, and day,
> See, search, shew, send some man, some mean that
>   may –   *A letter falleth.*
>
> (3.2.1–23)

The rhetorical poise of the deliberately patterned first half of the speech is ended by this letter: it is thrown down by Bel-Imperia and gives him new purpose. Moreover the letter, according to a stage direction, is written in red ink, which is meant to be a visible indication to the audience that it is written in Bel-Imperia's blood. Typically this is done for the practical reason that she has no ink in prison, and also for the symbolic link between blood and revenge. After the letter, the soliloquy continues for another 28 lines, but the style changes completely as the rational side of Hieronimo takes over and he resolves to be cautious and test what the letter tells him.

From what has been said so far it should be clear that the techniques of tragedy are much in evidence. Though there had been precedents· in many of the interludes like *Cambises*, as well as in the imitators of Seneca such as *Gorboduc,* and *The Misfortunes of Arthur,* Kyd's play focused the genre in a concentrated way, and his influence on what follows was to be emphatic, especially on account of the popularity of his play. He is strong in the conventional ingredients, as well as the use of tragic form to embody a view of life. At the end of the first scene Revenge invites Andrea:

> Here sit we down to see the mystery
> And serve for Chorus to this tragedy.
>
> (90–1)

In the last line of the play he refers to 'endless tragedy'. What he actually seems to mean is the endless suffering of Andrea's enemies, but this does not really divert attention from the sense that all within the play is tragic, even the cruel comedy of Pedringano's death (3.6.17–108).[3]

The play opens up the huge and highly popular question of revenge, which is found in interludes as well as in the ancient drama. The Elizabethan interest in this subject was complex but it was undoubtedly pervasive. It shows itself in the ruling passions which revenge generates, in great complexities of intrigue, and in the overpoweringly difficult topic of whether revenge could be justified. The predicament subsequently destroyed many theatrical avengers because they acquired guilt. In one of his most tormented speeches Hieronimo follows biblical indications that vengeance is properly the concern of God, but he converts this into a requirement that he should himself become an avenger:

> *Vindicta mihi!*   *Vengeance is mine!*
> Ay, heaven will be revenged for every ill,
> Nor will they suffer murder unrepaid:
> Then stay, Hieronimo, attend their will,
> For mortal men may not appoint their time.
>
> (3.13.1–5)

The disturbing feature here is that Kyd makes Hieronimo take the fatal step of becoming involved himself. There is a further irony in that Hieronimo is himself a justice. The abstract character of Revenge who appears in the framing episodes sheds very little light upon this predicament, but he does grimly and persistently assure the increasingly impatient Andrea that the violent and comprehensive revenge will certainly follow. Thus it is established that revenge tragedy will have an inevitable and destructive outcome. In the rest of his long speech Hieronimo prepares himself for possible death and for taking on the secrecy and circumspection necessary for the avenger:

> Thus therefore will I rest me in unrest
> Dissembling quiet in unquietness,
> Not seeming that I know their villainies.
>
> (3.13.29–31)

All these details may be recognised as elements which were to become part of the conventions of behaviour in revenge plays, as is, indeed, the extreme passion of the avenger which shades into madness. Possibly the terrible and unbalanced passions of Seneca's characters were contributory. Hieronimo's manifestation of them became a byword subsequently. Nevertheless, in this play madness is a positive technique, and it plays a significant part in the rejection of rationality which is Hieronimo's deliberate choice.

This last quotation also exemplifies Kyd's intense interest in introducing language which is crammed with double meanings and antitheses. The precedent for such poetic devices is again Seneca, whose work bore many indications that it was intended to be read as literature rather than performed as drama,[4] but it followed from the skill exemplified by Kyd that tragedy could establish a relationship between the perceived tricks and ambivalences of Fortune and subtleties and ingenuities of expression. At times the speech is heavy with irony. When Horatio sets up the performance, the audience already knows of his 'conceit' (scheme) to kill in earnest. He explains some of the plot to Lorenzo and Balthazar, and when asked what part he will play himself he replies:

> I'll play the murderer, I warrant you,
> For I already have conceited that.
>
> (4.1.133–4)

Alongside the metatheatrical aspects of the staging there goes also a concern with the difficulty of expressing passion. It is here that the classical convention of stichomythia is useful to Kyd. The device of having two or more characters speak alternate lines at moments of intense feeling may appear artificial, but it is in effect an isolating device which Kyd successfully uses to portray intimacy and close exchange. In this instance the dialogue of love between Bel-Imperia and Horatio is witnessed by the conspiring Balthazar and Lorenzo, showing that the watcher watched technique could be closely linked with language:

Bel-Imperia	Why stands Horatio speechless all this while?
Horatio	The less I speak, the more I meditate.
Bel-Imperia	But whereon dost thou chiefly meditate?
Horatio	On dangers past, and pleasures to ensue.
Balthazar	On pleasures past, and dangers to ensue.
Bel-Imperia	What dangers and what pleasures dost thou mean?
Horatio	Dangers of war and pleasures of our love.
Lorenzo	Dangers of death but pleasures none at all.

(2.1.24–31)

This form of exchange is further elaborated for the next love scene between Bel-Imperia and Horatio where they alternate couplets as well as single lines, and their words are accompanied by action:

Bel-Imperia	Nay then, to gain the glory of the field,
	My twining arms shall yoke and make thee yield.
Horatio	Nay then my arms are large and strong withal,
	Thus elms by vines are compassed till they fall.

(2.4.42–5)

It is perhaps not surprising that one contemporary commentator, seeking to denigrate the apparent literariness of plays, condemned 'Seneca by Candle-light'; but such devices are worked into some of the most telling parts of the play and are part of its inner experience and meaning. As it happens they also perform much better than they appear on the page, perhaps because they make the audience aware of different levels of appreciation.

Another aspect of Kyd's tragedy which became increasingly of interest to dramatists was the Machiavellian villain. Though the concept of this type of character originated in Machiavelli's *The Prince*, his stage presence and conduct had some similarities with those of the Vice of the interludes. But whereas the Vice operated in a cosmos which knew how to condemn him – by carrying him off to Hell on the Devil's back, for instance – the Machiavel is usually found in a world where he is only one of many conflicting evils and his presence gives little hope of a divinely appointed universe. We shall see this aspect exploited by Marlowe, who makes explicit reference to Machiavelli in somewhat ambiguous moral circumstances. Here, it is Lorenzo who is prepared to go to any lengths to achieve his political ambition and who threatens many of the other characters. The absence of any reference to a Christian God seems a significant aspect in a play in which the fortunes of the characters are so bleak. An expert in strategy backed up by violence, he extracts the truth by force from Pedringano about Bel-Imperia's love for Horatio, and comments upon his methods:

> Why so: *tam armis quam ingenio*;
> Where words prevail not, violence prevails.
>
> (2.2.107–8)

His later actions sustain his ruthless attitude as he takes the lead in the murder of Horatio, and then having used Pedringano to murder a possible witness has him hanged, playing a trick upon him about a pardon.

These elements which function so emphatically in Kyd's play are both technique and substance. They show him manipulating and developing conventional aspects which could have been accumulated from many different models, English or Continental. They became a way of advertising a tragedy from the outside, so to speak, but a special case can be made for Kyd's achievement. His pursuit of tragedy is single-minded, and though at times he seems to suggests that 'tragedy' is a synonym for violence, there is undoubtedly a consistency about his view of the human condition, and he marries this with a strong literary as well as theatrical sense of the power of this dramatic form. It may be that he was popular in his own time for the sensational violence of the plot of his play, together with his exceptional skill in producing emphatic and clever language. For us he is impressive not so much as an innovator but as one who could combine so many of the features of tragedy which others were conscious of in his time. Though to Kyd the concept of violence was synonymous with tragedy, it was primarily an art-form, a way of presenting.

Let us turn finally to his tragic vision, which is substantial even though it is based upon a single play. The plot itself presents a situation from which there is no escape. Although Hieronimo, as we have noted, makes a deliberate decision to take on the role of avenger, he remains a victim of the conspiracy of others, and he is impelled towards revenge by the intensity of his grief, and indeed that of Isabella, his wife (3.8). Even though he initiates action, his mastery of events is never complete. His internal conflict between reason and passion points to another constraining factor, and this is a significant development of a medieval trope which Kyd makes a part of the tragic predicament. But here there is a sense not of good against evil, but of a dislocation which can never be fully resolved. The surrounding circumstances, devised by Kyd, add much to the enclosed position in which Hieronimo is located. The King's refusal to hear his cry for help, the Machiavellian brutality of Lorenzo, his own madness and the prompting of the passionate Bel-Imperia are all contributing factors which operate causally.

In the strategy of the play there are also factors which do not operate causally. The presence of the supernatural does not compel things to happen, but it does embody a view of events which must affect the responses of the audience. The significant parallels between the two courts and the Princes who dominate them give structural emphasis. Kyd's poetic style will also affect the audience, since the presence of ironic commentary and the tendency to abstract from the flow of the play those concentrated observations in the form of *sententiae*, urge interpretation instead of simple chronological or causal sequencing. Indeed, Kyd's dramatic scheme seems to challenge realism by a process of raising consciousness about the issues involved and about the destructive world in which these events are shown. The plot is vital, but it is by no means all.

Though one should look upon the whole play as a tragedy, the management of the character of Hieronimo himself is poignant in that he is the victim of what goes on around him. It seems that Kyd has developed strongly our awareness of Hieronimo's states of mind. The soliloquies help to increase our sensitivity to these in such a way that even they are tragic. In Kyd's hands tragedy is developing a greater sense of the agony, which came to dominate the work of later tragedians. In many important ways Kyd is able to present and develop an individual consciousness which makes his tragedy more poignant. This is one of the chief links with Marlowe's work.

Christopher Marlowe (1564–93)

Marlowe's reputation has been growing steadily in the twentieth century to an extent which perhaps exaggerates his popularity among his contemporaries. Historically he has been much prized for his powerful language, but more recently the emphasis has shifted to the nature of his challenge to the accepted values of his time, a challenge which, out of circumspection, incorporated paradoxically a reflection of those values. This has led to a strong interest in the ambiguity in the world of his plays, and also it has led to an inquiry into the nature of his heroes. These have proved intriguingly ambiguous, and have produced much speculation about whether they should excite sympathy, revulsion, or indeed a mixture of both as their various deeds and feelings are unfolded. Recent stage productions, especially at the Swan Theatre in Stratford-upon-Avon which reproduces some of the features of early theatres, have also revealed much about the theatricality of the plays.[5]

Because it may be his earliest play, associated with his time in Cambridge which ended in 1587, *The Tragedy of Dido, Queen of Carthage* is in some respects untypical of the rest. Another factor may be that it was written for the boy actors of the Chapel Royal. It is not without physical action but it is less vigorous than most of the others: instead, it is much occupied by the rhetoric of troubled love. The play is rich in narrative, especially Aeneas's account, in about 160 lines, of the fall of Troy and his escape from it. The sequences of narratives here are full of horrific images of suffering and slaughter, and include terrified speeches by the participants. It is well known that Marlowe owed a debt to the popular school text of Virgil's *Aeneid* II, but much of the violent, even frenzied detail of the death of Priam is still brilliantly original. The following may have been parodied in the Player King's speech in *Hamlet* (2.2.464–514), but it has a dynamism which is Marlowe's own:

> At which the frantic queen leaped on his face,
> And in his eyelids hanging by the nails,
> A little while prolonged her husband's life.
> At last the soldiers pulled her by the heels,
> And swung her howling in the empty air,
> Which sent an echo to the wounded king:
> Whereat he lifted up his bed-rid limbs,
> And would have grappled with Achilles' son
> Forgetting both his want of strength and hands;
> Which he disdaining, whisked his sword about,
> And with the wound thereof the king fell down.
>
> (2.1.244–54)

But as Dido, to whom Aeneas tells the story, has already wept at reports about him before he arrived in Carthage, the story is presented in a fruitful dramatic context. Because a boy might well be skilled in playing a woman's role, her part is endowed with some fine speeches and has great emotional range. Indeed, so much initiative does she have that there is no doubt that this is her tragedy.

Another way in which Marlowe exploited his dramatic opportunity was his rather comic presentation of the Gods, who participate actively in these events. Thus Jupiter sports with Ganymede and there is a quarrel between Venus and Juno. Venus sets up the love affair by having Cupid disguise himself as Ascanius, the son of Aeneas, in order to have him touch Dido with the arrow of love. The emotional life of the play is extended by having Iarbas in love with Dido unsuccessfully, and having Anna, her sister, in love with him. The play ends with the death of all three, as Aeneas, summoned by the Gods, sets out for Italy and his destiny which he accepts not unwillingly.

The plot is neatly managed to give important climaxes in the narration of Troy, the tender union of the lovers in the cave during a storm, and the sensational last scene with its triple suicide. In spite of settling for the comic tones described, Marlowe does establish the love affair effectively, even though he follows Ovid, whose picture of Aeneas is less admirable than that of Virgil. Dido reveals her passion tentatively and with much grace:

Not sick, my love; but sick I must conceal
The torment that it boots me not reveal.
And yet I'll speak – and yet I'll hold my peace.
Do shame her worst, I will disclose my grief:
Aeneas, thou art he – what did I say?
Something it was that now I have forgot.

(4.1.25–30)

The tragedy turns upon the risk of this passionate love thwarted by destiny and to some extent by the character of Aeneas. Marlowe's plays allow such prominence to a woman's part nowhere else.

For his contemporaries *Tamburlaine the Great, Parts I and II* resonated emphatically. It was written in 1587–88, printed in 1590, and according to Henslowe performed many times in 1594–95. Like most of Marlowe's other heroes, Tamburlaine himself is not a superficially attractive figure, characterised by violence, ambition and cruelty. The story of his rise to world domination carries him through a series of military victories reflecting intense personal aspiration and complete disregard for the interests of others. But he is borne on by an exultation which seizes the imagination by its intensity and by its unrelenting excitement. He seeks irresistible military glory:

Our quivering lances, shaking in the air,
And bullets, like Jove's dreadful thunderbolts,
Enrolled in flames and fiery smouldering mists,
Shall threat the gods more than Cyclopian wars,
And with our sun-bright armour as we march
We'll chase the stars from heaven, and dim their eyes
That stand and muse at our admired arms.

(I.2.3.18–24)

His worldly ambition resonates with hyperbole:

Our souls, whose faculties can comprehend
The wondrous architecture of the world
And measure every wandering planet's course,
Still climbing after knowledge infinite,
And always moving as the restless spheres,
Wills us to wear ourselves and never rest,
Until we reach the ripest fruit of all,
That perfect bliss and sole felicity,
The sweet fruition of an earthly crown.

(I.2.7.21–9)

It may be difficult to like or admire him, but the story of his successes is written with a theatrical *bravura* that commands attention. In other words, his grasp upon us, or more correctly Marlowe's achievement in making Tamburlaine so compelling, is a function of the theatrical process by which he is presented rather than deriving simply from the narrative of his deeds. Most of these are unworthy and a deliberate challenge to typical chivalric values – his position as an outsider is continuously noted by himself and by others.

The action of the play is an intriguing blend of long speeches and vigorous physical activity which often assumes a symbolic force as Marlowe creatively devises ways of representing the power of Tamburlaine's activity before our eyes. Marlowe's powerful rhetoric, incorporating rich imagery and strong rhythms, invites performance skills and at a deeper level yields a way of representing a powerful complex of feelings. This extract is an example:

> I hold the Fates bound fast in iron chains
> And with my hand turn Fortune's wheel about;
> And sooner shall the sun fall from his sphere
> Than Tamburlaine be slain or overcome.
> Draw forth thy sword, thou mighty man-at-arms,
> Intending but to raze my charmed skin,
> And Jove himself will stretch his hand from heaven
> To ward the blow, and shield me safe from harm.
>
> (I.1.2.174–81)

The process is one of self-exposition not essentially dissimilar to the self-exposition in earlier plays, but Marlowe manages also to impose a measure of self-display and an attitude to it which makes it compelling, so that we are not sure that we are inside Tamburlaine's mind or being directed to his thoughts as it were from outside. In this speech it is notable that the register is fairly direct but the rhythm and the sentence structure are typically forceful.

There is a noticeable difference in the shape of the two Parts which increases the interest in this extraordinary characterisation. In *Part I* the movement is upwards to a position of authority, in which he is supported by Zenocrate, his adored and adoring wife, as well as by his faithful and devoted fellow warriors. In *Part II* his pursuit of tyrannical and comprehensive domination is marked by even greater cruelty, as in this climactic entry to 4.3:

Enter Tamburlaine drawn in his chariot by the Kings of Trebizon and Soria, with bits in their mouths, reins in his left hand, and in his right hand a whip with which he scourgeth them . . .

Tamburlaine: Holla, ye pamper'd jades of Asia!
What, can ye draw but twenty miles a day,
And have so proud a chariot at your heels,
And such a coachman as great Tamburlaine?

(II.4.3.1–4)

Nevertheless, as he enumerates further lands to be conquered, there is
a sense that the aspiration apparent at the beginning has become stale,
and this is compounded by the death of Zenocrate. In her memory he
condemns the place where she died:

This cursed town I will consume with fire,
Because this place bereft me of my love.
The houses, burnt, will look as if they mourned.

(II.2.4.137–9)

His end is a mixture of boasting and frustration:

And shall I die, and this unconquered?
Lo here, my sons, are all the golden mines
Inestimable drugs and precious stones,
More worth than Asia and the world beside.

(II.5.3.151–4)

Such words put the play some distance from tragedy since his end comes
because it is time to die, and though he has tried to prepare his sons to
succeed him the implication is that he cannot be followed. The Scourge
of God, as he several times describes himself, has finally worn himself out.
Thus Marlowe again poses the problem of aspiration which, though
splendid in itself, actually implies and achieves nothing of value, and the
end of the play remarkably carries no comment.

The chief characters of his other plays are sometimes seen more tragically than Tamburlaine, but they usually share with him an alienation from
the world in which they live and the action of the plays which they
inhabit. In *The Massacre at Paris* (printed in 1592, and performed in 1593,
according to Henslowe), the Duke of Guise, in a typically Marlovian
soliloquy, gives an account of himself which, like several in *Tamburlaine*,
is designed to create imagery about the character of the speaker as much
as to reveal inner thoughts:

What glory is there in a common good,
That hangs for every peasant to achieve?
That like I best that flies beyond my reach.
Set me to scale the high Pyramides,
And thereon set the diadem of France;

I'll either rend it with my nails to naught,
Or mount the top with my aspiring wings,
Although my downfall be the deepest hell.

(1.2.40–7)

The Guise, a fanatic, is shown trapped in an amoral world of secrecy and deception from which there is no escape. Marlowe's lack of sympathy for most of the characters is tempered only by his support for the Protestants in a play which seeks to exploit the inexorability of *realpolitik*. This is strengthened because he relies to some extent upon popular xenophobia here, especially against Catholic countries.

The development of soliloquy by Marlowe is a salient feature of his drama, both for its strength in characterisation and in revealing the function of the character in the dominating ideas of the play. However, this is not necessarily a realistic technique designed to tell us some truth about the character's inner thoughts so much as a demonstrative one which is dependent upon the kind of language which is employed, and also upon a certain distancing of the speaker from himself. In one way it may be seen as an increase in self-awareness, but it is also a development of diegetic techniques used by abstract characters in morality plays where the techniques of soliloquy had been evolved for moral purposes. The intention must always be to affect the audience: the imagery of flying beyond one's reach draws particular attention, and again, as in the moralities, it offered scope for emphatic performance.

In a similar way in *Dr Faustus* the protagonist begins with a long speech exploring the various kinds of learning he has experienced, and this in a play which has a number of other specific references to morality drama. These include the argument between the Good and Bad Angels, the encounter with the Seven Deadly Sins, and the devils carrying off the sinner to hell at the end: all these are found in *The Castle of Perseverance*. The Chorus preceding Faustus's first soliloquy describes in strictly moral terms how he was 'swol'n with cunning of a self-conceit'. (In medieval times 'cunning' meant knowledge, so the phrase means 'swollen with the knowledge of an idea about himself'.) It remains an issue throughout the play how far this medieval view is an adequate account of what happens to Faustus: much that follows is at odds with such a version. Indeed, one of the strengths of this play is that it ranges critically over a number of religious and philosophical issues. The use of medieval practices and concepts is inherent, but it is also a base for development.

Faustus's first speech is an assault upon traditional categories of learning, rejecting Aristotle, Galen the physician, Justinian the lawyer, and St Jerome, editor of the Vulgate – all of them pillars of medieval learning. In doing so, it is generally agreed, he reveals errors of scholarship which might have been detectable by some of the original audience: but this rejection may have been seen as both dangerous and, for some, inspiring. His intention to use medical knowledge to make himself rich (which may be an echo of Chaucer's Physician) suggests both the excitement of fantasy and day-dreaming, and a palpable corruption of the soul. He substitutes for the disciplines of scholarship the ambiguous power of magic, which could be good or bad. The division between what we now call science and a whole range of magical practices, whether trivial or cosmic, did not exist. But once again the form of the soliloquy suggests to us that the 'black' magic predominates, as his intention is now blasphemous. He concludes with this:

> A sound magician is a demi-god.
> Here, tire my brains to get a deity.
>
> (1.1.61–2)

The occurrence of this first soliloquy sets up an expectation of further self-examinations which are double-edged. This culminates in the last scene, which is played in the form of a monologue as Faustus is forced to face up to the final consequences of his pact with the Devil. As he speaks, the pressing sense that time is running out is underlined by the striking of the clock. The imagery of heaven and hell developed earlier in the play now resonates terribly. Instead of the Good and Bad Angels trying to persuade him, Faustus now seems to dramatise the conflict within himself, as though they were still speaking to him in rapid succession. He speaks alternately to Christ and Lucifer, but though he is terrified of what is to come he allows himself no hope, in spite of the signs which have made clear to the audience that repentance is still possible. It seems as though he has trapped himself into refusing to ask for mercy at the right time and he cannot bring himself to do so now. He is close to Wanhope, culpable despair. But if there is still a possibility that he might repent, the contract would not have been binding. Thus the conflict within Faustus, as one who aspired intellectually, and one who became fated to destruction because of the pact, is ended with the arrival of Lucifer to carry him off. The result is powerfully tragic, but once again the Chorus seems to restrict interpretation to a moralistic one which does not fit the enormity of the circumstances.

In the intervening episodes, which may not have all been written by Marlowe himself,[6] Faustus exploits his magical powers in a series of adventures which show his ambition – to achieve great things – but also reveal the futility of his magic in trivial and sometimes comic events. This is interwoven with a series of attempts by others, including the Good Angel, the Old Man, and other scholars, to bring about his salvation – but always Faustus, exercising free will, chooses not to repent, sometimes saying that he cannot, by which Marlowe almost certainly implies he *will* not. The ironic culmination of his aspiration is a series of empty tricks and a failure to repent.

Much of the play is ironic, though it is not always certain exactly how far this is sustained. Many things are done which undercut the aspirations of Faustus, such as the refusal of Mephistopheles to answer certain questions about the nature of Creation. At the same time, Marlowe's rhetorical skills give credibility to Faustus's aspirations, so that the audience may feel much sympathy for him in his attempt to understand the mystery of the universe: like the Guise, flying beyond his reach. As with Tamburlaine the aspiration is presented as two-edged: attractive, perhaps admirable, and yet fatally flawed by the limitations of the hero. In the case of Faustus there is more than one occasion when he seems cowardly.

The comic episodes show a good deal of ingenuity and can be made to work well on stage, but there is always a sense that they do not quite match the more serious and searching ironies of the tale of the damnation of Faustus. One special function is to undermine the magic and to show that it can be perverse, as in the episode of the horse which turns into a bale of hay because of the Horse Courser's insatiable curiosity (4.5.47–62): perhaps this man is a comic version of Faustus. The comic business of mocking the Pope (3.3) has a more far-reaching implication, however, because of its anti-Catholic intention. It suggests that although Marlowe is prepared to attack the Catholic Church and exploit a popular prejudice, he does not completely reject the Christian framework in which the story of Faustus is located. In spite of the commonly held view that he was an atheist (originating in contemporary accusations), the overwhelming terror of the fate of Faustus implies that Marlowe was at least prepared to accept the possibility of damnation as real, or that he expected it to be so for his audience. This position may be sustained elsewhere in his work, where we find a critical attitude to failure in religious practice, but not a sense that the whole theological system is mistaken.

In *The Jew of Malta* (1589, regularly performed at the Rose Theatre between 1592 and 1596) the Christian world is challenged through the excesses of Barabas, the Jew. Machevill speaks the Prologue, in which he throws doubt on the established order:

> I count religion but a childish toy
> And hold there is no sin but ignorance.

(ll. 14–15)

He makes a plea that he receive a sympathetic hearing in spite of his reputation, as Marlowe deliberately inverts the traditional moral Prologue focusing a morality play. His subsequent development of the plot is given a similar ironic twist as in the other plays. Barabas follows the principles of Machiavelli by infiltrating Abigail, his daughter, into a nunnery which has been established in his former house, filched from him by a legal device. His purpose is to recover treasure secreted there, but, having been successful in retrieving it, Abigail really does turn Christian. Barabas sees to it that she and all the other nuns are poisoned to ensure that his secret is not discovered.

Structurally Marlowe strengthens the position of the Machiavellian principles in the play by making Ferneze, the Governor of Malta, just as ruthless as Barabas. Though this man is a self-proclaimed Christian, he shows no pity and exploits Barabas for his wealth. Barabas also acquires in Ithamore, a Turkish slave, a fittingly wicked instrument for his villainy, yet when Ithamore is disloyal Barabas immediately kills him. In the end Barabas, in an egregious error of judgement, trusts the word of Ferneze that if he helps to expel the Turks he will be rewarded by the Christians. Thus he is caught by the very principles as outlined by Machevill in the Prologue, who declares that those who act by him,

> when they cast me off
> Are poisoned by my climbing followers.

(ll. 12–13)

The ironic programme of the play is sustained by the stage techniques and by many stylistic decisions on Marlowe's part. In spite of the horrors and cruelties, there is a pervading sense of the grotesque which almost amounts to farce, posing an interesting question of credibility. Not only are the actions of Barabas unbelievably destructive, as when he sets up the mortal combat between Abigail's two suitors, one of whom she loves, but there are also episodes where his evil intentions are communicated to the audience in a grotesque way. The following speech occurs as he simultaneously

(1)   negotiates with Friar Jacomo for Abigail's entry to the nunnery, while at the same time he
(2)   pretends to be scolding her for her (feigned) conversion, and
(3)   gives her instructions in whispered asides about the treasure:

> (1) Blind friar, I seek not thy persuasions –
> (3) The board is marked thus [*gesture*] that covers it –
> (1) For I had rather die than see her thus.
> (2) Wilt thou forsake me too in my distress,
> Seduced daughter? –
> (3) Go, forget not. –
> (1) Becomes it Jews to be so credulous? –
> (3) Tomorrow early I'll be at the door. –
> (2) No, come not at me! If thou wilt be damn'd
> Forget me, see me not! And so be gone! –
> (3) Farewell. Remember tomorrow morning. –
> (2) Out, out, thou wretch!

(1.2.367–78: stage directions abbreviated)

The physical appearance of Barabas would have added strong visual elements to this reliance upon farce. His costume may well have included a red wig, a Jewish hat, large beard, and exaggerated nose;[7] but at one point in order to trick Ithamore he appears 'disguised as a French musician, with a lute and a [poisoned] nosegay in his hat' (4.4.39, s.d.). The stage business he has to present involves the strangling of Friar Barnardine with the help of Ithamore's girdle, followed by propping the corpse on a stick so that Friar Jacomo can quarrel with it, strike it and then be carried off to the magistrates as a murderer (4.1.145–208). Disbelief is overcome by comic outrage.

Because of the extensive rhetorical splendour of much of the play Marlowe is successful in setting up strongly conflicting impressions of the action. Barabas can be very persuasive, yet the context always pressures us not to trust him even though the contemptible actions of the Christians may sometimes make for sympathy for him. There is a strong sense that here, as in the other plays, Marlowe has invented a hero who is less than admirable, and then he proceeds to manipulate the response of the audience both in terms of credibility as well as how he should be judged. When Barabas is finally boiled in oil by Ferneze's trick, the sense that he has deserved it is undercut by the baseness of Ferneze's behaviour. This final act has a comic appropriateness, but its major achievement is Marlowe's attempt to keep shifting the response of the audience.

In *Edward II* (composed 1591–93, printed 1593) Marlowe again picks up on the ideas of Machiavelli by showing the ruthlessness of the power struggle around the King, though he does not particularise this by having an abstract Machiavel. The movement away from myth and legend and towards a more realistic theatre may well be significant, and there is a notable lack of comic scenes in this play. This grim world is presented with virtually no supernatural dimension: Marlowe does not offer us either a cyclic or a theological pattern for history. The fortunes of Edward, who relies upon the authority innate in kingship rather than upon political craft, are successively challenged by the nobles, and by Mortimer. This political realism, which is developed without much reference to moral values and significantly avoids inner commentary, is echoed in the texture of the play. Marlowe compressed the events of more than twenty years with a remarkable selection of key incidents.

Alongside this political plot are set the personal wishes of the characters, so that there is an extensive private dimension which revolves around Edward's homosexual love for Gaveston and his consequent neglect of Queen Isabella. Once again, there is a starkness about the way in which these emotional aspects are presented, but there is a notable absence of the rhetorical and imagistic language we have noted in the other plays. Many of the scenes are quite short, and the play reads as though Marlowe was trying to make an impression of speed and to create sharp theatrical images, some of which are intensely visual. It is in this play therefore that we can see that Marlowe's contribution to English theatre and his high reputation should relate as much to his capacity to write for theatrical situations as to his ability to draw upon his rich and versatile ability with words.

The play fits into the developing genre of the history play, which we can further trace in the next chapter with Greene, Peele and others. It is thought to have been written after Shakespeare's first work in the genre, the *Henry VI* trilogy and *Richard III*, and may have been influenced by his interest in weak kings.[8] But because of the personal side of Edward's emotional life – his absolute will not to give up Gaveston when it would be politically expedient to do so – the play also has important tragic dimensions; and in this matter of will, the play can be seen as a development from the positions demonstrated in *Tamburlaine* and *Dr Faustus*.

Marlowe shaped his source material accordingly. The structure, with its rise in Edward's fortune in Act III concurrent with Gaveston's execution and Isabella's news of the loss of lands in France, shows precisely that his victory is short-lived, and the second half of the play is concerned with his political defeat at the hands of Mortimer and his decline into imprisonment and a horrific death. But this may well be seen not as a causal sequence so much as one which works by the juxtaposition of stage images: Edward accoutred for war (3.2), disguised as a monk (4.6), and being washed and shaved in puddle water (5.3.37, s.d.).

There is a strong concentration upon Edward himself throughout the play, and his private emotional life is exploited to make him both cause and victim. Early in the play his devotion to Gaveston excites a strong reaction from members of the nobility on the grounds of the latter's low status, but even after the death of this favourite another takes his place in the form of the Younger Spencer. Edward's love takes the form of bribery and self-indulgence, and it expresses itself in intense concentration upon personal satisfaction, though it is not often given a sensual tone:

> Live where thou wilt, I'll send thee gold enough;
> And long thou shalt not stay, or, if thou dost,
> I'll come to thee; my love shall ne'er decline.
>
> (1.4.114–16)

In the second half of the play he becomes a figure of loneliness and despair, and his misfortunes are dominated by the cruelties of Mortimer and those who serve him. Psychologically he is unable to resist death; indeed he welcomes it – 'all places are alike, / And every earth is fit for burial –' (5.1.145–6) – and his last scenes show that he has been unable to learn from the horrors that surround him.

Among the cross influences between Marlowe and Shakespeare at this point it may well be that the intensely personal agonies of Edward are

reflected in Richard II. Nevertheless Marlowe also develops the personalities of lesser figures as well as questioning their social identities as wife,
brother, son or rival, so that they too are part of the tragedy. Gaveston is
seen by others as ambitious and self-seeking, and he makes it clear himself
that he does intend to exploit his opportunities with the King, perhaps in
adaptation of the Vice. To a certain extent, like the Vice, he is also an
embodiment of Edward's self-seeking passion. But this possible morality-
play manner does not account for all that he does and is, especially as he
shows genuine affection for the King. Isabella, the disappointed wife, tries
for a long while to recover her place in the King's affections, and her
emotional connection with Mortimer only rises late in the play. Mortimer
is used especially to develop the atmosphere of tragedy: the title page
refers to his 'Tragical Fall'. At one point he stands 'as Jove's huge tree',
and shortly afterwards he pointedly says:

> Base Fortune, now I see that in thy wheel
> There is a point to which men aspire,
> They tumble headlong down.
>
> (5.6.59–61)

One of the most striking theatrical successes is the young son of Edward
and Isabella, the future Edward III. Though he is vulnerable through the
play, he takes power enigmatically on his father's death, and in a remarkable way the tragedy ends not with the death scene but with Prince
Edward's imposition of his will upon Mortimer and Isabella. Sentencing
the former to beheading and quartering, he sends his mother to the
Tower pending further trial, and then in a grim theatrical icon, he has
Mortimer's head placed on his father's coffin. His very last word, the last
in the play, carries a strange irony:

> And let these tears, distilling from mine eyes,
> Be witness of my grief and innocency.
>
> (5.6.101–2)

Not only has Edward II failed to learn much from his sufferings except
despair, but it looks as though his son, though politically more decisive
and even efficacious, will not rule a better world. This stark realisation
is underscored by Marlowe's refusal to moralise either about Edward's
homosexuality or about his political ineptitude: it is a striking evolution
of the mismatch between moralising and actuality observed in his other
plays, including Dr Faustus. Thus Edward II offers a great deal as a history
play and there are grounds for assuming that Marlowe significantly enlarged the genre, but there is also a very close perception of personal and
public tragedy which make ascription to both genres perfectly appropriate.

It is remarkable that there are several plays in the Elizabethan corpus which note them both on their title pages.

Marlowe's dramatic achievement is predicated upon a radical approach to the art of theatre, as well as to the society in which he lived and worked. His plays are immensely inventive: though we have suggested some links between them, they start from markedly different premises and develop quite different styles of characterisation and plot. The contrast between the Jew and Edward as farcical and tragical is paralleled by the distinction between the episodic repetition of *The Jew of Malta* and the carefully reciprocal halves of *Edward II,* balanced as they are around his fragile triumph in the middle of the play. Marlowe's astonishing and justly famed poetic skills are effectively and appropriately modulated from play to play, and they are closely integrated into the dramatic structures, and adapted to the exploitation of the physical characteristics of the theatres in which they were performed.

Notes

1. Thomas Kyd, *The Spanish Tragedy*, ed. J.R. Mulryne (London, 1989), p. xxx; all references are to this edition.

2. *The First Part of Hieronimo* (printed 1605) has been attributed to Kyd on slender evidence: its style and dramatic effects are markedly different.

3. One of the most interesting aspects of the RSC's 1997 production was the idea that revenge was an endless cycle.

4. This is a matter difficult to resolve, but it does not directly affect the enormous influence of Seneca in the sixteenth century: see G. Braden, *Renaissance Tragedy and the Senecan Tradition* (New Haven, 1985), pp. 230–1, n. 1.

5. References are to J.B. Steane (ed.) *Christopher Marlowe: The Complete Plays* (Harmondsworth, 1969).

6. Collaborative authorship is discussed by David Bevington and Eric Rasmussen (eds) *Christopher Marlowe: Doctor Faustus* (Manchester, 1993), pp. 70–2. My comments are based upon the so-called A-text which was printed in 1604: an enlarged version, the B-text, appeared in 1616. Both versions are given by Bevington and Rasmussen, who favour the date 1588–89 for composition and first performance, pp. 1–3.

7. The hat appears at 4.4.89, and the nose at 3.3.10 and elsewhere: see N.W. Bawcutt (ed.) *The Jew of Malta* (Manchester, 1978), p. 2.

8. There is a helpful revaluation of this chronology in C.R. Forker, 'Marlowe's *Edward II* and its Shakespearean Relatives: the Emergence of a Genre', in *Shakespeare's English Histories: A Quest for Form and Genre*, edited by J.W. Velz (Binghampton, 1996), pp. 55–90.

Chapter 13

Greene, Peele and Some Popular Plays, 1580–95

In this chapter we shall be concerned with a number of plays which show the versatility of the English stage in the 1580s and early 1590s. Once again the precise chronology is difficult to determine, and in the case of Greene and Peele at least there are overlaps in time apparently, and in subject matter. There is, however, a persistent sense that the plays of these dramatists, working at close quarters with one another, evidence parallels which may indeed be signs of rivalry or simply emulation. But whichever way influence may have flowed, we find here an intensive playmaking culture in which it must have been stimulating to work, and this in spite of some very vociferous cross-criticism like Greene's characterisation of Shakespeare, in *A Groatsworth of Wit*, as

> an upstart Crow, beautified with our feathers, that with his
> Tiger's heart wrapped in a Player's hide, supposes he is as
> well able to bombast out a blank verse as the best of you:
> and . . . is in his own conceit the only Shake-scene in a
> country.[1]

Several of the other plays considered in this chapter have become famous because they were used by Shakespeare, but it is important to preserve the perspective that they have discernible qualities of their own, and it is possible to see them as successful parts of the vigorous life of the English stage at this time. Some of them became very popular and were acted or printed repeatedly. Most of them are preoccupied with morality or romance, or both.

Robert Greene (1558–92)

Greene, born in Norwich, studied at St John's College, Cambridge, where he was M.A. by 1583, and he was also M.A. at Oxford by 1588. This learned background shows itself in the resourceful variety of his writings. He lived an immoral life and died in wretched circumstances in London in 1592, aged 34, but moral issues became more and more important to him as a writer. Indeed at one point, in 1590, he speaks of a moral transformation, and rejects the tales of love he had written earlier on the grounds of their immorality. There is a good deal of his own writing, as in *A Groatsworth of Wit* (1592), and accounts by others which describe his reformation, but which also make much of the squalid circumstances in which he died, and of the excesses and depravity of his life. Such work bears indirectly upon the plays, though we may regard the reported excesses of his life with some scepticism as they make such a good contrast with moral improvement. For him and for others his life story was marketable. He wrote a good deal of fiction in which fate and fortune played a strong part and in which he showed a considerable interest in the moral position of women. In *Penelope's Web* (1587), the supremacy of female virtue over men is celebrated when Penelope, wife of Ulysses, outwits her would-be seducers. He was attracted to stories which exemplified such chastity, as can be seen from his telling of the tale of Susanna in *A Mirror of Modesty* (1584). His tale of *Pandosto* (1588) is one of Shakespeare's sources for *The Winter's Tale*. Such stories also had their darker side in that women were threatened by tyrannous, ruthless and lustful men, aspects which also had a prominent place in his fictions. In his pamphlet *Never Too Late* (1590) there is a debate between Chaucer and Gower over the moral aspects of Greene's story-telling in which Chaucer approves the didactic value of Greene's work while Gower concentrates upon its pecuniary objectives. These tales often had supernatural elements, such as the dispute between Venus and Saturn in *Planetomachia* (printed 1585). This feature parallels the framing device of Venus and the Muses in his play *Alphonsus*.

His output of fiction is matched by his production of pamphlets and books about contemporary affairs, such as the three issues of the *Cony Catching* pamphlets (1590–92). These set out to expose realistically the follies and crimes of contemporary society, dwelling particularly upon the common realities of trickery and cynicism which he portrayed as ubiquitous. He was a very prolific writer, producing more than thirty pamphlets in the decade 1584–94. Such an output was indeed necessary if writing was to produce enough to live on. Perhaps it was this which led him to turn to writing for the theatre. Greene would have shared the contemporary sense of the ephemerality of writing plays, but it was an opportunity which struggling professional writers could not afford to disregard.

Seven plays have been attributed to him, the first chronologically being *The Comical History of Alphonsus King of Aragon* which is thought to have appeared in 1587.[2] The subject of this play is the military ambitions of Alphonsus, and in a number of ways the play recalls *Tamburlaine*, which is thought to have been produced in 1587. Tamburlaine himself is specifically mentioned at l. 1444. A few lines later comes a stage direction which seems to echo the triumphing of Marlowe's hero:

> *Enter Alphonsus with a canopie carried over him by three Lords, having over each corner a Kings head crowned.*
>
> (l. 1450, s.d.)

But the character of Alphonsus is different from Tamburlaine's as he is high born and, for a time at least, follows chivalric ambitions in trying to put right the wrongs done to his father, and the play is given a framework in which Venus traces the rise of Alphonsus on Fortune's wheel. Although there is a consciousness of tragedy in the play, the end is a happy union between Alphonsus and Iphigina the daughter of Amuracke, the Great Turk. This reflects the growing theatrical interest in exotic settings, and is perhaps to be associated with *Tamburlaine*. The upshot of the plot is that Venus is seen to have conquered Mars. Thus Greene apparently uses historical material, but his real purpose is to explore the possibilities of romance and to lead to an ending which is outstandingly comic, in the sense of being the fortunate outcome of difficult adventures.

This comic objective remains consistent in the other six attributed plays, especially concerning the outcome of romantic love. Thus *James the Fourth* (1590), though ostensibly dependent upon an alliance by marriage between the English and Scottish crowns, is substantially concerned with the relationship of James with Dorothea, his wife, and with Ida, who is the daughter of the Countess of Arran and whom he loves persistently through the play. One of the chief purposes is to demonstrate the virtue of both women. *The Honourable History of Friar Bacon and Friar Bungay* (1589) also has a royal initiative in that Lacy is sent to woo the country keeper's daughter Margaret on behalf of Prince Edward, son of King Henry III. In the event Lacy and Margaret fall in love and once again the story is turned into a celebration of the course of true love against many difficulties. The play introduces the use of magic by the two Friars which in its 'good' manifestation fits in well with the love story. However, it also has some bad effects reminiscent of its role in *Dr Faustus*, with the result that Bacon repents of his studies and relinquishes magic. He admits that in the course of these studies he has travelled to hell, and his pupil Miles is taken off to hell riding on the Devil's back in imitation of the morality-play motif.

The History of Orlando Furioso (1591), derived from Ariosto, reveals the victory of love over madness and war. In spite of troubles and the wild behaviour of Orlando, who is induced by Sacrepant to think that his beloved Angelica loves another, she remains true to him. Greene alters her character from the inconstant model in Ariosto. In his afflicted state Orlando judges women harshly, and it is an important part of the development of the plot that he comes to revise this judgement.[3] Greene's management of his female characters may be a touch sentimental, and somewhat idealised, but it is a constant feature of his plays that he seeks to present women in a favourable light. While one may take this disposition at its face value, it also offers obverse opportunities which allow women to be misrepresented, insulted and abused. The discourse of gender is thus a salient feature.

The attribution of the remaining three plays is less certain than those discussed so far, but they do have sufficient material in common with the others to make it probable that Greene was involved. *A Looking Glass for London* (1590) is a collaboration with Thomas Lodge. It has a biblical setting, using Babylon as an image for London and attempting to show up the weaknesses and moral decay of London through the voices of biblical figures, the prophets Hosea and Jonah. In this play the moral tone is persistent and the rebukes of the prophetic figures are given strong emphasis, often embodied in sermons urging repentance.

The full title of *Selimus* (1592) shows that Greene was interested to elaborate the increasingly popular exploitation of the terrible Turks, which probably became theatrically fashionable after the success of the spectacular *Tamburlaine*:

> *The First part of the Tragicall raigne of Selimus, sometime*
> *Emperour of the Turkes, and grandfather to him that now*
> *raigneth. Wherein is showne how hee most vnnaturally raised*
> *warres against his owne father Baiazet, and preuailing therein,*
> *in the end caused him to be poysoned: Also with the murthering*
> *of his two brethren, Corcut, and Acomat.*

The story of this play sticks to the Turkish setting and makes much of the mayhem allegedly present in the Turkish court, a sensational and appealing subject. The idea that, in the struggle for power, patricide and fratricide were normal became a commonplace.

In *The Pleasant and Conceited Comedy of George a Greene, the Pinner of Wakefield* (1590) Greene substitutes patriotism for chauvinism. Like *Friar Bacon* it has a rural setting and makes much of local customs. It brings in material derived from folk entertainment, specifically using Robin Hood and his band in the plot. Indeed some aspects of the fighting in the plot are drawn from well-established narratives about the adventures of this folk hero who was a frequent subject of village plays in the sixteenth century, as we have seen above in Chapter 10.

Some of Greene's plays were owned by Philip Henslowe at the Rose Theatre, and there is considerable evidence of continuing success in the following years. According to Henslowe, *Friar Bacon*, for example, was performed nine times in 1593 and 1594 before its printing in 1594, and it was revived and enlarged after 1602.[4] The aspects which follow may account for Greene's popularity.

He was a significant contributor to the development of comedy. Indeed he sticks quite closely to treating the subject of love by means of virtuous heroines who are challenged in various ways by circumstances and yet triumphantly achieve their aims in love. In *Friar Bacon*, once Margaret has made a commitment to Lacy, partly as a result of the intervention of magic, she is threatened because he decides to test her. In fact he has no need to doubt her, but Greene apparently saw a special advantage in showing her as successful in a Griselda-like predicament. Lacy tells her in a letter that he has chosen to marry someone else. Her response is to return the money he has sent her and to prepare to enter a nunnery. The scene ends with her heroic stoicism as she instructs the messenger to

> Say that she joys his fancies be at rest
> And prays that his misfortune may be hers.
>
> (ll. 1525–6)

But in this and other plays the virtuous way to happiness is threatened by a variety of forces, showing that Greene was interested in presenting moral principles in this romantic universe. Not only do the men act dishonourably or cruelly, as does Prince Edward in *Friar Bacon* in pursuit of Margaret; there are also some characters in these plays who are intensely evil, presenting the sort of challenge to the moral order to be found in the morality-play Vice or the Machiavel who inherited some of his function. Characters such as Ateukin in *James IV* and Sacrepant in *Orlando Furioso* carry out destructive attacks upon others. Ateukin urges the murder of Dorothea in order to promote the King's adulterous pursuit of Ida (ll. 1293–1301). Sacrepant is instrumental in deluding Orlando. He arranges that roundelays shall be hung up on trees to show that someone else loves Angelica, and arranges for his servant to assume the disguise of an honest shepherd who will convince Orlando of the truth of what he has read. Sacrepant is very scornful of the 'lunacies of love', claiming that his real interest is war. Some of his language is reminiscent of Senecan emotionalism. Greene's handling of these outstanding villains is, however, concerned with amelioration, and he avoids the traditional morality-play assumption that such characters are supernaturally evil: Ateukin has a change of heart, and Sacrepant dies in a guilty state saying of the trick with the roundelays, 'O that's the sting that pricks my conscience' (l. 1255). As he dies he calls for apocalyptic destruction:

> Heaven, earth, men, beasts and every living thing
> Consume and end with Countie Sacrepant.
>
> (ll. 1291–2)

Both endings are appropriate to Greene's conception of comedy. These are not Vices at the end but humanised characters, and in spite of rhetoric about fate and disaster there is a strong sense of justice.

The other ingredients of Greene's plays show that he had a good sense of theatre and also that he knew how to combine different theatrical effects successfully. It is striking that in common with other early Elizabethan dramatists except Kyd and Marlowe, there have been few attempts to assess his dramatic skills in their own right: his principal role in the critical canon has been as a rather inept forerunner of Shakespeare, especially in comedy. Thus he uses Clowns in *Friar Bacon* and in *Orlando*, where the Clown is dressed up as the heroine for a time. The magic of Bacon is used theatrically to show up two scenes at once:

> But come with me; we'll to my study straight
> And in a glass prospective I will show
> What's done this day in merry Freshingfield.

> (ll. 603–5)

The device of the Brazen Head, monitored by Miles, the incompetent and foolish student, while the exhausted maestro sleeps, speaks prophetically and cryptically, and it plays a significant role in the discrimination between good and bad magic. Apart from the purely moral aspects within the play, this was a serious intellectual problem since the division between magic and science was a matter of contemporary concern and debate: yet Greene puts the problem very neatly into stage terms. The spectacle must have been most entertaining:

> *Here the Head speaks and a lightning flasheth forth, and a hand*
> *appears that breaketh down the Head with a hammer.*

> (l. 1604, s.d.)

It is important that Bacon subsequently renounces all magic, good as well as bad.

There are various manifestations of patriotism in the plays attributed to Greene. Perhaps it is significant that much of his stage work came after the defeat of the Armada in 1588. His interest in country life is idealised and he rarely seems interested in Hogs Norton stereotypes. His heroine Margaret embodies country virtues, and there are worthy huntsmen in *James IV*. In the *Pinner of Wakefield* the extended use of Robin Hood gives scope for a celebration in the ritualised combat of the local Privilege of the Vail Staff whereby none could enter the town carrying his stave on his shoulder.

In addition to the magic discussed above, there is also scope for fairies in the form of Oberon in *James IV*, who provides jigs and onstage entertainment, a commentary which acts as a Chorus, and who intervenes in the plot. Medea, in a long scene in *Alphonsus* (ll. 998–1120), prophesies the success of the heroine, Iphigina, and advises her mother what to do, giving a warning:

> That which the fates appoint must happen so,
> Though heavenly Jove and all the Gods say no.
>
> (ll. 1119–20)

The destruction of the self-admiring Remilia, in *Looking Glass*, is brought about by magic forces acting in accordance with moral objectives. Courted incestuously by her brother, she enters an arbour raised from the ground by the Magi and there is destroyed (ll. 491–549, and especially l. 494, s.d.). These devices add a supernatural dimension which is not simply moralistic, but provides a way of introducing tension and suspense. They widen the emotional range of the art of theatre. Indeed the presentation of stress and psychological disorder is a strong characteristic. It suggests that Greene needed to reflect some of the suffering of his own life in them, even though they are not directly autobiographical.

George Peele (1556–96)

Peele will always be closely associated with Greene because there are marked similarities in his life and in his works. It may be as well to set out differences as strongly as possible before returning to the point made above that they both worked in an environment which must have been stimulating to the writing of plays. Peele came from a more educated background. His father was Clerk of Christ's Hospital and George attended the school there between 1562 and 1570. At Oxford he went first to Broadgates Hall, and then to Christ Church, where he was M.A. in 1579. During his time at Oxford he was recognised as a poet of some distinction, as well as being interested in plays. When he left, he returned to London to write tilt pageants for the Earl of Essex, and street pageants for the Lord Mayor in 1585, 1588 and 1591. This interest in public shows followed the precedent of his father, and it has an effect upon the content of his plays for the court and the public theatres during the 1580s and up to 1596. It is revealed in spectacular stage effects, and in the highly allusive nature of his poetry which often draws directly upon classical and other learned sources.

The intent and subject matter of his poetry point towards patriotic objectives and suggest that Peele wrote in the ambience of the court.

Though his wife brought him money on their marriage in 1580, he was soon without means, and died in poverty, but it appears from his poems that he had reason to hope for patronage from the highest social groups. He celebrated *The Honour of the Garter* (1593), the birthday of Queen Elizabeth in *Anglorum Feriae* (1595), and in *Polyhymnia* (1590), the tilt at which thirteen pairs of named antagonists were engaged, culminating in the change of the Queen's Champion.[5] An interest in matters of chivalry was supported by his exploitation of myths, among which there was the important theme of the supposed inheritance of England and particularly London from Troy (Troy Novant) via the mythical descendants of Brutus, great grandson of Aeneas. He showed his interest in the matter of Troy in *A Tale of Troy*, written while he was still at Oxford, as well as in *The Arraignment of Paris* (printed in 1584). His poetry is distinguished by its easy grace. He does not appear to attempt too much, but writes well within the bounds of propriety and conformity. On the Queen's birthday he tastefully recalls her earlier sufferings in smooth couplets:

> Clio, record how she hath been preserved
> Even in the gates of death and from her youth
> To govern England in the ways or truth;
> Record heaven's goodness to this gracious queen,
> Whose virtue's peer what age hath ever seen?
>
> *Anglorum Feriae* (p. 237)

The socially acceptable subject matter of his poetry, combined with the continuing elegance of much of its expression, separates it markedly from the more disturbed, even pathological substance and the vigorous intensity of much of Greene's work.

Nevertheless, the five surviving plays which can be attributed to him share with those of Greene a remarkable variety of theatrical effects. For example, *The Battle of Alcazar* (written after 1588 and printed 1594) works over some exotic material concerning the attack 'in Barbarie' upon the Moorish kingdom by Sebastian, the King of Portugal, perhaps echoing Greene's *Selimus*; and Peele's *Edward I* (printed 1593), though it begins with a spectacular ceremony to mark the King's return from Jerusalem, presents much romantic intrigue under the historical circumstances of the King's wars with Balliol of Scotland and Lluellen of Wales in a manner not unlike the elaborate love stories in *James IV*. Both dramatists pick up on patriotic themes in their plays and, in accordance with widespread national taste, find the matter of Robin Hood irresistible. Peele's episode involves the somewhat unlikely disguise of (Welsh) Lluellen and his followers:

Ile be maister of misrule, ile be Robin Hood thats one,
cousin Rice thou shalt be little John, and heres Frier David
as fit as a die for Frier Tucke, now my sweet Nel if you
will make up the messe with a good heart for Maid Marian
and doe well with Lluellen under the greene wood trees . . .

(*Edward I*, ll. 1182–7)

The culmination of the device is that King Edward arrives incognito and
confronts Lluellen, still as Robin Hood, so that the traditional motif of
Robin's fight with a real King is invoked, ending in a conventional
stalemate.

The patriotism and the appeal to popular subject matter has some other
outcomes in Peele's plays, but in considering these we should bear in
mind the complexity of his dramatic effects. Probably his two most successful plays are *The Old Wives' Tale* (printed in 1595) and *The Love of
King David and the Fair Bethsabe, with the Tragedy of Absalom* (written 1587
and printed 1599).

The first of these claims to have been acted by the Queen's Majesty's
players, but because it draws upon a range of narratives, some of a type
associated with folk stories, and because it is rather shorter than usual it
seems likely that the play was meant to be performed by boys, perhaps at
court (though the printed text offers no compliment to Elizabeth). The
idea that stories or tales have a magnetic but also enigmatic effect seems to
underlie much that goes on. The framework of the play suggests that
Peele was specially interested in the process of story-telling as it could be
enacted. We have seen in other plays of the period, including *The Spanish
Tragedy*, that to tell a story onstage is highly effective, for it raises questions about the teller as well as the tale. In Peele's play Madge, the Old
Wife, begins to tell a tale to entertain Frolic and Fantastic, two lost pages
to whom she gives food and shelter. As she introduces the story, a certain
confusion on her part is apparent. Describing how a conjurer (magician)
turned dragon had carried off a king's daughter in his mouth, she continues with a remarkable transition:

O, I forget! she (he I would say) turned a proper young
man into a bear in the night, and a man in the day, and
keeps by a cross that parts three several ways; and he made
his lady run mad. – gods me bones, who comes here?

(ll. 125–8)

Whereupon the two brothers of the abducted princess enter her house,
and Frolic remarks, 'Soft, gammer, here some come to tell your tale for
you.' Madge subsides and the dramatisation of the narrative takes over. The
tale lasts all night, and Madge concludes with another enigmatic comment:

When this was done I took a piece of bread and cheese and
came my way; and so shall you have, too, before you go,
to your breakfast.

(ll. 906–8)

Possibly we might fall back upon the critic's resource and say the text
is corrupt, and yet throughout the enactment of the tale there is a sense
that the magic or fantastical is the central concern, and is indeed very
entertaining.

The plot is much too complex to summarise in full. Besides the wicked
magician, the abducted maiden, her two brothers searching for her, and
the old man turned into a nocturnal bear, there is another wandering
knight called Eumenides, and a test of his love for the abducted princess,
as well as two half sisters, one beautiful but proud and the other ugly but
good-hearted, and the demented wife of the man turned into a bear (who
is himself most likely a manifestation of the 'monster bridegroom' folk-
story motif). The interweaving of these fairy-tale characters and fragments
of narrative into a magical story reaches a climax when Eumenides, who
had given his last coppers to pay for the burial of Jack, a good man
neglected by the parish, finally rescues the princess by a magic trick. In
this he is helped by the Ghost of Jack (who never appears as a living
person) on the understanding that Eumenides will share all he gains with
him. To keep his word he must now divide the princess in two, which
he is prepared to do until the Ghost stops him saying that this was the test
of true love. The Ghost then 'leaps down into the ground' (s.d.).

The effect of these interwoven tales is remarkable for surprise, and for
the inexplicable. The plot is much closer to myth than allegory, and it
works, as myths often do, by means of a compelling incredibility. What
happens cannot be explained in purely moral or realistic terms. The framework as well as the pervading sense that the inexplicable events are all of
a piece helps to sustain our attention. Perhaps even more striking, the
play is an indication that the moral terminology of so many of the plays
discussed here is now superseded by dramatic effects which draw upon
quite different ranges of experience.

There remains the potential for performance. There is a good deal of
humour and mockery in the play, especially in Madge's part and in the
behaviour of the pages, but that is not necessarily a reason to suggest, as
some have, that it should be played as a burlesque. No doubt a good deal
might depend upon the ambience of the place of performance. The
sudden appearance of the unexpected and incredible may also seem to
verge on the ludicrous, but this may have been an intentional device by
Peele. While it will not do to be over-pretentious in interpretation, the
unfolding of the magical plot, with suitable attention to stage effects such
as the business around the Well of Life, and the villain Sacrapant's magical

light under the hill, would seem to have given considerable opportunity to the performers. Perhaps the most impressive aspect of the text is that, once launched upon this particular mode of dramatisation, the author sticks to it throughout: there seems little doubt that he is in earnest.

In *David and Bethsabe* (1587), there is a comparable uniformity of texture, but the interpretation of the events in the plot is altogether more palpable. This play shares with *Alcazar* a grim sense of political intrigue and a good deal of ruthless and violent political action and manoeuvring. It is a blending of biblical and classical cultures and touches upon a variety of private and public issues. Deriving from the biblical account in 2 Samuel 10–19 and 1 Kings 1–2, David is presented as a flawed hero, and Peele achieves a powerful sense of the conflicts which his love for Bethsabe produces. The affair is passionate, exciting and understandable, but it is also sinful and outrageous because of David's fatal plot against Uriah, the husband of Bethsabe. It is remarkable that Peele gives due weight to both these aspects. Though the story in itself was well known, it is apparent that the dramatisation by Peele provides a number of distinctive qualities.[6] Not only is the emotional depth brought out by some fine writing, there is also intrigue, death and repentance. David's sensuality is ecstatic, and Peele's verse moves towards a climax with its clever repetitions:

> Bright Bethsabe shall wash, in David's bower,
> In water mixed with purest almond-flower,
> And bathe her beauty in the milk of kids:
> Bright Bethsabe gives earth to my desires;
> Verdure to earth; and to that verdure flowers;
> To flowers sweet odours; and to odours wings
> That carry pleasure to the hearts of kings.
>
> (87–93)

Peele commits himself also to the story of Absalom and his rebellion against David in such a way that the emotional register of the play is much enriched. The death of Absalom, caught by his beautiful hair, and stabbed twice by Joab and then by other soldiers, is spectacularly managed, and his burial poetically envisaged by an unnamed soldier:

> Come, let us take the beauteous rebel down
> And in some ditch, amidst this darksome wood
> Bury his bulk beneath a heap of stones
> Whose stony heart did hunt his father's death.
>
> (1558–61)

David's heroic response to the double blows of the deaths of Bethsabe and Absalom transforms suffering into faith, and in Absalom's apotheosis the poet David is inspired:

Thou shalt behold thy sovereign face to face
With wonder knit in triple unity,
Unity infinite and innumerable.

(1914–16)

This is supported by the development of the admirable character of Solomon in the last Act.

Peele's concept of David may be considered alongside some other major characterisations of the 1580s and early 1590s, notably Faustus, Edward II and Hieronimo. As in Marlowe's characters, the depth of personality is achieved partly by means of Peele's strong poetic techniques, which include eulogy and elegy. This linguistic authority enables him to express a range of emotions. David is given the capacity to love, but also to fall short of the moral standards appropriate to a king. He is not a tragic hero since the programme of the play is redemptive, but in the range and complexity of his emotional life he has tragic potential. It may well be that the moral condemnation of David inherent in the biblical story provided the means by which the private dimension of this great and famous figure could be extended. In this way Peele moves into the rich type of characterisation which brings these aspects into contrast: it is one of the most compelling features of kingship.

There is also a dramatic skill which enables Peele to select key incidents for enactment and to arrange the episodes in the plot so as to set off the character of David. An example of this is the way Peele intercuts scenes in David's palace with the war scenes involving Uriah at Rabbah, and later in the way in which the dangerously proud character of Absalom is built up as he seeks to avenge the rape of his sister Thamar. The three-fold structure of the play, comprising the stories of Bethsabe, Thamar and Absalom, is used to deepen the emotional range. The misdirected sexuality of Thamar's rape reflects upon David's shame in his seizure of Bethsabe, and the egotistic rebellion of Absalom is placed alongside the intense selfishness of David. There are also the dramatic condemnations of David by Nathan (2.1), Sadoc (3.1), and Semei, who stones him (3.3).

Peele's sense of the stage as a vehicle for narrative and for commentary upon it is apparent in this play. It is introduced by a Prologus who is daunted by the task of celebrating Israel's greatest singer, and then opens the first scene by drawing back a curtain to reveal Bethsabe. This theatrical enterprise can be paralleled by the destructive Ate, whose Prologue to *The Arraignment of Paris* foretells the fall of Troy in fateful terms:

and so the twine
That holds old Priam's house, the thread of Troy
Dame Atropos with knife in sunder cuts.

(Prol. 21–3)

The dramatic style of this play is, however, rather different from the others. It was played before the Queen by the Children of the Chapel and is somewhat earlier. The presence of music and dancing, the mellifluous nature of much of the verse, and the culminating compliment whereby Diana, given the onerous task of adjudicating between those claiming the golden apple, awards it to Elizabeth make it more like a masque than a popular play.

The framing devices in *The Battle of Alcazar* (1589) are even more elaborate. The Presenter introduces each Act, usually with emphasis upon the violence to come. His speeches are interwoven with dumb shows involving characters from the play which he explicates. In this play the exotic horrors of the Moors are set off by a moral commentary with allegorical overtones:

> *Enter a banket [banquet] brought in by two Moores. Enter to the bloudie banket Sebastian, Muly Mahamet, the Duke of Avero, and Stukley. To them enter Death and three Furies, one with blood, one with Dead mens heads in dishes, another with Dead mens bones.*
>
> (l. 984, s.d.)

It is worth noting that this kind of representation has affinities with the emblematic aspects of street pageants, though the Lord Mayor's pageants written by Peele were not so awesome or bloodthirsty. It is in episodes like these that we can perceive the most important quality of Peele's dramatic imagination: his ability to exploit language in close association with visual effects.[7]

Popular plays, 1580–95

No one has ever satisfactorily defined what a 'popular' play is, but we may use the term here to indicate that there were a large number of plays which, for the most part, were performed by professional companies before audiences drawn from different social levels. Some of them were also taken to court, and it is often only a brief reference to the expenditure there on some related item of staging or costume which tells us that a play once existed. The indications are that the largest category was romance plays but there were also tragedies, and history or chronicle plays, as well as plays defying any category. Because we can find so many similar aspects in them it seems reasonable to suppose that the authors recognised public demand, and presumably increased it by their response.

Romance plays

Most of these we know anything about are lost: references have survived to twenty-seven titles of apparent romances without text in the years 1570–85.[8] Of the ones that survive up to 1595 there are elements already discussed in Marlowe's *Dido, Queen of Carthage*, Peele's *The Arraignment of Paris*, and Greene's *James IV* which bear some relationship to other plays in the genre. But some of the titles of lost plays, such as *A Knight in the Burning Rock* (1579), and *The Mad Priest of the Sun* (1587), indicate other preoccupations: conspicuous here are chivalry and enchantment.

As examples we shall consider *The Rare Triumphs of Love and Fortune* (1582), *Mucedorus* (1588), and *A Knack to Know a Knave* (1592), but before doing so we should recall two plays of the 1570s to show a slightly earlier taste. As it happens, there are so many similarities between *Clyomon and Clamydes* (1570) and *Common Conditions* (1576) that some scholars have suggested that they are by the same author. Though this view cannot be fully endorsed, it is possible that one was developed from the other in the active circumstances of playmaking. Both are tales of knights who fight battles and have noble ladies as their idealised lovers. Honour is a keynote, but there are passages of extensive lamentation about the (frequent) harshness of Fortune, as well as complex courting scenes. One rhetorical characteristic they share is an elaborate, figurative description of such a thing as a vine or a shipwreck which can then be applied to the real situation in which the characters find themselves. At the end of such a description Clyomon tells Neronis, his beloved:

> thus I wish it were,
> That you would me accept to be, that ship, O Lady faire.
>
> (1081–2)

Further indications of a dramatic taste that was passing away comes in the versification in fourteeners; and in the Vice who in both plays indulges in many stage tricks, including changing his names for different circumstances, generally misleading the principal characters and providing comic and inconsequential upsets. But it seems likely that the interest in duels on stage, the incredible and complicated plots involving disguise and cross-dressing, being kidnapped, impersonation, losing one's beloved or one's parents, being the victim of evil enchantment, and frequently being threatened with death, torture and the loss of honour, were ingredients which would have a long life in the theatre, as the 1997 production of *Cymbeline* by the RSC has suggested. Things usually end up favourably for the good protagonists, but evil people and monsters tend to lose their heads and become stage properties. The mode was mocked by some contemporaries such as Stephen Gosson who, vainly seeking moral values in the theatres, condemns

> adventures of an amorous knight, passing from country to
> country for the love of his lady encountering many a
> terrible monster made out of brown paper.[9]

The sources for these two early plays lie in prose romances such as *Perceforest* which, though printed in 1528, originated in the early four-teenth century, and may well have reflected much older chivalric stories.

In various ways *Love and Fortune*, *Mucedorus* and *A Knack* pick up on the dramatic style and subject matter of the earlier romances, but it is important not to make them into clones – variety within the mode is a characteristic. Their differing stage histories, insofar as we can ascertain them, are enough to keep them somewhat apart, and this may well depend on many individual choices. The performance of *Love and Fortune* at court before the Queen is attested on the 1589 title page, and it can be sustained by a note in the Revels accounts recording the provision of a 'city' and battlements for scenery when it was enacted by the Earl of Derby's Men in December 1582. That these particular players were involved suggests that the play had a popular context, but the text itself shows a very firm organising hand as though exacting structural criteria were in mind.

The dominating issue is a dispute in the presence of Jupiter between Venus and Fortune as to who is the more powerful: this takes up the whole of Act 1 and most of Act 5, and the five-act structure is strictly managed. The details of performance in the text call for special effects. As the plot develops, these two rivals demonstrate their influence on the romance plot which tells the story of the love affair between two humans, Fidelia and Hermione (a gentleman). At the end of Act 2 Fortune is on top and the stage direction reads, '*Strike up Fortune's triumphs with drums and trumpets*' (ll. 554–5). At the end of Act 3 it is the turn of Venus: '*Strike up a noise of Viols, Venus Triumph*' (l. 978: *noise* – band). After Act 4 it looks as though Fortune is going to run away with the contest: '*Fortunes Triumph, sound trumpets, drums, cornets and guns*' (ll. 153–4). It is time for the Gods to intervene again, and the contestants are required at last to work together, relieving the pressure on their human victims. Though this divine framework looks like similar packages in other plays we have discussed, this one is remarkable for the ways in which the conflicting interests are reflected and referred to throughout in the story of the lovers.

The human affairs here have many familiar romance ingredients, such as the banishment of Hermione, the hero, his eventual discovery of his father who is also exiled and living in the woods, practising magic. Fidelia has a cruel brother who is struck dumb, and she herself is banished by her father for loving Hermione, but she fails a rendezvous with him in the wilds, and is fortunately befriended by his father. He protects her and eventually saves her reputation at court by his magic skills. Although the versification is often the old-style fourteeners, there is no doubt that this particular version has strong characteristics of court performance. One of the most striking is the sequence of so-called 'shows' in Act 1. Here, Jupiter asks for examples of the power of Venus, whereupon Mercury and Vulcan comment successively upon dumb shows, with music, about Troilus and Cressida, Alexander, Dido, Pompey and Caesar, and Leander and Hero in a masque-like sequence (ll. 218–45).

There are some comic episodes in *Love and Fortune*, but they are nothing like those developed in *Mucedorus*. This highly successful play is a little later, but it has such a long history of performance and publication that it must have gone through all sorts of changes, especially as it is known to have been given by several different companies at different locations, in and outside London. There is a reference to a performance at Witney, Oxfordshire, as late as 1654, and there were at least fifteen quartos printed between 1598 and 1668. Indeed it may well be that the various surviving printed versions bear valuable witness to the now neglected concept of text as a basis for improvisation and development. The part of Mouse was no doubt conceived for a skilful clown. As the play was performed at an early point by the Queen's Men, it is likely that this role was taken by Richard Tarlton, their famous clown who died in 1588. His first appearance is to introduce himself and the Bear.[10] Having revealed his terror, he has a pratfall exit:

> *As he goes backwards the Bear comes in, and he tumbles over her, and runs away and leaves his bottle* [bundle] *of hay behind him.*
> (2.15, s.d.)

His next appearance is a long conversation with Segasto, the cowardly and unwanted lover of the heroine. Mouse becomes his servant, but the scene is a series of verbal and physical jokes, and once again one suspects that improvisation may have been a factor. Segasto plays the 'straight man':

Segasto   But tell me sirra, where dost thou dwell?
Mouse   Why, do you not know me?
Segasto   Why no, how should I know thee?
Mouse   Why then you know no body, and you know not me.
(1.4.63–8)

There is also a game about his name, with an accompanying action, a variation of 'kiss my arse':

> But do you hear, sir, I am a very young mouse, for my tail
> is scarce grown out yet: look you here else.
>
> (1.4.80–2)

Some of his comedy is the folk nonsense patter:

> a was a little, low, broad, tall, narrow, big, well-favoured
> fellow.
>
> (4.2.55–6)

These devices are very like those used by the Vice, but Mouse's part has the significant difference that, though he is mischievous, he is not an embodiment of evil, and it looks as though the part is a personal vehicle for the virtuosity of an individual actor.

The framework of this play is a dispute between Comedy and Envy. Their costumes are allegorical but they may also suggest the crude extravagance of folk-drama: she is '*joyful, with a garland of bays on her head*', while he has '*his arms naked, besmeared with blood*'. It appears that Envy is identified with tragedy, and is expected to do everything he can to thwart Comedy:

> I'll thunder music shall appal the nymphs
> And make them shiver their clattering strings
> Flying for succour to their dankish caves.
> *Sound drums within and crie, 'stab! stab!'*
>
> (Induction 21–3)

But at the end Comedy triumphs, her success depending upon another story of misfortunes and true love. Mucedorus, the hero, leaves home secretly for love of Amadine and he goes through disguises as a shepherd, a hermit, and finally a servant to his beloved. At this point, she is enslaved by Bremo, a wild man who, however, is unable to harm her chastity in spite of his cannibal inclinations. The plot turns on the audience's knowing all about the disguises, but as they are kept from most of the characters, including Amadine, there is always the potential of recognition and revelation until the final reconciliation is reached. One of the factors here is a loss of social status, and it would be interesting to know whether Mucedorus changed his speech with his costumes. Disguise becomes a main thread of the entertainment, taking over from credibility. We do not know whether the audience cheered when true identities were at length revealed, but it must all have been fun. The entertainment was enhanced by plenty of music, including a lyric by the wild man, with a refrain from Amadine, his captive, undercutting it – 'You may, for who but you'.

Though there are distinct romance elements in *A Knack to Know a Knave*, there is no framing device and the play has a strong morality flavour. This is somewhat surprising since the play is not traceable until performances by Strange's Men at the Rose in 1592. Two years later its title page advertises that it has been played sundry times by Edward Alleyn and it includes Will 'Kemps applauded merrimentes'. The moral pace is determined by Honesty, who seeks, with Dunston's help, to show King Edgar the faults of many of his subjects. One of these is a Cutbert Cutpurse, a Conycatcher. While this name can be traced as far back as Fulwell's *Like Will to Like*, the role of Conycatcher would probably have been suggested by Greene's pamphlets of 1590–92.

That the inspiration is traditional is clear from the death of the Bailiff. As he is making a speech explaining how he takes bribes to temper justice he sees a vision of death. Like Faustus he is unable to repent because of his hard heart (l. 269) and he realises he is damned: whereupon – *Enter Deuil, and carie him away* (l. 323, s.d.). But the author could not resist the current pressure for romance: he adopts the wooing by proxy like that found in Greene's *Friar Bacon and Friar Bungay*. Once again the proxy, here Ethenwald, decides to serve himself first, deceiving the King, his master. His speech is in the newer blank verse idiom:

> . . . Ile tel the king the maid is fair
> Of nut browne cullour, comelie and fair spoken,
> Worthie companion to an Earle or so:
> But not a bride for Edgar, England's King,
> This will alay the strong effects in loue.
>
> (ll. 919–23)

For the purpose of trapping the Conycatcher the King himself adopts a disguise, but he is quick to discard it when the fraud is exposed (l. 881). However, he is on the receiving end of deception when Alfrida, now married to Ethenwald, disguises herself as a kitchen maid, and the kitchen maid as herself to woo Edgar. He refuses to pardon Ethenwald in spite of Dunston's entreaties and his own rectitude in other matters, but the saintly bishop uses his power with the Devil to persuade Edgar of Ethenwald's contrition. This episode does not fit the chivalric mode of the other romance plays, and yet the manipulation of the incredible for an acceptably optimistic end is quite in line with the others. Honesty, however, strikes a discordant note, for his treatment of the social malefactors is severe. Walter, the erring farmer, is

> To be caried to a corne field, and there haue your legs and
> hands cut off, because you loued corn so wel, and there
> rest til the crowes pick out thine eies.
>
> (ll. 1851–3)

He offers dire warnings to the audience, suggesting that the author was
particularly incensed about social evils. His objectives are quite similar to
those of Greene and Lodge in *A Looking Glass for London.*

The individual exploitation of the romance elements in these plays
suggests that they were widespread and acknowledged as good theatrical
entertainment. Like modern soaps, they make the best of the market for
economic as much as for dramatic reasons, and, like the soaps, they
operate on the basis of skilled presentation, using extreme predicaments,
standard characters and a few star turns. However, the element of fantasy
seems much more developed, especially in respect of popular magic and
the supernatural.

Tragedies and histories

The popular plays used both these terms, but definition is a tricky matter.
The contrast between *The Lamentable and True Tragedie of M. Arden of
Faversham in Kent* (written after 1587 and printed in 1592) and *The True
Chronicle Historie of King Leir and his Three Daughters* (acted before 1594,
and printed in 1605) is indicative. Both are 'true': the former being based
upon a documented scandal of 1551 found in Holinshed's *Chronicles*, and
the latter a part of the history of the ancient Kings of Britain which was
still held to be authentic and formed part of the traditional Troy Novaunt
narrative.[11] But *Arden of Faversham* turns into death and disaster while
King Leir goes much nearer to tragicomedy: its events are serious and
heart-rending but it results in reconciliation and a happy ending with no
deaths among the principals.

The main thrust of *King Leir* is to make the most of the emotional
contrast between the two cruel daughters, Gonorill and Ragan, and the
virtuous Cordella. The cruelty of the first two sends Leir on the run, and
his own acts lead Cordella to poverty and suffering. There is however a
concern to see her happily married, this being the chief purpose of the
initial love-test. Leir is supported in his misery and exposure by Perillus,
an elderly courtier, and much is made of their adventures together. Ragan
seeks to have them murdered, but the intervention of heaven in the form
of thunder and lightning stirs the would-be murderer's conscience and
they escape (sc. 19): it superimposes a sense of an ordered and beneficent
universe. In disguise they cross to France in search of Cordella, an event

which gives an opportunity for a mariners scene common in romances (sc. 23).

Disguise itself also supports the romance atmosphere. Perhaps this is one of the ways that the play is kept within the limits of tragicomedy, for there is a notable scene in which Leir and Perillus in disguise encounter Cordella and her husband, also in disguise. The latter gradually recognise the former who are in extremes of suffering, and they are able to applaud the loyalty of Perillus offering his blood to revive his master. When Cordella, still unrecognised by Leir and Perillus, provides food and drink, Perillus offers his own doublet in recompense (l. 2212, s.d.). The dramatic effect of the disguises is taken further:

Leir	Ah, who would think such kindnes should remayne
	Among such strange and unacquainted men:
	And that such hate should harbour in the brest
	Of those which have occasion to be best?
Cordella	Ah, good father, tell to me thy griefe,
	Ile sorrow with thee, if not adde reliefe.
Leir	Ah, good young daughter, I may call thee so;
	For thou art like a daughter I did owe. *own*
Cordella	Do you not owe her still? what, is she dead?
Leir	No, God forbid.

(ll. 2214–23)

The irony in Leir's words turns upon the audience's being fully aware of the identities of all four participants, but it is not a tragic one even though there are intense emotions here. Full recognition is implied and anticipated, and when this takes place later in the scene the playwright turns his back upon disaster; things get progressively better. Thus the double disguise is an important part of audience management: it allows intense emotions but directs them towards a happier solution.

There is another significant contribution to the tragicomedy in the comic elements. The invasion of Britain by Cordella and her French troops is successful chiefly because the British soldiers at Dover would rather be in the alehouse enjoying ale and rashers of bacon. But this minor comic episode is strengthened by the ambiguous presence of Mumford, a French courtier. On his first appearance he volunteers to accompany the King of Gallia on the latter's quest to marry one of Leir's daughters, and his playfulness will lighten their mission incognito (another disguise here): 'Thy pleasant company will make the way seem short' (l. 390). Using the names Will and Jack, they encounter the dispossessed Cordella who is about to seek her living as a sempstress (ll. 619–20). Hearing this Mumford comments:

O brave! God willing, thou shalt have my custom,
By sweet St Denis, here I sadly swear   *earnestly*
For all the shirts and night-gear that I weare.

(ll. 621–3)

His jokes about wenching re-appear later in the play and he accompanies Gallia and Cordella in their disguise '*like Country folke*' (l. 2091, s.d.). At the invasion he is appointed the general and promises to 'gall' the British (ll. 2417–27). He personally overwhelms the besotted Watch, and is thanked by Leir (l. 2656). The role is an interesting adaptation of fool techniques and would give scope to a competent actor.

Arden of Faversham (1591) has little room for comedy. It is a single-minded, almost claustrophobic dramatisation in a middle-class setting of a crime involving both violent passion and socio-economic matters of property and status. There is no doubting the vehemence of Alice Arden's desire for Mosbie, and although he returns her feelings at times he is enough of a social upstart to be aware of the financial advantages of marrying her once her husband is ultimately disposed of. The tension in the play is built up because these lovers quarrel and reproach one another from time to time, but there are other significant elements. Arden himself, a prosperous farmer with influential friends, perceives much of what his wife is doing, but he is also involved in avaricious acquisition of land to the great discomfort of those living on it. When challenged by Reede, who is dispossessed, Arden is pitiless (xiii.18–27), and this occurs at a point in the play when the private conspiracy against him initiated by Alice and Mosbie is well advanced. It is a significant balancing of sympathy for and against him, and it makes for a grim impression of the playwright's viewpoint.

A further increase of tension is achieved by the assassins hired by Alice and Mosbie. Shakebag and Black Will are desperate criminals who are eager to kill for money. Socially, they are examples of the Elizabethan underworld which gave much anxiety to local and national authorities. But for a variety of reasons they are unsuccessful and all their schemes are thwarted. When they finally kill Arden onstage it is a desperately violent and clumsy business in which Alice herself also stabs him. The author's skill in creating tension is then turned to the process of detection, as Franklin, Arden's friend and confidant, investigates and exposes the murderers. Violent punishments are envisaged.

The writer has Providence constantly in mind and there is a series of strong moral impulses as the failings of most of the characters are revealed; again the author is relentless. In his remarks on tragedy he claims rather ingenuously to use no art, when in fact the play is full of skilful work, as we have seen. He says:

> Gentlemen, we hope you'll pardon this naked
>   tragedy,
> Wherein no filed points are foisted in,
> To make it gracious to the ear or eye;
> For simple truth is gracious enough
> And no other points of glozing stuff.　　　　　　　*specious*
>   (Epil. 14–18)

The play succeeds by sticking to such limited objectives and yet it is a subtle presentation of destruction in private and public affairs. At times it is melodramatic in its violent language and actions, and yet such extremes seem to contribute much to the grim, tragic effect. There is also a good deal of attention to the inner struggles and conflicting emotions of the principal characters, especially Mosbie, Alice and Arden himself. But it is not Arden's marital tragedy alone: the play brilliantly points out the failures of contemporary society.

The last three histories to be discussed here show much less interest in romance material than most of those considered earlier: together they stand for a more restricted and perhaps purposeful concentration on actual historical events, with indications of how these should be interpreted. In this way they are developments rather of the thematically directed morality play than of the romances. Such purposes may be linked to some contemporary issues, but there is also a strongly theatrical aspect to them, and this can be shown to operate differently in each context. *The Famous Victories of Henry V* (?1583, printed 1598) has a narrow agenda and it is thought that the extant text may be rather abbreviated, perhaps cut for touring. It concentrates very closely on the popular view of Henry himself which was derived from the chroniclers. Thus he appears in the first half as an irresponsible villain and petty thief, with a well-developed group of discreditable followers, including Ned and Oldcastle, attacking the established representatives of prosperity and justice. The best that can be said for him is that he is energetic and bold, and these qualities re-appear after his conversion to virtue and the values of kingship at his accession. In his reformed role he promotes the Lord Chief Justice, whom he had struck in open court, to the role of Protector while he is to be away on the French campaign. He now exposes, somewhat chauvinistically, the vanity of the French courtiers, and he scores a strong personal triumph in his dominance over the French king.

Theatrically there is a good deal of word-play, and the Dolphin's clumsy insult over the tennis balls is much extended by Henry as his superiority develops. The play has an extensive underclass, including Dericke, the clown, who was played by Tarlton. After Prince Henry is committed to prison, Dericke and John Cobbler play an imitation:

Dericke	Faith John, Ile tel thee what, thou shalt be my
	Lord Chiefe Justice, and thou shalt sit in the chaire,
	And Ile be the young prince, and hit thee a boxe on the eare,
	And then thou shalt say 'to teach you what prerogatives
	Mean, I commit you to the Fleete.'
John	Come on, Ile be your judge,
	But thou shalt not hit me hard.

(386–92)

Later he proposes to come and live with Cobbler, but his claim that he will not eat much seems to be a self-directed visual joke:

> I am none of those great slouching fellowes that devoure
> these great peeces of beefe and brewes [meat broth]; alass a
> trifle serves me.

(427–9)

The Troublesome Raigne of King John (acted 1587, printed 1591) has an ancestry in anti-papal propaganda, dramatic and non-dramatic, including Bale's *King Johan*. Its dramatic texture is altogether more complex than *The Famous Victories* in terms of language as well as well-developed dramatic and indeed dynamic situations. There is plenty of historical detail, which is arranged to cover the loyalty of Falconbridge, illegitimate son of Richard I, to King John in the face of repeated challenges from France over the inheritance of young Prince Arthur, John's nephew. Between them, John and Falconbridge sustain a patriotic line against the French and against the papacy, including John's excommunication over Langton. Part One ends with John welcoming the news that Arthur has escaped death, but Part Two starts by referring to John's fatal tragedy. The narrative continues with the death of Arthur and the invasion of England by King Louis, who is largely supported by the English barony. It is here that the political sophistication is best seen. Pandulphus, the papal legate, supports John in return for his submission to Rome and curses the rebel nobles. In the battle, Meloun, a leading French warrior, is fatally wounded, and he reveals that if Louis were to win he would turn against his English allies. His powerful speech turns the campaign: 'The smiles of Fraunce shade in the frownes of death' (2.755). John's fortunes recover slightly and the two Kings reach an accommodation. The anti-papal programme climaxes with John's death, as he is poisoned by a monk of Swinstead Abbey who has been forgiven in advance for his crime by the hierarchy, as in Bale's *King Johan*.

The texture of the play depends upon the criss-crossing of interests and the shifting moods of the characters. John, in great difficulty over the confederation of the nobles at Bury St Edmunds, speaks tragically and reveals with striking imagery and rhetoric the sense of overwhelming odds. His thought develops from a kind of *sententia*:

> Why so it must be: one hower of content
> Matcht with a month of passionate effects.   *suffering*
> Why shines the Sunne to favour this consort?
> Why doo the windes not breake their brazen gates,
> And scatter all these perjurd complices,
> With all their counsells and their damned drifts?
> But see the welkin rolleth gently on,
> Theres not a lowring to frowne on them;
> The heaven, the earth, the sunne, the moone and all
> Conspire with those confederates my decay.
>
> (2.197–206)

The dramatist has a good eye for a dramatic scene. As death approaches, John reviews his crimes and despairs of forgiveness, but in line with Tudor propaganda and, in imitation of King David, he prophesies great offspring 'Whose armes shall reach unto the gates of Rome' (2.1085).[12] As the now compliant nobles are persuaded to submit, they are brought in by Prince Henry while the King is succumbing to the effect of the poison. Falconbridge points up the action:

> O piercing sight, he fumbleth in the mouth,
> His speech doth faile: lift up yourself my Lord,
> And see the Prince to comfort you in death.
>
> (2.1103–5)

The Prince then presents the lords in submission before John dies.

Thomas Lodge's *The Wounds of Civil War* (before 1589, printed 1594) is another well-organised historical play, based upon the rivalry of Marius and Sulla using material from Appian and Plutarch. The play shows classical restraint in its pursuit of its main message, which is to portray the horrific consequences of tyranny and civil war. The character of Marius is presented strongly, especially his crabbed and eccentric personality, and he is given a bravura soliloquy in which he laments his misfortune as, isolated in the Numidian mountains, he feeds on roots:

> Thou that hast walk'd with troops of flocking friends
> Now wand'rest 'midst the labyrinth of woes,
> Thy best repast with many sighing ends,
> And none but fortune all these mischiefs knows.
>
> (3.4.1–4)

This develops into a dialogue with Echo, who copies his last syllables to make a prophecy, a popular stage device at the time:

Sweet nymph draw near, thou kind and gentle Echo.	*Echo.*
What help to ese my weary pain have I?	*I*
What comfort in distress to calm my griefs?	*griefs*
Sweet nymph, these griefs are grown before	
I thought so.	*I thought so*
Thus Marius lives disdain'd of all the gods,	*O ods*
With deep despair late overtaken wholly.	*O ly*
	(3.4.39–44)

The influence of *Tamburlaine* appears in Sulla's entry '*in his chair triumphant of gold, drawn by four Moors before the chariot*' (3.3.1, s.d.), but the main effect is to portray the destructive effect of civil war in which survival cannot be guaranteed even to the most doggedly persistent. The extremities of suffering which civil war induced may have been part of the theatrical attraction of this subject: it seems to fit in with the preoccupation with violence which persisted in popular drama, and which may not have been gratuitous so much as a means of coming to terms with grim aspects of sixteenth-century public life.

The achievements of the popular stage in the 1580s and early 1590s are remarkable. We can perceive that there may have been a measure of uniformity in what was offered to audiences, and yet it was a period of very rapid development and cross-influences as more and more people sought their livelihood from theatrical ventures. The opening of Burbage's Theatre in 1576 may have drawn upon many features of the earlier drama, but it brought in a new and expandable theatrical environment which the playwrights discussed in this chapter were able to develop. The many individual decisions about stage presentation embodied in the surviving texts of their plays, together with such records that have come down to us, also show that there were many others who contributed.

Notes

1. A.B. Grosart (ed.) *The Life and Complete Works in Prose and Verse of Robert Greene*, 15 vols (London, 1881–6), 12.144.

2. References for six of the plays discussed here are to J. Churton Collins (ed.) *The Plays and Poems of Robert Greene*, 2 vols (Oxford, 1905). For *Selimus* see the edition by W. Bang, Malone Society Reprint (Oxford, 1908).

3. Orlando was played by Edward Alleyn: his written part survives at Dulwich College: see *ES* 3.329.

4. See D. Selzer (ed.) *Friar Bacon and Friar Bungay* (London, 1963), p. x.

5. References are to C.T. Prouty (ed.) *The Life and Works of George Peele, 3 vols* (New Haven, 1952–70). In this edition the plays have through line numbering.

6. For a detailed discussion of Peele's selection from the sources in 2 Samuel 10–19 and 1 Kings 1–2 see R.H. Blackburn, *Biblical Drama under the Tudors* (The Hague, 1971), pp. 171–6.

7. Perhaps one of Peele's most spectacular effects is the suit of glass provided for Edward I which can be traced in Henslowe's *Diary* in 1598 (Prouty 2.7).

8. See Harbage for the titles in these years; for details of editions used here, see Bibliography.

9. From *Plays Confuted in Five Actions*, quoted *ES* 4.215. Ben Jonson was still laughing at such plays in *The Magnetick Lady* (1632) through the critique of Mr Damplay; see I Chorus, 15–24.

10. Bears turn up commonly, perhaps because they were popular for their dancing: they could be borrowed from the bear-baiting pits near the theatres. Sometimes, however, actors wore skins instead.

11. See Geoffrey of Monmouth, *The History of the Kings of Britain* (1136) ed. and trans. Lewis Thorpe (Harmondsworth, 1966), pp. 81–6.

12. There are strong iconographical links between King David and Henry VIII; see John N. King, *Tudor Royal Iconography* (Princeton, 1989), figs 20, 21.

Chapter 14
Epilogue

> As Plautus and Seneca are accounted best for comedy and
> tragedy among the Latins; so Shakespeare among the
> English is the most excellent in both kinds for the stage.

Francis Meres was already in 1598 trumpeting the arrival of Shakespeare.[1]
The eulogy continued through Ben Jonson who, though he said, 'Shakespeare was not of an age but for all time,'[2] was temperate in his appreciation. Dryden moved things up a gear, desiring to increase Shakespeare's
reputation at the expense of Jonson and to bring his achievement into line
with the emphatic principles of the new civilisation of the Restoration. In
this he was followed by Dr Johnson.[3] To some extent this was increased
by neoclassical criticism, which sought to fortify the critique of genre,
especially comedy and tragedy.[4] In this book we have tried to move
against the tide which is still current today and to see the work of the
many makers of early plays in its richness and variety. Fortunately, we are
not alone in this enterprise. Work carried out in the past twenty-five
years has done much to recognise the nature and importance of the drama
before 1590 and new perspectives have emerged.

The art of the early theatre has been explored by editors concentrating
upon establishing the texts themselves in terms of the physical properties of
manuscripts and early printed books. This work has been complemented
by implications of modern critical theory, which has led to a discussion of
the nature of text and its instabilities, together with its relationship to author
and reader or audience. Through the study of iconography the visual
aspects of early plays have become much clearer. Modern live performance
of many medieval plays has recreated their dynamics, and shown how the
place and circumstances of performance contribute to the total experience
of a play. Much can be done, whether or not one specifically pursues an
accurate historical reconstruction. Such performances have reminded us
that the text is by no means all and they urge that a proper understanding
and enjoyment of these plays will follow attempts to explore them by
active participation. The word and the visual image interact, and part of
what we have to rediscover is how they complement one another.

During recent years with the changes in the contexts of literary study, the relationship between history and theatre has come into question and it has affected the appreciation of the early drama. The study of the records of drama has done much to clarify where and when plays were performed, and there also arise some implications from when and where they were not performed. In this process the astonishing variety and quantity of dramatic activities have become more apparent. Among these, many paradramatic events are far from a literary text or even an actor's script and they rely principally for their effect and significance on participation and occasion, as in royal entries or parish drama. As the complexity of historical contexts has unfolded, we need to notice that it is no longer a matter of history but of histories. The narrative of the practical exploration of theatrical space, insofar as we can compose one, has to be considered alongside that of the development of dramatic language, including both prose and verse forms. Such narratives can no longer be progressivist even though some events like the opening of Burbage's Theatre are landmarks.

The interrelationship between theatre and history is being re-interpreted through the perception that plays had a special role in the negotiation of power.[5] In a period of enormous change, even revolution, Renaissance and Reformation transformed personal and social life. Such changes gave opportunities for power as well as taking them away. Plays like Heywood's *Wether* and Bale's *King Johan* are not just commentaries but contributions to a perceived need to halt or promote change by influencing those in authority. In these and other plays it is now evident that there are very many minute but significant details which bear upon the political contexts and the purpose of playmaking. Even the sixteenth-century presentations of the mystery cycles were occasions for political manipulation. Part of the literary task is to try to evaluate how far text and performance of the early plays were about sustaining a political/religious hegemony and how far they were the expression of aspiring discontent expressed directly or by implication.[6] To do this it is necessary to look steadfastly and closely at the surviving texts whatever the limitations surrounding them.

Given the vigour and interest of the historical enquiry in these differing forms, it remains an important task to describe accurately the texts that have survived so that the relationship with historical context may be clearer. There is also a need, which we have tried to address, for the aesthetics of the early drama to be revisited. This may be in terms of the critical thinking active in those times, which in itself went through significant changes; but the heart of the matter is how far the dramatic effects can be described and appreciated. This has to do with some traditional categories of criticism including structure, pace and characterisation. It has been one of our preoccupations to show that realism and verisimilitude, indeed the whole question of probability, was not of the highest emphasis in the early drama. Instead, such things as the creation of images, visual and verbal, which comprise theatrical imagery, together with the dynamics of change within a dramatic plot, had the priority. We need to look more and more at the audience, as no doubt the compilers and actors did, for it is the audience who had to be moved, convinced and entertained. To describe a medieval or Elizabethan audience is very difficult indeed, but we can paradoxically see them mirrored in the plays themselves and in the expectations which the playmakers had of how their audiences might react and what they might appreciate. When the metatheatrical Vice in *Cambises* says, 'How like ye now, my maisters? Doth not this gear cotton?' (l. 694, *this affair prosper*) he speaks better than he knows: in making us think about theatrical illusion he draws us into it. Does the Vice or the audience have the 'maistry'?

Notes

1. *Palladis Tamia, ES* 4.246. Cf. the praise given by Will Kempe speaking to Richard Burbage in the anonymous *Second Part of the Return from Parnassus* (1601): 'Few of the university men pen plays well, they smell too much of that writer Ovid and that writer Metamorphosis (*sic*), and talk too much of Proserpina and Jupiter. Why here's our fellow Shakespeare puts them all down', in J.B. Leishman (ed.) *The Three Parnassus Plays* (London, 1949), 4.3.1766–70.

2. Dedicatory verse prefixed to Shakespeare's First Folio, 1623.

3. I. Donaldson, *Jonson's Magic Houses* (Oxford, 1997), pp. 182–7.

4. Simon Shepherd rightly notices that the mixed form of most Elizabethan plays has been much denigrated and its quality undervalued, *Marlowe and the Politics of Elizabethan Theatre* (Brighton, 1986), p. 71.

5. Stephen Greenblatt's comment is symptomatic: 'Marlowe's protagonists rebel against orthodoxy, but they do not do so just as they please; their acts of negation not only conjure up the order they would destroy but seem at times to be themselves conjured up by that very order', *Renaissance Self-fashioning: From More to Shakespeare* (Chicago, 1980), p. 197.

6. Cf. 'To British historicist critics in the Eighties, Renaissance texts were sites of conflict, not containment', R. Wilson, 'Introduction: Historicising New Historicism', in R. Wilson and R. Dutton (eds) *New Historicism and Renaissance Drama* (London, 1992), p. 13.

Chronology

DATE	PLAYS	OTHER WORKS	HISTORICAL/CULTURAL EVENTS
965–75	*Quem Quaeritis* (Winchester)		Edgar (959–75)
12 cent.	*Le Mystère d'Adam* (*c.* 1160)	*Ancrene Riwle*	Murder of Becket (1170)
		Laʒamon, *Brut*	
		Winchester Bible	
		Geoffrey of Monmouth, *History* (1136)	
		Comestor, *Historia Scholastica* (1155–58)	
		Benediktbeuern Passion (*c.* 1180)	
13 cent.	*La Seinte Resureccion* (*c.* 1275)		Magna Carta (1215)
			Marco Polo in China (1275)
14 cent.	*Interludium de Clerico et Puella*	*Cursor Mundi*	Corpus Christi established (1311)
		Dante, *Divina Commedia*	
		Holkham Bible Picture Book (1326–31)	
c. 1350	*The Pride of Life*	Boccaccio, *Decameron* (*c.* 1353)	Edward III (1327–77)
		Sir Gawain and the Green Knight (*c.* 1360)	Hundred Years War (1338–1453)
			Black Death (1348)

DATE	PLAYS	OTHER WORKS	HISTORICAL/CULTURAL EVENTS
c. 1375	Cornish *Ordinalia*		
Before 1376	*York Cycle*		
Before 1377	*Beverley Plays* *Chester Cycle*		
1377	*Coronation of Richard II*	Langland, *Piers Plowman*	Richard II (1377–99)
Before 1378	*York Pater Noster Play* (lost)	Chaucer, *Canterbury Tales* (1387–1400) Gower, *Confessio Amantis* (1390)	Peasants' Revolt (1381) Wyclif d. (1384)
Before 1392	*Conventry Plays*		Chaucer d. (1400)
1405–25	*Shrewsbury Fragments* *Castle of Perseverance*	*Tretise of Miraclis Pleyinge* (1405–10)	Henry IV (1399–1413)
Before 1400	*Abraham and Isaac* (Brome)		
Before 1410	*Towneley Plays*	Lydgate *Troy Book* (*c.* 1412–20)	
1415	*Entry of Henry V*		Henry V (1413–22) Battle of Agincourt
Before 1426	*Newcastle Plays*		Henry VI (1422–61)
c. 1430	Lydgate, *Mummings*		
1432	*Entry of Henry VI*	*The Book of Margery Kempe* (1438) *Paston Letters* (1440–86)	
c. 1445	*Abraham and Isaac* (Dublin) *Entry of Margaret of Anjou*	Gréban, *Passion* (1452)	Fall of Constantinople (1453) Wars of the Roses begin (1455)
c. 1460	*Wisdom*	*Biblia Pauperum*	
1460–1500	*N Town Cycle*		

DATE	PLAYS	OTHER WORKS	HISTORICAL/CULTURAL EVENTS
1461–1500	*Play of the Sacrament* (Croxton)		Edward VI (1461–83)
1465–70	*Mankind*	Malory, *Morte D'Arthur* (1469–70)	Caxton printing at Westminster (1476)
		Seneca printed, 1474	
1475	*Robin Hood* (frag.)		
1480–1520	*Conversion of St Paul*	Caxton, *Golden Legend* (*c.* 1483)	Richard III (1483–85)
	Killing of the Children	Brant, *Ship of Fools* (1494)	Columbus' voyages (1492–1504)
	Mary Magdalene (Digby MSS)		Henry VII (1485–1509)
	Beunans Meriasek		
c. 1495	Medwall, *I & II Nature*		Bosch, *Temptation of St Antony*
			Leonardo, *Last Supper*
c. 1497	Medwall, *I & II Fulgens and Lucres*		Cabot reaches Canada
			Da Gama rounds Good Hope
1502	*Receyt of the Ladie Katherine*	Sophocles printed	Leonardo, *Last Supper* (1503)
			Michelangelo, *David* (1504)
c. 1508	*The World and the Child*	Erasmus, *The Praise of Folly* (1509)	Michelangelo begins Sistine Chapel
			Henry VIII (1509–47)
1510–16	*Everyman* printed		
c. 1513	*Hickscorner*	Machiavelli, *Il Principe*	Flodden
	Youth	More, *Utopia* (1516)	
1517	Rastell, *Four Elements*		Luther, *95 Theses*
c. 1519	Skelton, *Magnyfycence*	Erasmus, *Colloquies* (1519)	Field of the Cloth of Gold (1520)
		Skelton, *Speke, Parrot* (1521)	Magellan rounds Cape Horn

DATE	PLAYS	OTHER WORKS	HISTORICAL/CULTURAL EVENTS
1522	*Entry of Charles V into London*		
1523	Rastell, *Calisto and Melebea*; *Gentleness and Nobility*	Tyndale, *New Testament* (1525)	Titian, *Bacchus and Ariadne*
Before 1528	John Heywood, *Witty and Witless*; *The Pardoner and the Friar*		
1528–33	John Heywood, *The Four PP*; *Johan Johan*; *The Play of the Weather*; *A Play of Love*		Royal divorce begins (1528)
1530	*Terens in Englysh*	Rabelais, *Pantagruel* (1531) Elyot, *Governor* (1531) Erasmus, *Terence* (1532)	Death of Wolsey
1533	*Coronation of Anne Boleyn*		Act of Supremacy (1534)
1535	*Temperance and Humility*	Coverdale *Bible*	Execution of More and Fisher Holbein, *Henry VIII*
1536–38	Bale, *Three Laws*; *God's Promises*; *The Temptation of Our Lord*; *John Baptist's Preaching*; *I & II King Johan*		Pilgrimage of Grace (1536–37) Dissolution of monasteries begins (1536) Tyndale burned (1536) Erasmus d. (1536)
1537	*Albion Knight* *Thersites*		Michelangelo, *Last Judgement*
1539	*Godly Queen Hester* Redford, *Wit and Science*		Six Articles

DATE	PLAYS	OTHER WORKS	HISTORICAL/CULTURAL EVENTS
1540	Lindsay, *Ane Satire of the Thrie Estaitis* (first version)		Fall of Thomas Cromwell
1541	Buchanan, *Baptistes sive Calumnia*		
1542	*Four Cardinal Virtues*	Hall, *Chronicles*	Inquisition established Scots defeated at Solway Moss
1544	Christopherson, *Jepthes*		
1545	*Resurrection of Our Lord*		Council of Trent Luther d. (1546)
1547	*Coronation of Edward VI* *Impatient Poverty* Grimald, *Archipropheta*	Bale, *Summarium* (1548) Cranmer, *Book of Common Prayer* (1549 and 1552)	Edward VI (1547–53) Ket's rebellion (1549)
1550	*Nice Wanton* *Love Feigned and Unfeigned* *Somebody, Avarice and Minister* Wever, *Lusty Juventus*	Vasari, *Lives of the Artists*	
1552	Lindsay, *Ane Satire of the Thrie Estaitis* (at Cupar) Udall, *Ralph Roister Doister*		
1553	*Coronation of Mary* W.S., *Gammer Gurton's Needle* Udall?, *Republica*		Mary (1553–58)
1554	*Jacob and Esau* *Wealth and Health*		Wyatt's rebellion Mary marries Philip II

DATE	PLAYS	OTHER WORKS	HISTORICAL/CULTURAL EVENTS
1555	*Jack Juggler*		
1556	Foxe, *Christus Triumphans*	Baldwin, *Mirror for Magistrates* Grafton, *Chronicle* Tottel, *Songs and Sonnets* (1557)	Cranmer executed Charles V abdicates
1558	*Coronation of Elizabeth I* Lumley, *Iphigenia in Aulis* L. Wager, *Life and Repentance of Mary Magdalene*		French take Calais Elizabeth I (1558–1603)
1559	Phillip, *Patient and Meek; Grissil* Jasper Heywood, *Troas* (trans.) W. Wager, *The Longer Thou Livest the More Fool Thou Art*		Act of Uniformity
1560	*Tom Tyler and his Wife* *Robin Hood* Jasper Heywood, *Thyestes* (trans.) Ingelend, *The Disobedient Child* W. Wager, *Enough is as Good as a Feast*		
1561	*The Pedlar's Prophecy* Preston, *Cambises* Jasper Heywood, *Hercules Furens* (trans.)	Castiglione, *Courtier* (trans.) Calvin, *Institutes* (trans.)	
1562	Norton and Sackville, *Gorboduc*		
1563	Neville, *Oedipus* (trans.)	Foxe, *Acts and Monuments*	39 Articles

DATE	PLAYS	OTHER WORKS	HISTORICAL/CULTURAL EVENTS
1564	R.B., *Apius and Virginia*		Elizabeth I visits Cambridge
			Michelangelo d.
			Marlowe b.
			Shakespeare b.
1565	*King Darius*	Golding, *Metamorphoses* (trans.)	
	Edwards, *Damon and Pithias*	Stow, *Chronicles*	
	W. Wager?, *The Cruel Debtor*		
1566	Gascoigne, *Supposes* (trans.)		Elizabeth I visits Oxford
	Wilmot, *Gismond of Salerne*		Royal Exchange founded
	Gascoigne & Kinwelmershe, *Jocasta* (trans.)		
	Nuce, *Octavia* (trans.)		
	Studley, *Agamemnon* (trans.); *Hercules Oetaeus* (trans.); *Medea* (trans.)		
1567	Pickering, *Horestes*		Red Lion theatre
	W. Wager?, *The Trial of Treasure*		
	Studley, *Hippolytus* (trans.)		
1568	*The Marriage of Wit and Science*		Mary, Queen of Scots flees to England
	Fulwell, *Like Will to Like*		
	Cheke, *Free-Will* (trans.)		
1569	Garter, *Susanna*		Last performance of York Cycle
			Palestrina *Motets*

DATE	PLAYS	OTHER WORKS	HISTORICAL/CULTURAL EVENTS
1570	*Misogonus* *Clyomon and Clamydes* *Juli and Julian*	Ascham, *Schoolmaster*	Elizabeth excommunicated
1571	*New Custom*		Ridolphi plot Battle of Lepanto
1572	Woodes, *The Conflict of Conscience*		Massacre of St Bartholomew Statute against vagabonds
1574			Players restricted in London
1575	*Processus Satanae* Gascoigne, *Glass of Government*; *Princely Pleasures at Kenilworth* Golding, *Abraham's Sacrifice* (trans.)		Last performance of Chester Cycle
1576	*Common Conditions* Wapull, *The Tide Tarrieth No Man*		Burbage's Theatre First Blackfriars
1577	Lupton, *All for Money*	Holinshed, *Chronicles*	Drake circumnavigates globe (1577–80)
1578	Whetstone, *I & II Promos and Cassandra*	Lyly, *Euphues*	
1579	Merbury, *A Marriage between Wit and Wisdom*	Gosson, *School of Abuse*	
1580	Legge, *Richardus Tertius*	Montaigne, *Essays*	
1581	Peele, *The Arraignment of Paris* Wilson, *Three Ladies of London* Watson, *Antigone* (trans.) Newton, *Thebias* (trans.)		

DATE	PLAYS	OTHER WORKS	HISTORICAL/CULTURAL EVENTS
1582	*Rare Triumphs of Love and Fortune* W. Gager, *Maleager*	Sidney, *Defence of Poesie* Gosson, *Plays Confuted*	
1583	W. Gager, *Dido*	Stubbes, *Anatomy of Abuses*	Throckmorton plot Queen's players formed
1584	*Fidele and Fortunio* W. Gager, *Oedipus* Lyly, *Campaspe; Sappho and Phao*		Teatro Olimpico, Vicenza Raleigh to Virginia
1585	Lyly, *Gallathea* Peele, *Pageant before Woolstone; Dixie*		
1586	*The Famous Victories of Henry V* Lyly, *Love's Metamorphosis* Peele, *Hunting of Cupid*		Babington plot Sidney d.
1587	*I & II The Troublesome Reign of King John* Greene, *Alphonsus, King of Aragon* Kyd, *The Spanish Tragedy* Marlowe, *I Tamburlaine; Dido, Queen of Carthage* Peele, *David and Bethsabe*	Greene, *Penelope's Web*	Mary, Queen of Scots executed Henslowe's Rose
1588	*Mucedorus* Hughes, *The Misfortunes of Arthur* Lodge, *The Wounds of Civil War*	Marprelate tracts	Spanish Armada Guise assassinated Tarlton d.

DATE	PLAYS	OTHER WORKS	HISTORICAL/CULTURAL EVENTS
	Lyly, *Endymion*		
	Marlowe, *II Tamburlaine*		
	Porter, *I The Two Merry Women of Abingdon*		
	Wilson, *Three Lords and Three Ladies of London*		
1589	*The Taming of a Shrew*		
	Greene, *Friar Bacon and Friar Bungay*		
	Lyly, *Midas; Mother Bombie*		
	Marlowe, *The Jew of Malta*		
	Munday, *John a Kent and John a Cumber*		
	Peele, *Battle of Alcazar*		
1590	*Edward III*	Spenser *Faerie Queene* I–III	
	Fair Em	Lodge, *Rosalynde*	
	King Leir	Greene, *Cony Catching pamphlets* (1590–92)	
	Soliman and Perseda		
	Greene, *James IV; George a Greene*		
	Greene and Lodge, *A Looking Glass for London and England*		
	Peele, *The Old Wives' Tale*		
	Wilson, *The Cobbler's Prophecy*		
1591	*A New Northern Jig*	Sidney, *Astrophel and Stella*	
	Arden of Faversham		
	Jack Straw		
	Locrine		
	True Tragedy of Richard III		

DATE	PLAYS	OTHER WORKS	HISTORICAL/CULTURAL EVENTS
	Greene, *Orlando Furioso*		
	Peele, *Edward I*		
	Shakespeare, *II Henry VI*; *III Henry VI*		
1592	*A Knack to Know a Knave*	Greene, *Groatsworth of Wit*	Plague closes theatres until 1593
	Woodstock	Henslowe's *Diary* starts	
	Gager, *Ulysses Redux*		
	Greene, *Selimus*		
	?Greene, *John of Bordeaux*		
	Marlowe, *Dr Faustus*; *Edward II*; *Massacre at Paris*		
	Nashe, *Summer's Last Will and Testament*		
	Shakespeare, *Comedy of Errors*; *I Henry VI*		
1593	Lyly, *The Woman in the Moon*		Marlowe killed
	Shakespeare, *Richard III*; *Two Gentlemen*		

General Bibliographies

(i) Historical and cultural background

Altman, J.B. *The Tudor Play of Mind* (Berkeley and Los Angeles, 1978) (Place of debate in education and drama.)

Anglo, S. *Spectacle, Pageantry and Early Tudor Policy* (Oxford, 1969) (Public display as an instrument of power.)

Axton, R. *European Drama of the Early Middle Ages* (1974) (Places earliest English drama in Continental context.)

Brigden, S. *London and the Reformation* (Oxford, 1989) (Presents concentration of struggle and change in the capital.)

Bristol, M.D. *Carnival and Theatre: Plebeian Culture and the Structure of Authority in Renaissance England* (New York, 1985) (Seminal account of containment and subversion in popular culture.)

Dickens, A.G. *The English Reformation*, 2nd edition (1989) (Close examination of development of Protestant change.)

Duffy, E. *The Stripping of the Altars* (Yale, 1992) (Detailed and sympathetic account of agonies of religious change.)

Elton, G.R. *England under the Tudors* (Cambridge, 2nd edition 1974) (Standard political history.)

Fox, A. *Politics and Literature in the Reigns of Henry VII and Henry VIII* (Oxford, 1989). (Wide-ranging survey of Tudor writers.)

Gibson, G.M. *Theatre of Devotion* (Chicago, 1989) (Rich account of late medieval piety in East Anglia, including iconography.)

Haigh, C. (ed.) *The Reign of Elizabeth* (Basingstoke, 1984) (Considers aspects of government, the court and social class.)

—— *English Reformations* (Oxford, 1993) (Centres on insecurity and religious change by exploring documentary material.)

Hardison, O.B., Jr *Christian Rite and Christian Drama in the Middle Ages* (Baltimore, 1965) (Explodes evolutionary theories about liturgical drama.)

Herman, P.C. (ed.) *Rethinking the Henrican Era* (Urbana and Chicago, 1994) (Part of the revaluation of the literary quality of Tudor authors.)

Hoskins, W.G. *The Making of the English Landscape* (1957) (Studies development of towns and cities.)

King, J.N. *English Reformation Literature: The Tudor Origins of the Protestant Tradition* (Princeton, 1982) (Examines literary achievement of polemical work.)

Laroque, F. *Shakespeare's Festive World*, translated by J. Lloyd (Cambridge, 1991) (Useful for calendar of rites and festivals.)

Loades, D.M. *Politics and the Nation: Obedience, Resistance and Public Order* (1974) (Concentrates on the monarchy and tensions with the aristocracy.)

MacCulloch, D. *The Reign of Henry VIII: Politics, Policy and Piety* (New York, 1995) (Considers evangelical issues, and the reception of religious changes.)

Mason, H.A. *Humanism and Poetry in the Early Tudor Period* (1959) (Importance of the humanist interpretation of the classics.)

Owst, G.R. *Literature and Pulpit in Medieval England* (Oxford, 1961) (Seminal work revealing links between sermons and literature, including drama.)

Rubin, M. *Corpus Christi: the Eucharist in Late Medieval Culture* (Cambridge, 1991) (Systematic account of nature and development of this rite: covers procession and drama.)

Thomas, K. *Religion and the Decline of Magic* (1970) (Points up relationship between religion, and black and white magic.)

Tillyard, E.M.W. *The Elizabethan World Picture* (1943) (Hierarchical view of structure of society, with medieval retrospect.)

Welsford, E. *The Fool: His Social and Literary History* (1935) (Provides invaluable social background for development of fools on stage.)

(ii) Theatres, actors and audiences

Bevington, D. *From 'Mankind' to Marlowe* (Cambridge, 1962) (Examines composition of interludes in the light of performance requirements.)

Cook, A.J. *The Privileged Playgoers of Shakespeare's London, 1576–1642* (Princeton, 1981) (Evidence about social mix of audiences.)

Elliott, J. *Playing God* (Toronto, 1989) (Role of modern performances revealing dramatic values of medieval plays.)

Feuillerat, A. (ed.) *Documents Relating to the Office of the Revels at Court in the Time of Queen Elizabeth* (Louvain, 1908).

—— (ed.) *Documents Relating to the Revels at Court in the Time of Edward VI and Queen Mary* (Louvain, 1914) (Two invaluable compilations of day-to-day expenditure.)

Foakes, R.A. and R.T. Rickert (eds) *Henslowe's Diary* (Cambridge, 1989) (Expenditure and receipts of a theatrical entrepreneur, from 1592.)

Gair, R. *The Children of Paul's* (Cambridge, 1982) (History of composition, management and theatres for boy companies.)

Gurr, A. *The Shakespearean Stage, 1574–1642*, 2nd edition (Cambridge, 1980) (Explores physical nature of theatres, and stage practice.)

—— *Playgoing in Shakespeare's London* (Cambridge, 1987) (Sheds light upon audiences from documentation about performance.)

Harbage, A. *Shakespeare's Audience* (New York, 1941) (Reviews evidence for composition of audiences.)

King, T.J. *Casting Shakespeare's Plays: London Actors and Their Roles, 1590–1642* (Cambridge, 1992) (Examines distribution of parts in acting companies: detailed charts of plays.)

Mill, A.J. *Medieval Plays in Scotland* (St Andrews, 1927) (Pioneering examination of documentation of early plays.)

Meredith, P. and J.E. Tailby (eds) *The Staging of Religious Drama in Europe in the Later Middle Ages* (Kalamazoo, 1983) (First-hand documents about stage practices, with translations.)

Mullaney, S. *The Place of the Stage* (Chicago, 1988) (Political implications of the physical location of theatres at city perimeter.)

Murray, J.T. *English Dramatic Companies*, 2 vols (1910) (Documents early companies and their movements.)

Robinson, J.W. *Studies in Fifteenth-century Stagecraft* (Kalamazoo, 1991) (Detailed and sensitive account of stage practices in some cycle plays.)

Shapiro, M. *Children of the Revels* (New York, 1977). (History of boys' acting companies.)

Smith, B.R. *Ancient Scripts and Modern Experience on the English Stage, 1500–1700* (Princeton, 1988) (Examines how the Renaissance theatre approached classical precedents.)

Smith, I. *Shakespeare's Blackfriars Playhouse* (1966) (Useful detail about First Blackfriars.)

Southern, R. *The Medieval Theatre in the Round* (1957) (Seminal, but controversial theory about in-the-round performance of *Castle of Perseverance*.)

—— *The Staging of Plays before Shakespeare* (1973) (Detailed consideration of possible staging for many interludes, with drawings.)

Tydeman, W. *The Theatre in the Middle Ages* (Cambridge, 1974*)* (Valuable European perspective for many stage practices.)

—— *English Medieval Theatre, 1400–1500* (1986) (Studies performance characteristics.)

White, P.W. *Theatre and Reformation: Protestantism, Patronage and Playing in Tudor England* (Cambridge, 1993) (Studies details of the theatre as propaganda.)

Wickham, G. *Early English Stages 1300–1660*, 4 vols (1959–81) (Encyclopaedic survey with much invaluable documentation and illustration.)

(iii) General criticism

Barrol, J.L., A. Leggatt, R. Hosley and A. Kernan *The Revels History of Drama in English, III, 1576–1613* (1975).

Baskervill, C.R. *The Elizabethan Jig* (Chicago, 1929) (Standard work on popular and successful dramatic genre.)

Bergeron, D. M. *English Civic Pageantry 1558–1642* (London, 1971) (Centres upon political implications of this theatrical form.)

Bakhtin, M. *Rabelais and his World*, translated by H. Iswolsky (Bloomington, 1984) (Seminal work on subversion.)

Beadle, R. (ed.) *The Cambridge Companion to Medieval English Theatre* (Cambridge, 1994) (Efficient, up-to-date compendium of research and bibliography up to *c.* 1530.)

Belsey, C. *The Subject of Tragedy* (1985) (Centres upon social context and subjectivity, including the position of women.)

Bentley, G.E. *The Jacobean and Caroline Stage*, 7 vols (Oxford, 1941–68) (Standard work, thoroughly well-documented.)

Bevington, D. *Tudor Drama and Politics* (Cambridge, Mass., 1968) (Discussion of political dimension of most extant interludes.)

Blackburn, R. *Biblical Drama under the Tudors* (The Hague, 1971) (Brings together a remarkable variety of plays in this mode.)

Boas, F.S. *University Drama in the Tudor Age* (Oxford, 1914) (Useful summary of range of university drama, chiefly in classical mode.)

Bradbrook, M.C. *The Rise of the Common Player* (1962) (Studies of Laneham, Tarlton, Wilson and Alleyn: sensitive to medieval continuities.)

Braden, G. *Renaissance Tragedy and the Senecan Tradition* (New Haven, 1985) (Re-examination of appeal of Seneca from a classicist's standpoint.)

Braunmuller, A.R. and M. Hattaway (eds) *The Cambridge Companion to English Renaissance Drama* (Cambridge, 1990) (Valuable on playhouses and dramatic genres.)

Briscoe, M.G. and J.C. Coldewey (eds) *Contexts for Early English Drama* (Bloomington and Indianapolis, 1989)

Brody, A. *The English Mummers and their Plays* (1970) (An account of survivals.)

Cawley, A.C., M. Jones, P.F. McDonald and D. Mills *The Revels History of Drama in English, I, Medieval Drama* (1983).

Chambers, E.K. *The English Folk-play* (Oxford, 1933) (Concentrates upon St George play.)

Craik, T.W. *The Tudor Interlude* (Leicester, 1958) (Investigation into allegory and theatrical characteristics.)

Cushman, L.W. *The Devil and the Vice in the English Dramatic Literature before Shakespeare* (Halle, 1900) (Distinguishes the functions of these roles.)

Davenport, W.A. *Fifteenth-century English Drama* (Cambridge, 1982) (Concentrates upon the early moralities.)

Davidson, C. (ed.) *The Saint Play in Medieval Europe* (Kalamazoo, 1986) (Examines the few survivals of this once important and widespread genre.)

Dollimore, J. *Radical Tragedy* (Brighton, 1989) (Re-examination from a cultural materialist viewpoint.)

Doran, M. *Endeavors of Art: A Study of Form in Elizabethan Drama* (Madison, 1954) (Study of theatrical conventions.)

Dutka, J. *Music in the English Mystery Plays* (Kalamazoo, 1980) (Catalogues music items systematically.)

Dutton, R. *Mastering the Revels: The Regulation and Censorship of Elizabethan Drama* (1991)

Farnham, W. *The Medieval Heritage of Elizabethan Tragedy* (New York, 1956) (Draws upon poetic as well as dramatic sources for tragedy.)

Greenblatt, S. *Renaissance Self-fashioning: From More to Shakespeare* (Chicago, 1980) (Examines images and concepts of the self.)

Happé, P. *Song in Morality Plays and Interludes* (Lancaster, 1991) (Catalogues music cues, performance groups and lyrics.)

Harbage, A. *Shakespeare and the Rival Traditions* (New York, 1952)

—— *Annals of English Drama 975–1700*, revised by S. Schoenbaum (1964) (Widely accepted as the most reliable chronology in spite of many uncertainties.)

Hattaway, M. *Elizabethan Popular Theatre* (1982) (In-depth re-creations of performance potential.)

Helm, A. *The English Mummers' Play* (Woodbridge, 1981) (Useful for details of types and their distribution.)

Houle, P. (ed.) *The English Morality and Related Drama* (Hamden, 1972) (Valuable reference work covering criticism play by play.)

Hunter, G.K. *English Drama, 1586–1642* (Oxford, 1997) (Uses much recent research and editing.)

Johnston, A.F. and Wim Hüsken (eds) *English Parish Drama* (Amsterdam and Atlanta, 1996) (Drawing upon local records these essays address the vigour of drama in parishes.)

Kipling, G. *The Triumph of Honour: Burgundian Origins of the Elizabethan Renaissance* (Leiden, 1977) (Landmark study of processions and entries.)

—— *Enter the King: Theatre, Liturgy, and Ritual in the Medieval Civic Triumph* (Oxford, 1998).

McAlindon, T. *English Renaissance Tragedy* (1986) (Studies tragedy in terms of its recurring paradox.)

Muir, L. *The Biblical Drama of Medieval Europe* (Cambridge, 1995) (Rich reference work with comparative studies of episodes.)

Nelson, A.H. *The Medieval English Stage* (Chicago, 1974) (Uses local documents to reveal variety of staging practices.)

—— *Early Cambridge Theatres* (Cambridge, 1994) (Using new evidence, proposes re-examination of hall staging.)

Norland, H. *Drama in Early Tudor Britain, 1485–1558* (Lincoln, Neb., 1995). (Series of studies of intellectual and educational contexts.)

Potter, R. *The English Morality Play* (1975) (Examines relationship between spiritual and theatrical objectives.)

Rastall, R. *The Heavens Singing: Music in Early English Drama* (Cambridge, 1997) (Musicology applied to a wide range of theatrical situations.)

Righter, A. *Shakespeare and the Idea of the Play* (1962). (Studies similarities between medieval and Shakespearian stage concepts.)

Rossiter, A.P. *English Drama from Early Times to the Elizabethans* (1950) (Deals with the function of comic and improper aspects.)

Sanders, N., R. Southern, T.W. Craik and L. Potter *The Revels History of Drama in English, II, 1500–1576* (1980)

Shepherd, S. and P. Womack *English Drama: A Cultural History* (Oxford, 1996)

Spivack, B. *Shakespeare and the Allegory of Evil* (New York, 1958) (Centred upon 'the Vice', traces continuity from medieval drama to Shakespeare.)

Taylor, J. and A.H. Nelson (eds) *Medieval English Drama: Essays Critical and Contextual* (Chicago, 1972).

Tiddy, R.J.E. *The Mummers' Play* (Oxford, 1923) (Invaluable fieldwork on pre-1914 survivals.)

Twycross, M. (ed.) *Festive Drama* (Cambridge, 1996) (Illustrates widening scope of study of early survivals.)

Velz, J.W. (ed.) *Shakespeare's English Histories: A Quest of Form and Genre* (Binghampton, 1996) (Exploration of medieval origins and later development.)

Walker, G. *The Politics of Persuasion* (Cambridge, 1991) (Close examination of political context and purpose of several interludes.)

Weimann, R. *Shakespeare and the Popular Tradition in the Theatre* (1978) (Politically conscious analysis of popular theatre.)

Wilson, F.P. and G.K. Hunter *The English Drama: 1485–1585* (Oxford, 1969).

Young, K. *The Drama of the Medieval Church*, 2 vols (Oxford, 1933) (Standard work on liturgical drama, with many texts.)

Individual Authors

Notes on biography, major works and criticism

Each entry has three sections:

(a) *Biographical information.* There are no full-length biographies for most of the authors. In a few cases editions giving the most reliable information are cited. *The Dictionary of National Biography* usually provides more detail.
(b) *Details of plays written,* and selected information about *non-dramatic works* where relevant. The dates are based on A. Harbage, *Annals of English Drama 975–1700,* though there is often uncertainty about composition, publication and performance.
(c) *Selected critical works,* listed chronologically. The place of publication is London, unless specified.

BALE, JOHN (1495–1564) Born at Cove in Suffolk, he became a Carmelite Friar and was educated at Jesus College, Cambridge. After his conversion in about 1534 he wrote polemical plays for Cromwell and apparently led and acted in a troupe of players. He went into exile twice (1540–47, and 1553–58) and was (Protestant) Bishop of Ossory in Ireland. Of his own list of more than twenty plays the following survive: *A Comedy concerning the Three Laws of Nature, Moses and Christ* (1531–8); *King Johan* (1536–58); *A Tragedy of Interlude manifesting the Chief Promises of God* (1538); *John Baptist's Preaching* (1538); *The Temptation of Our Lord* (1538). He compiled a monumental British bibliography – *Scriptorum Illustrium Maioris Britanniae . . . Catalogus* (Basle, 1557–59). He died in Canterbury.

> See: Harris, J.W. *John Bale* (Urbana, 1940)
> McCusker, H. C. *John Bale* (Bryn Mawr, 1942)
> Blatt, T.B. *The Plays of John Bale* (Copenhagen, 1968) (Valuable work on the sources of the plays.)
> Fairfield, L.P. *John Bale: Mythmaker for the English Reformation* (West Lafayette, 1976) (Thorough and illuminating on Bale as historian and polemicist.)
> Happé, P. *John Bale* (Boston, 1996) (Discusses the plays in detail and places them in the context of the non-dramatic work.)

BURBAGE, JAMES (d. 1597) Originally a carpenter, he became a player and was in Leicester's company in 1574. He is known to have put a stage into the Red

Lion Inn in 1567, before his major achievement, the building and managing of the Theatre in Shoreditch from 1576. He began further enterprise at the Blackfriars in 1596. He was supported by his sons Cuthbert and Richard, the latter being a leading actor in Shakespeare's plays.

See: Smith, I. *Shakespeare's Blackfriars Playhouse* (1964), pp. 137–43
    Leongard, J.S. 'An Elizabethan Lawsuit: John Brayne, his carpenter, and the Building of the Red Lion Theatre', *Shakespeare Quarterly* 34 (1983), 298–310

EDWARDS, RICHARD (?1523–66) Studied music at Corpus Christi College, Oxford, and Law at Lincoln's Inn. He was a Gentleman of the Chapel Royal and Master of the Chapel Children. He performed a tragedy for the Queen at Richmond, and his *Palamon and Arcite* (lost, but based on Chaucer's *Knight's Tale*) was performed at Christ Church during her Oxford visit in 1566. His play, *Damon and Pithias*, was printed in 1571. His poems were much praised.

See: Bradner, L. (ed.) *The Life and Poems of Richard Edwards* (New Haven, 1927)
    Le Huray, P. *Music and the Reformation in England, 1549–1660* (1967)

FULWELL, ULPIAN (1546–86) Born in Wells, ordained in 1566, he became Rector of Naunton, Gloucestershire, from 1570 until his death. His mismanagement of the parish attracted a fine in 1576. He pursued public recognition after the publication of *Like Will to Like* in 1568. He published *The Flower of Fame* (1575), a miscellany in support of the Tudor dynasty, and *Ars Adulandi* (1576), a satire on flattery and preferment, for which he had to make a public recantation. He was admitted to St Mary's Hall, Oxford, at the age of 33, and proceeded to M.A. in 1584.

See: Ribner, I. 'Ulpian Fulwell and his family', *Notes and Queries* 195 (1950) 444–8
    Happé, P. (ed.) *Two Moral Interludes* (Oxford, 1991) (Dramaturgy and life.)

GASCOIGNE, GEORGE (*c.* 1534–77) Was educated at Trinity College, Cambridge, where he was known for his extravagance, and at Gray's Inn. He became an M.P. and lived at St Giles, Cripplegate. His adventurous life included shipwreck and a period in the Netherlands. His dramatic work comprised *The Glass of Government* (1575), contributions to the *Princely Pleasures* at Kenilworth, and *The Queen's Entertainment* at Woodstock (1575), and translations of *Jocasta* and *Supposes* (1566) for performance at Gray's Inn. He also wrote poetry: *The Posies* (1575), *The Steel Glass* (1576), *A Hundred Sundry Flowers* (1572), and fiction: *A Pleasant Discourse of the Adventures of Master F[erdinando] J[eronimi]* (1573). He was buried at St Mary's, Stamford.

See: Schelling, F.E. *The Life and Writings of George Gascoigne* (Boston, 1893)
    Cunliffe, J.W. *The Works of George Gascoigne*, 2 vols (Cambridge, 1907, 1910) (Standard text.)
    Prouty, C.T. *George Gascoigne* (New York, 1942)
    Johnson, R.C. *George Gascoigne* (New York, 1972)

GREENE, ROBERT (1558–92) Born in Norwich and educated at St John's College, Cambridge (B.A. in 1580, and M.A. in 1583; also M.A., Oxford, 1588). He deserted his wife and lived an unsavoury life in London, seeking his living by writing. He produced as many as forty books including novels and ephemera, and the *Cony-Catching* pamphlets (1590–92). From about 1587 he began to write plays: *Alphonsus, King of Aragon*; *Friar Bacon and Friar Bungay*; *George a Green, the Pinner of Wakefield*; *James IV*; *Orlando Furioso*; and possibly *Selimus*. He collaborated with Lodge in *A Looking Glass for London* (1590). His work took a moral tone after his 'repentance' (*c.* 1590), but he died wretchedly in poverty.

See: Clemen, W. *English Tragedy before Shakespeare* (1961), pp. 178–91
   Muir, K. 'Robert Greene as Dramatist', in R. Hosley (ed.) *Essays on Shakespeare and the Elizabethan Drama in Honor of Hardin Craig* (New York, 1962), pp. 45–54
   Sanders, N. 'The Comedy of Greene and Shakespeare', *Stratford-upon-Avon Studies* 3 (1962), 35–53
   Jordan, J.C. *Robert Greene* (New York, 1972)
   Senn, W. *Studies in the Dramatic Construction of Robert Greene and George Peele* (Bern, 1973)
   Crupi, C. W. *Robert Greene* (Boston, 1986)

HEYWOOD, JASPER (1535–98) Son of John Heywood, he was born in London and had a distinguished career at All Souls College, Oxford. His translations of Seneca, *Troas* (1559), *Thyestes* (1560) and *Hercules Furens* (1561), were republished in 1581. He became a Jesuit and died at Naples.

See: De Vocht, H. *Jasper Heywood and his Translations of Seneca* (Leuven, 1913)
   Daalder, J. (ed.) *Thyestes* (1982) (Valuable and sympathetic study, especially of language and Senecan tradition.)

HEYWOOD, JOHN (1497–*c.* 1578) Born in London or Coventry, was probably a boy chorister in London and at court, and studied at Broadgates Hall, Oxford, *c.* 1513–14. He made a prosperous living at court from about 1519 until 1564, a staunch Catholic throughout; his activities were both musical and dramatic. He married Joan, daughter of John Rastell, and probably collaborated with him in *Gentleness and Nobility* (1526–30). He composed the manuscript of *Witty and Witless* for performance at court *c.* 1525. In the critical years of the Reformation and the King's divorce, he published the following plays: *Johan Johan* (1533), *The Pardoner and the Friar* (1533), *The Play of the Wether* (1533), *A Play of Love* (1534), and *The Four PP* (1544). His non-dramatic works include *The Spider and the Fly* (1556), a political allegory about Queen Mary, his patroness, and *A Dialogue of Proverbs* (1546, with three further expansions). He spent his last years impoverished in exile, and died at Leuven.

See: Bolwell, R.S. *Life and Works of John Heywood* (New York, 1921)
   Reed, A.W. *Early Tudor Drama* (1926) (Seminal study of Medwall, Heywood and the Rastells.)
   Maxwell, I. *French Farce and John Heywood* (Melbourne, 1946)
   Milligan, B.A. *John Heywood's 'Works' and Miscellaneous Short Poems* (Urbana, 1956)
   Habenicht, R.E. *John Heywood's 'A Dialogue of Proverbs'* (Berkeley and Los Angeles, 1963)
   Johnson, R.C. *John Heywood* (Boston, 1970)
   Walker, G. *Plays of Persuasion* (Cambridge, 1991) (Political context.)
   Axton, R. and P. Happé (eds) *The Plays of John Heywood* (Cambridge, 1991) (Interprets Catholic commitment.)

KYD, THOMAS (1558–94) Born in London, son of a scrivener, attended Merchant
Taylors' School, under Richard Mulcaster. From 1587 he was working with a
group of players. *The Spanish Tragedy* was probably written *c.* 1587 and printed
c. 1592. He translated Robert Garnier's *Cornélie* (1594). An associate of Marlowe,
he fell foul of the authorities and was probably tortured in 1593. He died the
following year, perhaps as a result.

See: Edwards, P. *Thomas Kyd and Early Elizabethan Tragedy* (1966)
  Murray, P.B. *Thomas Kyd* (New York, 1969)
  McAlindon, T. *English Renaissance Tragedy* (Basingstoke, 1986)
  Ardolino, F.R. *Thomas Kyd's Mystery Play: Myth and Ritual in 'The Spanish
  Tragedy'* (New York, 1986)

LINDSAY, SIR DAVID (1486–1555) Was educated at St Andrews, a lifelong
courtier. He was tutor to the boy James V, and went on diplomatic missions to
England and France. He wrote a good deal of poetry, including *Squire Meldrum*
(1579). *Ane Satire of the Thrie Estaitis* is first recorded at Linlithgow Palace in
1540. In 1552 it was enlarged and produced at Cupar, Fife, where he was the
laird, and again with the patronage of Mary of Guise, the Queen Regnant,
at the Greenside in Edinburgh in 1554. He died in 1555.

See: Hamer, D. (ed.) *The Works of Sir David Lindsay of the Mount 1490–1555*,
  4 vols, Scottish Text Society (Edinburgh, 1931–36) (Unsurpassed edition
  with encyclopaedic annotation and commentary.)
  Murison, W. *Sir David Lindsay* (Cambridge, 1938)
  Kantrowitz, J.S. *Dramatic Allegory: Lindsay's 'Ane Satyre of the Thrie Estaitis*
  (Lincoln, Neb., 1975) (Outstanding discussion of use of allegory.)
  Edington, C. *Court and Culture in Renaissance Scotland: Sir David Lindsay of
  the Mount, 1486–1555* (East Linton, Mass., 1995)

LODGE, THOMAS (*c.* 1557–1625) Educated at Merchant Taylors', Trinity
College, Oxford, Lincoln's Inn, and later at Avignon where he qualified in
medicine. He went on several voyages and lived in the Netherlands, being a
recusant. Besides the romance *Rosalynde* (1590) he wrote *The Wounds of Civil War*
(*c.* 1588) and collaborated with Greene in *A Looking Glass for London and England*
(*c.* 1590). He died in London, probably from plague.

See: Burton, P.N. *Thomas Lodge: The History of an Elizabethan* (New Haven,
  1931)
  Sisson, C.J. *Thomas Lodge and other Elizabethans* (Cambridge, Mass., 1933).
  Walker, A. 'The Life of Thomas Lodge', *Review of English Studies* 9 (1933),
  410–32
  Bradbrook, M.C. *The Growth and Structure of Elizabethan Comedy* (1955).
  Eccles, M. 'Brief Lives: Tudor and Stuart Authors', *Studies in Philology*
  79 (1982), 81–6

LYLY, JOHN (*c.* 1554–1606) Educated at Magdalen College, Oxford (B.A. 1573,
M.A. 1575), but failed to get support for his academic aspirations. His romance
Euphues (1578) secured patronage from the Earl of Oxford. Using boy actors at
the First Blackfriars, he prepared court plays which reflect his continuing ambition
there: *Campaspe* and *Sappho and Phao* (1584), *Gallathea* (1585), *Love's Metamorphosis*
(1586), *Endymion* (1588), *Mother Bombie* (1589) and *The Woman in the Moon*
(1593). Failing advancement at court he became an M.P. and died disillusioned.

See: Hunter, G.K. *John Lyly: The Humanist as Courtier* (1962)
     Saccio, P. *The Court Comedies of John Lyly* (Princeton, 1969)
     Houppert, J.W. *John Lyly* (New York, 1975)
     Pincombe, M. *John Lyly* (Manchester, 1996) (Discussion of Lyly's court
       ambitions.)

MARLOWE, CHRISTOPHER (1564–93) Born in Canterbury, son of a
shoemaker, and educated at King's School. Parker Scholar at Corpus Christi
College, Cambridge, 1580: B.A. 1584, M.A. 1587. He wrote poems, including
Hero and Leander (published 1598); and his plays were performed by the Chapel
Boys: *The Tragedy of Dido, Queen of Carthage*; and by the Admiral's Men: *I & II
Tamburlaine* (1587–88), *Dr Faustus* (1588–92), *The Jew of Malta* (1589–90), and
Edward II (1591–93). He engaged in espionage for Walsingham and was stabbed
in a tavern fight in Deptford.

See: Steane, J.B. *Marlowe: A Critical Study* (Cambridge, 1964)
     Maclure, M. *Christopher Marlowe: The Critical Heritage* (1979)
     Shepherd, S. *Marlowe and the Politics of Elizabethan Theatre* (Brighton, 1986)
       (Studies Marlowe's interest in political power.)
     Barber, C.L. *Creating Elizabethan Tragedy: The Theatre of Marlowe and Kyd*
       (Chicago, 1988)
     Friedenreich, K., R. Gill and C.B. Kuriyama (eds) *'A Poet and a Filthy
       Play-maker': New Essays on Christopher Marlowe* (New York, 1988) (Lively
       collection of essays in re-valuation.)
     Tydeman, W. and V. Thomas *The State of the Art: Christopher Marlowe*
       (Bristol, 1989) (Survey of critical approaches.)
     Cole, D. *Christopher Marlowe and the Renaissance of Tragedy* (Westport, Conn.,
       1995)
     Proser, M.N. *The Gift of Fire: Aggression in the Plays of Christopher Marlowe*
       (New York, 1995) (Psychological study.)
     Grantley, D. and P. Roberts *Christopher Marlowe and English Renaissance
       Culture* (Aldershot, 1996)

MEDWALL, HENRY (?1461–?1501) Studied at Eton and King's College,
Cambridge. Took an interest in entertainment at the college for some years after
1483. Qualified as a notary, but entered minor orders and served Archbishop
Morton through the 1490s. The date of his death is conjectural. His *Fulgens and
Lucres* was printed by John Rastell (*c.* 1512), and *Nature* by William Rastell (*c.* 1530).

See: Reed, A.W. *Early Tudor Drama* (1926)
     Nelson, A.H. (ed.) *The Plays of Henry Medwall* (Cambridge, 1980), pp. 163–9
     Godfrey, R.A. 'Nervous Laughter in Henry Medwall's *Fulgens and Lucres*', in
       Tudor Theatre 3 (Bern, 1996), pp. 81–97

MORE, SIR THOMAS (1478–1535) After training at Oxford and the New Inn,
he had a very distinguished career as a lawyer, rising to be the first lay Lord
Chancellor in 1529. He was a determined prosecutor of heretics and his staunch
Catholic beliefs led him into conflict over the divorce with Henry VIII. He
was beheaded in the Tower for high treason. He was an influence on other
dramatists, rather than a playwright himself. As a youth he took extempore roles,
and he was an associate of Erasmus with whom he translated Lucian's *Dialogues*
(1506). He was related by marriage to the Rastells and the Heywoods, and may
well have influenced them. His works include *Utopia* (1516, in Latin), and
religious and polemical work such as *A Dialogue of Images* (1529), his *Apology*

(1530) and *A Dialogue of Comfort* (1532). His interest in drama became legendary, as shown in the manuscript play *The Book of Sir Thomas More* (1595) by Munday, Shakespeare and others.

See: Reed, A.W. *Early Tudor Drama* (1926)
   Hogrefe, P. *The Sir Thomas More Circle* (Urbana, 1959)
   Marius, R. *Sir Thomas More* (1985) (Outstanding biography.)
   Norland, H.B. *Drama in Early Tudor Britain, 1485–1558* (Lincoln, Neb., 1995), pp. 111–27 (Detailed work on More's interest in drama.)

NORTON, THOMAS (1532–84) Thought to have gone to Cambridge with help from the Grocer's Company. He attended the Inner Temple and was called to the bar. He was known for his English and Latin poems. He collaborated with Sackville in writing *Gorboduc* (1562), which was performed at the Inner Temple. He became an M.P. in 1558 and later was appointed a Censor of Catholics, and was involved in persecution.

See: Baker, H. *Induction to Tragedy* (Baton Rouge, 1939)
   Walker, G. 'The Politics of *Gorboduc*', *English Historical Review* CX (1995), 109–21.

PEELE, GEORGE (1556–96) Born in London, educated at Christ's Hospital where his father worked. Attended Broadgates Hall, Oxford: B.A. 1577, M.A. 1579. After a period at Christ Church when his reputation as poet was established, he wrote London pageants, as his father had done. Of his plays *The Arraignment of Paris* (1581–82) and *The Old Wives' Tale* (1588–94) were performed by the Chapel Boys, while *The Battle of Alcazar* (1588–99), *The Love of King David and the Fair Bethsabe* (1589–92) and *The Famous Chronicle History of Edward I* (1591) were given by the Admiral's Men.

See: Campbell, L.B. *Divine Poetry and Drama in Sixteenth-century England* (Berkeley and Los Angeles, 1959), pp. 252–60
   Clemen, W. *English Tragedy before Shakespeare* (1961), pp. 163–77
   Senn, Werner *Studies in the Dramatic Construction of Robert Greene and George Peele* (Bern, 1973)
   Axton, M. *The Queen's Two Bodies* (1977) (*Alcazar* and *Edward I*).
   Marx, J.C. ' "Soft who have we here?": The Dramatic Technique of *The Old Wives' Tale*', *Renaissance Drama* 12 (1981), 117–23
   Braunmuller, A.R. *George Peele* (Boston, 1993)

PIKERYNG, JOHN, (*fl.* 1567) possibly identified with John Puckering of Lincoln's Inn, called to the bar in 1567. Later he became Speaker of the House of Commons, presenting a petition for the execution of Mary Queen of Scots.

See: Axton, M. (ed.) *Three Tudor Classical Interludes* (Cambridge, 1982) (Valuable for attention to debt to classics.)
   Robertson, K. and J-A. George (eds) *Horestes* (Dublin, 1996) (Introduction relates to Scottish politics.)

PRESTON, THOMAS (1537–98) Educated at Eton and King's College, Cambridge, he became Master of Trinity Hall in 1584, and served as Vice-Chancellor. Besides writing *Cambises, King of Persia* (1561), he played in a tragedy of *Dido* and delivered a Latin oration for the Queen's visit in 1564. He also published broadside ballads (lost).

See: Johnson, R.C. (ed.) *A Critical Edition of Thomas Preston's 'Cambises'*, *Salzburg Studies in English Literature* 23 (Salzburg, 1975)

RASTELL, JOHN (?1475–1536) Son of the city coroner at Coventry, he attended the Middle Temple, and married Elizabeth, sister of Sir Thomas More. He took up printing by 1510, and was involved in merchant voyages, as well as helping prepare the Field of the Cloth of Gold (1520), and erecting pageants in London, including one for Emperor Charles V in 1522. He built a stage at his house in Finsbury Fields. His printing output included plays, works by More, and his own *The Pastime of People*. Engaging in religious controversy as a rather lukewarm Catholic in his *A New Book of Purgatory* (1530), he was converted to Protestantism by John Frith's reply. His known plays are *The Interlude of the Four Elements* (1517), *Calisto and Melebea* (1523) and *Gentleness and Nobility* (1523), to which John Heywood may have contributed. He spent the last two years of his life in the Tower and died there. William, his son (1508–65), remained a Catholic and was the printer of most of John Heywood's plays.

See: Reed, A.W. *Early Tudor Drama* (1926)
   Hogrefe, P. *The Sir Thomas More Circle* (Urbana, 1959)
   Axton, R. (ed.) *Three Rastell Plays* (Cambridge, 1979) (Valuable for life and for dramatic qualities.)
   Geritz, A.J. and A.L. Laine, *John Rastell* (Boston, 1983)
   Geritz, A.J. (ed.) *The Pastime of People* and *A New Book of Purgatory* (New York, 1985) (Comprehensive Introduction.)

REDFORD, JOHN (*fl.* 1535) a trained musician, became Master of the Children of Paul's. In this post he produced instrumental music and motets. Some of his lyrics are found in the same manuscript as John Heywood's. He would also have been under an obligation to produce court entertainment, for which he wrote *Wit and Science* (*c.* 1539).

See: Stevens, J. *Music and Poetry in the Early Tudor Court* (1961)
   Velz, J.W. and C.P. Daw, Jr 'Tradition and Originality in *Wyt and Science*', *Studies in Philology* 65 (1968) 631–46.

SACKVILLE, THOMAS (1536–1608) Inherited wealth, and studied at the Inner Temple. An active Protestant, he was knighted and raised to the peerage in 1567, and went on diplomatic missions. He became Lord Treasurer and was created Earl of Dorset in 1603. He died at the council table, and was buried at Withyham. Besides collaborating with Norton over *Gorboduc* (1562), he contributed the *Induction and Complaint of Henry Duke of Buckingham* to *The Mirror for Magistrates* (1562).
   For bibliography, see NORTON.

SKELTON, JOHN (?1460–1529) Was a laureate of Oxford and Cambridge. He was tutor to Henry VIII, but lost his position at court and became Rector of Diss. His extensive poetic output included *The Bowge of Court* (1499), *Speke, Parrot* (1521), *The Garlande of Laurell* (1523), and *Colin Clout* and *Philip Sparrow* which were published posthumously. Most of his work is highly satirical. He translated *Speculum Principis*, advice to a monarch. His one surviving play, *Magnyfycence* (*c.* 1519), was an attempt to reassert his influence over the youthful King Henry. He claims to have written other plays, but only a fragment of *Good Order* is attributed to him. He took sanctuary in Westminster where he died.

See: Heiserman, A.R. *Skelton and Satire* (Chicago, 1961)
    Harris, W.O. *Skelton's 'Magnyfycence' and the Cardinal Virtue Tradition*
    (Chapel Hill, 1965) (Essential allegorical interpretation.)
    Pollet, M. *John Skelton, Poet of Tudor England* (1971)
    Edwards, A.S.G. *John Skelton: The Critical Heritage* (1981)
    Scattergood, J. *John Skelton: The Complete Poems* (Harmondsworth, 1983)
    Kinney, A.F. *John Skelton: Priest as Poet* (Chapel Hill, 1987)
    Walker, G. *John Skelton and the Politics of the 1520s* (Cambridge, 1988)
    (Relocates Skelton's political activities.)

TARLTON, RICHARD (d. 1588) Born at Condover, Salop., is thought to have
been an innkeeper who did 'turns'. He joined the Queen's Men in 1583 and
became the most celebrated clown of his day, winning patronage from the
aristocracy. He was successful with his *Play of the Seven Deadly Sins* (lost),
and with inspired extempore rhyming and jigs.

See: Bradbrook, M.C. *The Rise of the Common Player* (1962)

UDALL, NICHOLAS (1505–56) Was educated at Winchester College, and Corpus
Christi College, Oxford (B.A., 1524). By 1534 was Headmaster of Eton.
Dismissed with ignominy by the Privy Council, he was imprisoned in the
Marshalsea, before becoming Vicar of Braintree in 1537. In spite of his strong
support for Protestants, he was favoured by Queen Mary and charged with
producing interludes for her. He became Headmaster of Westminster School in
1554 and died in office. He produced *Flowers for Latin Speaking* (1534), a school
textbook based upon Terence, and translated the *Apothegmes* of Erasmus (1542).
His dramatic works include *Ralph Roister Doister* (1552), and also attributed to
him are *Thersites* (1537), *Respublica* (1553) and *Jack Juggler* (1555).

See: Egerton, W.L. *Nicholas Udall* (New York, 1965)
    Axton, M. (ed.) *Three Tudor Classical Interludes* (Cambridge, 1982)
    Norland, H.B. *Drama in Early Tudor Britain, 1485–1558* (Lincoln, Neb.,
    1995), pp. 199–209

WAGER, LEWIS (d. 1562) A Franciscan Friar at Oxford, he and was made a
subdeacon in 1521. The date of his conversion is unknown, but he became
Rector of St James, Garlickhithe, in 1560, where he was buried. His only known
play, *The Life and Repentaunce of Marie Magdalene* (1558), was intended for
performance by a travelling company, and was influenced by Calvin.

See: Eccles, M. 'Brief Lives: Tudor and Stuart Authors', *Studies in Philology*
    79 (1982), 123–4
    Happé, P. 'The Protestant Adaptation of the Saint Play', in C. Davidson
    (ed.) *The Saint Play in Medieval Europe* (Kalamazoo, 1986), pp. 205–40
    White, P.W. *Reformation Biblical Drama in England* (New York and London,
    1992) (Informative Introduction; includes an edition.)

WAGER, WILLIAM (c. 1537–91) Probably the son of Lewis Wager, was married
at St James, Garlickhithe, in 1562, where four of his children were subsequently
christened. He was Rector of St Benet at Gracechurch, where he was buried on
29 March 1591. His ministry included hearing petitions from debtors, acting as
a school governor, as well as a lectureship at St Mary Woolnoth and a licence
to preach throughout London. He sent one of his sons to Oxford, and one to

Cambridge. His confirmed plays are *The Longer Thou Livest the More Fool Thou Art* (1559) and *Enough is as Good as a Feast* (1560), and he may have written *The Cruel Debtor* (1565) and *The Trial of Treasure* (1567). He was licensed to publish a ballad in 1589.

See: Benbow R.M. (ed.) *The Longer Thou Livest the More Fool Thou Art* and *Enough is as Good as a Feast* (1968)

Eccles, M. 'William Wager and his Plays', *English Language Notes* 18 (1981), 258–61

WILSON, ROBERT (d. 1600) Was a comic actor in Leicester's Company, 1574, and the Queen's Men, 1583. He was an associate of Tarlton, as well as a playwright: *The Three Ladies of London* (1584), *The Three Lords and Three Ladies of London* (1590), *The Cobbler's Prophecy* (1594) and *The Pedlar's Prophecy* (1595). He died in the parish of St Giles, Cripplegate.

See: Bradbrook, M.C. *The Rise of the Common Player* (1962)

Mithal, H.S.D. *An Edition of Robert Wilson's 'Three Ladies of London' and 'Three Lords and Three Ladies of London'* (New York, 1988) (The most comprehensive account of his work.)

Anonymous Plays

For the principal editions see Abbreviations.
Selected critical studies, in chronological order for each text.

Mystery cycles

Travis, P. *Dramatic Design in the Chester Cycle* (Chicago, 1982)
Lumiansky, R.M. and D. Mills *The Chester Mystery Cycle: Essays and Documents* (Chapel Hill, 1983)
Mills, D. *Staging the Chester Cycle* (Leeds, 1985)
Harty, K.J. (ed.) *The Chester Mystery Cycle: A Casebook* (New York, 1993)

Longworth, R. *The Cornish Ordinalia* (Cambridge, Mass., 1965)
Bakere, J.A. *The Cornish Ordinalia: A Critical Study* (Cardiff, 1980)
Higgins, S. *Medieval Theatre in the Round* (Camerino, Marche, Italy, 1995)

Collins, P.J. *The N-Town Plays and Medieval Picture Cycles* (Kalamazoo, 1979)

Gardner, J. *The Construction of the Wakefield Cycle* (Carbondale and Edwardsville, 1974)

Collier, R.J. *Poetry and Drama in the York Mystery Play* (Hamden, 1977)
Davidson, C. *From Creation to Doom: The York Cycle of Mystery Plays* (New York, 1984)

Gardiner, H.C. *Mysteries' End* (New Haven, 1946)
Prosser, E. *Drama and Religion in the English Mystery Plays* (Stanford, 1961)
Kolve, V.A. *The Play Called Corpus Christi* (Stanford, 1966)
Woolf, R. *The English Mystery Plays* (1972)
Stevens, M. *Four Middle English Mystery Cycles* (Princeton, 1987)

Castle of Perseverance

Pederson, S.I. *The Tournament Tradition and the Staging of 'The Castle of Perseverance'* (Ann Arbor, 1987)

Mankind

Coogan, M.P. *An Interpretation of the Moral Play 'Mankind'* (Washington, DC, 1947)
Neuss, P. 'Active and Idle Languages: Dramatic Images in *Mankind*', in N. Denny (ed.) *Medieval Drama* (1973), pp. 252–63.

Wisdom

Smart, W.K. *Some English and Latin Sources and Parallels for the Morality of 'Wisdom'* (Menasha, Wis., 1912)
Molloy, J.J.A. *A Theological Interpretation of the Moral Play 'Wisdom, who is Christ'* (Washington, DC, 1952)
Riggio, M.C. *The Play of Wisdom: Its Text and Contexts* (New York, 1986)
Riggio, M.C. (ed.) *The Wisdom Symposium* (New York, 1986)

Index

Note: authors and titles are shown separately. Some titles have been abbreviated. References in bold are to the Individual Authors section.